OUR LAST BACKPACK

A MEMOIR

Other Books by Daniel Doan

The Crystal Years (1952)
Amos Jackman (1957)
50 Hikes in the White Mountains (1973)
50 More Hikes in New Hampshire (1978)
*Dan Doan's Fitness Program for Hikers and
Cross-Country Skiers* (1978)

OUR LAST BACKPACK

⊠ ⊠ ⊠ *A MEMOIR*

BY DANIEL DOAN

BACKCOUNTRY PUBLICATIONS
WOODSTOCK, VERMONT

PUBLISHER'S NOTE

The Mousley Brook Trail on Smarts Mountain, located in the towns of Orford and Lyme, New Hampshire, has recently been renamed the Daniel Doan Trail. The Dartmouth Outing Club made the change in recognition of Doan's efforts "to stimulate interest and involvement in hiking and the out-of-doors."

Library of Congress Cataloging-in-Publication Data

Doan, Daniel, 1914-
    Our last backpack : a memoir / Daniel Doan.
        p. cm.
    ISBN 0-88150-273-1
      1. Backpacking—New Hampshire. 2. Hiking—New Hampshire
3. Appalachian Trail. I. Title
GV199.42.N4D63 1993
796.5'1'09742—dc20   93-15766
                                                      CIP

Published by Backcountry Publications
A division of The Countryman Press, Inc.
Woodstock, Vermont 05091

Printed in the United States of America
Cover design by Karen Savary
Text design by Ann Aspell

10 9 8 7 6 5 4 3 2 1

In Memoriam
My Friend of Sixty-four Years,
Claud Sharps

WHY WE WENT

ONCE UPON A TIME THERE WAS A CAMPFIRE IN A SPRUCE FOREST. IT almost got away. An act of God stopped it.

This was so long ago that I hesitate to put a date on it. The four figures might scare off readers who have not lived 78 years. But you see, Claud Sharps and I began camping out that year. And we kept right on camping out. (There was no such term as "backpacking.") And so it was that early in our lives we formed the foundation for what later became, in 1966 at age 52, our adventure in the Mahoosucs.

In 1929—there, I've let the date slip—two boys, aged 15, while learning the woods east of Orford, New Hampshire (the Connecticut River and Vermont bounded Orford on the west), discovered a new and joyous experience.

Even earlier, their world had begun to expand in the pastures and pines behind the big houses on the "Ridge."

A mention of social strata is necessary here, and then it can be forgotten. Claud lived in Orford year-round, the son of the caretaker for my Uncle Addison Fay's place near my parents' summer home. My aunt called Claud's father "Sharps." My uncle called him "Joe." This puzzled me. I was a summer bastard until 1929, when my mother moved from Winchester, Massachusetts, to Hanover, and I became a permanent, life-long resident of New Hampshire.

Claud and I had gone on one overnight camping out with a Scout troop organized for a brief time by the postmaster's son, Louis Conant, a summer or two before, maybe three, say 1926. That overnight to a shelter at the base of Mount Cube with half a dozen other boys was our last organized camping out.

We had progressed, however, to some skill in building campfires. By ourselves, mind you. No adult help, other than that of authors on woodcraft, such as Ernest Thompson Seton. We called our excursions into the woods for a noon meal "cooking our dinner out." We were too young to be allowed out overnight. And I'm not sure that the building of fires was with permission. But we longed to explore farther than the woods behind our houses.

The absorbing desire to explore ever-widening countryside came not from my father, a Unitarian minister and trout fisherman, who died in 1927 when I was 13. We were not a hiking family, although my three older sisters climbed Moosilauke. Nor did Claud receive the urge from his father, a Welsh gardener trained at Kew. (His parents had come to America before World War I.) Wherever the drive came from, we shared it.

After we had a falling out one summer, we continued to share woods interests and continued amicably to learn woods lore together—but no camping out alone until 1929. Age 15 was not considered responsible, but my poor mother gave in with good grace to endless teasing. Claud, somewhat of a revolutionary, yet persuasive, presented his parents with a chance for temporary relief from one son. They were on the way to producing six. (Or was it seven?)

As a destination we chose the "Meadows."

This wild stillwater on the north branch of Jacobs Brook between Mount Cube and Smarts Mountain was fabled among fishermen, including my Uncle Fred and Uncle Earl. We weren't sure where we'd end up, though I had verbal directions from Uncle Fred; Claud had talked to a deer hunter who knew the territory.

Claud's father drove us in his Model T Ford to Quinttown and a vacant Four Corners, our jumping-off place, a valley of abandoned farms and logging camps. What bewildered thoughts he must have had about this son and the nephew of his employer, but without parental admonitions he backed around and left us with our makeshift packs, bedrolls, and a large hand ax borrowed from his toolshed. (We scorned Boy Scout hatchets.)

We started for the Meadows. The logging road petered out at the fork of Jacobs Brook. Our route up the north branch became steep on an old sled-road trace. It ended at a tangle of swampy spruce-fir forest and a slowing of the brook, which abruptly appeared as a channel through an expanse of low bushes and a broad greenery that we didn't know was sphagnum moss interspersed with bunches of lambkill shrubs and pitcher-plant. A strange bird called from a dead stub, saying as I later learned, "Hic, three beers."

We stood on a ridge about two feet high. I, the romantic, announced it had been a beaver dam. Claud said, "More likely the remains of a dam for an old shingle mill. I've heard about Lamprey Mill."

There were no beavers in 1929. Beavers didn't return until the late forties, when they connected flowage of ponds.

We had discovered the Meadows.

Remoteness took over as we pushed our way into the open bogland. An unknown hill rose low in the east; on the left Mount Cube sloped up, covered with hardwoods, then evergreens, to its crown of quartzite at 2,909 feet. On our right a long ridge led up with hardwoods to the final humped summit in spruce-fir woods and a crude pole tower...that too we were to climb in 1929. Smarts Mountain, elevation 3,238 feet.

Following books written by Seton, Dan Beard, and Horace Kephart, we explored for a campsite and chose a knoll overlooking the slow dark water of the channel. With the ax, we laid down some dead spruce poles to frame a shelter in the best book tradition. Thatching with plenty of spruce boughs and shingling a bed with balsam boughs for fragrance and no-prickly comfort, we made ready for the night as instructed before going fishing for the legendary trout predicted by Uncle Fred.

Over the years we learned how to catch trout in bog channels. To wit, don't expect a bite on a worm or a rise to a fly until your patience is worn out. Then wait some more. You can't walk close enough to a bog channel without scaring the trout. They must feel vibrations for a hundred yards.

This time, we caught none of the wary speckled beauties I had visualized.

Back at camp we started a fire on top of the forest duff. I collected more wood for the night. Claud chopped pieces. He liked to chop. There was plenty of dead spruce, from twigs to standing trees 10 feet high, which had succumbed to natural thinning.

I opened a can of beans. Claud fried bacon. A can of pears would be dessert. We had a cob pipe to share, found on the rock of an old stone wall. Claud had swiped some tobacco.

As darkness filled the space between the evergreens, we didn't admit being scared, but took turns loading the pipe and smoking the Prince Albert tobacco which made me feel sick.

The fire kept back the dark. Nearby trunks were familiar.

Thunder rolled off in the distance, first toward Cube, then toward Smarts.

We were about to improve on our book learning.

An evergreen shelter is not waterproof. It turns rain all right, but into a very wet mist that's not only wet but cold. I drew my blanket around me and lay down, then remembered that Kephart advised covering up with the blanket after you lie down, tucking in edges. I must have dozed because I awoke to a red glare. I was wet and cold. I poked Claud.

He mumbled, "Leemealone," as though at a brother.

"Get up!" I hollered. "Woods afire!"

He raised up on one elbow. "Nothing but the wood I threw on."

I made out a pile of those dead spruces.

He said sleepily, "Gotta keep warm somehow."

I lay back and watched the flames illuminate the combustible branches over my head—and all their dripping needles. I fell asleep. Fitfully, I recall, though I became fully aware as a cloudburst poured on us sometime toward morning. Claud slept on.

By daylight I saw what that act of God had done: extinguished the fire in the foot and half of dry duff, leaving a mammoth hole in the forest floor. Our boots were on the edge of it, wet but safe.

The day of exploration began cool and relatively bugless as we made our way up the brook, pushing our way through evergreens. Sun out, and blackflies found us. Our citronella bug repellent, Kimball's Salve, smelled effective but wasn't. Wet spruces slapped us with dripping branches. Soon we were soaked and bitten.

But we found Lamprey Pond, also called Pickerel Pond. We were discoverers like Balboa at the Pacific. Someday we would camp at the inlet and build a log shelter…catch monster pickerel….

Our second lesson in woodcraft began the next day.

I asked Claud, "Do you feel like you're walking three feet off the ground?"

"No, I feel like I'm going to puke."

"We better get out of here while we can."

Babes in the woods, we had been drinking bog water.

Through bleary eyes, with packs on our backs, we pushed across a tangle of sheep laurel into evergreens and headed downstream. Camped far down the brook, we soon recovered.

(Not drink water from brooks and streams? Ridiculous! We knew enough about pollution not to drink from the Connecticut River, though we swam in it. But at watering boxes for horses along the roads, such as the one on the way to Orfordville, we relished the cool sweet water running in along the gouged-out log that conducted it from the side-hill spring. If there was giardiasis then, nobody warned us. And of course the beavers had not returned.)

And so we became woodsmen in time and lived to tell, as I am now.

Hunting, fishing, and mountain climbing were part of the experience.

There were boys like us all over the country, learning the hard way. We happened to be lucky in our countryside, the foothills of the White Mountains.

And also all over the country were mothers worrying about their sons who might be lost in the wilds.

My poor mother. After my father died, she had the sole responsibility for a difficult son. This son's penchant for lone walks and nature study seemed to her fairly normal. But strange were his urges to explore unknown wilderness, inexplicable, as was his association in such excursions with her sister's gardener's son who tended to be a wild one and eccentric.

I was never sure what Claud's parents thought of this peculiar passion of American youth. His father took a dim view of our wearing moccasins and imitating the walk of Indians. With resignation he drove us in the Model T to the borders of Orford's hinterland—resignation at least in my presence—then returned to his gardens and lawns and the greenhouse and rose beds. In his spare time he was reading all of Thomas Carlyle's works from my father's library.

Yes, my poor mother. Yet her ears never heard the really serious complications of our excursions, such as our getting lost several times.

Glory be, however, she could relax later that summer of 1929. I became the overjoyed member of a group aiming to climb Mount Washington. My father's friend, Dr. Speight, a professor at Dartmouth, asked me to go with him and his daughter, Ray, and her friend Doris Gilbert, both about my age.

Sometimes at Pinkham Notch Camp and the AMC's elaborate buildings I still feel that blend of ecstasy and excitement I felt at this opportunity, all of a sudden, to climb Mount Washington.

What was Mount Washington like in 1929? This is what it was like:

To get there I first waited for a small touring car with its top down to turn up the long driveway from Orford's "street." I paced the concrete walkway of our big white house and eyed my woefully inadequate knapsack and my blanket roll which I had wrapped in an old army poncho and tied with a rope at both ends to form a strap. Dr. Speight had told me to bring plenty of warm clothing and heavy socks. My blanket roll contained wool socks and a heavy wool sweater with a big collar. My mother had insisted on a change of underwear.

I wore long pants and a cotton shirt. Proudly on my feet I wore my leather woodsman's shoepacs, new that spring—moccasin-toed, leather soles. Nobody told me to bring a hat or gloves. Nor warned of the butterflies in my stomach.

I knew the mountains from summer tours and the places to see like the Old Man, the Flume, Lost River, and the vast set of peaks beyond the Mount Washington Hotel, where my father had announced, "Far enough. We must turn around and head for Orford."

At 35 miles an hour, that was a day's tour, up and back. I had never been through Crawford Notch.

But this was not to be an annual family picnic with parents and three older sisters. A climb up mighty Mount Washington! Could I make it? Suppose my strength failed, dashing my dream of becoming a mountain climber?

No more time for worry about outfit or strength. The touring car had appeared in the driveway. The two girls sat in back; I knew that I'd have trouble talking to them. Dr. Speight jumped out, all smiles and business as he took up my knapsack and said, "I've brought a larger one for you." He was a smallish man, neat and lithe, his fair hair thinning in front. His kindly manner relaxed me. My mother came out to kiss me good-bye.

As a break in the long drive to the AMC Pinkham Notch Camp, and to give us time to organize packs, Dr. Speight drove to a cabin in the Dartmouth Outing Club's chain—Agassiz Cabin, just off the Kinsman Notch Road west of North Woodstock.

The next day with packs ready early, we left North Woodstock and headed into Franconia Notch. The car labored up the steady grade. Trees joined over the narrow blacktop road, and I saw only a quick glimpse of the Old Man. Farther on, trees almost hid the cliffs of Crawford Notch. I did look up at a railroad trestle below the sheer rock face of Mount Willard. Snow sheds like long covered bridges protected the tracks. A large house appeared up there. Dr. Speight said it was a boarding house for track crews.

When we entered Pinkham Notch, where I noticed only three cars, woods again bordered the road closely, northern evergreen forest beyond a last steep, narrow pitch up Spruce Hill. Then a clearing and the AMC log cabins of Pinkham Notch Camp. My mountain loomed up huge and forbidding, but challenging. How would I attack it?

Dr. Speight parked in the row of three cars. I followed him and the girls into the cabin for lunch with the trail crew and their boss, Joe Dodge. Dr. Speight exchanged trail information with the other hikers. We ate beef stew and fresh-baked bread and canned peaches. I drank for the first time a mug of tea with the distinctive flavor of canned milk, a strange and delightful beverage (now nostalgic of many cabins and campfires). I heard the names of our trails for the afternoon, Old Jackson Road, Madison Gulf Trail, and the Great Gulf Trail.

There was initial surprise when I felt the weight of my pack and the bedroll looped over my shoulder. This eased on the Old Jackson Road, which was apparently long out of use for horses and wagons. Then the slope up to the crossing of the Carriage Road made me realize I was in for hard work and gasping breath. Madison Gulf Trail was a relief as it slabbed around a contour. But the downhill grade pushed my load into me. A footbridge took us over the West Branch of the Peabody River to the Great Gulf Trail.

The path became rougher. I was ready to rest at a look-off up the Great Gulf. I knew the Gulf had been named by Ethan Allen Crawford during his explorations of the mountain. I also knew from my reading that geologically it was a gouged-out glacial cirque from which the gnawing crunching ice of the Ice Age had melted maybe 10,000 years before. But I was not prepared for the vastness and the steepness of the headwall beyond whose rim rose the sky's blue dome, belittling me—a tired speck in a tremendous new world.

My main concern was that I would not get enough rest to keep up with the girls. And Dr. Speight was once again swinging up his loaded Trapper Nelson pack.

Descending to brook crossings, I learned that trout fishing had not prepared me for negotiating stream-bed rocks with a pack and bedroll. The trail became a tortuous way among roots and boulders. Evergreens hung close in places. My shoulders ached. The bedroll chafed the back of my neck. Occasional little white AMC signs notified us that we were into a section of the Gulf where trails led up to the Carriage Road and to Mount Jefferson. And Dr. Speight and I had to stop and help the girls over a ledge and across a stream. But they were game and laughed about muddy sneakers and legs.

Suddenly I felt good, strong and ready for more real mountain trail. Yet such climbing demanded more than a spurt of energy. Where was the shelter? A sharp-edged can had shifted in my pack and the corner dug into my back. My legs were columns of water. My breath came in gasps.

At one rest stop for another stream crossing, I noticed a large pool down at the main West Branch. It must have trout in it. I'd have to come here with Claud and fish it.

Not far beyond the pool there loomed a heap of rocks. I was bent over so far under the pack that I peered up and over the rocks at logs laid up on top of each other to form a gable end of what?

The Great Gulf Shelter was more like a cabin than the open-front shelter of my Scout trip to Mount Cube. The bottom logs were monsters; the gable end covered a porch and a wide door into the dark interior. Not a soul was in sight. This did not seem strange. I had arrived at the remotest place in the mountains. I had done it.

The pile of stones, I realized, was the fireplace. And I knew how to find wood and how to build a cooking fire. I told Dr. Speight I could, I would. Water? Right down there a few yards in the West Branch—pure mountain water. The girls were going inside to explore accommodations. I saw the end of a low, bough-filled bunk, fir boughs held in by a long log. I shed my bedroll and pack. The relief of arriving gave way to more sensations of joy at having done it, yes, having conquered that horrendous two miles from the Madison Gulf Trail, which had seemed like 10 miles of scrambling, panting. Would I feel so wonderful in the morning? Up the headwall, Dr. Speight had said. I went about gathering firewood.

And that night in the log cave, on the fragrant boughs, I listened to the wind outside and I was snug in a mountain fastness and knew the feeling that went with the strange word: fastness. Peaks out there in the darkness. Mount Washington, Jefferson, Adams, Madison.

In the morning, a glow of light outside the doorway. Up betimes, firebuilder, never mind the complaining muscles, I had the wings of a bird. I went out in my untied boots. As I smelled the ashy pungency of the fireplace, I looked up and above the mist of the Great Gulf. I saw the future of this big day, blue sky and sunlight.

The term "headwall" was a challenge, and during breakfast of buttered toast, tea with evaporated milk and heavy on the sugar, then oatmeal, and bacon and eggs, the talk was of this most difficult route up Mount Washington. I thought: "Let's pack and get at it."

We were to travel light, mutual rucksack, jackets, sweaters, canteens, and lunch. I conceived the urge to be able to say, "I carried a pack up the headwall of the Great Gulf." Dr. Speight humored me with a smile and a nod. I shouldered the pack, hoping to impress the girls.

The trail soon became a twisting way between boulders, past waterfalls, sparse spruce trunks, past tiny Spaulding Lake in mist, then the headwall. And easy, though the trail was obscure among the loose stones and alpine turf. Paint blazes were rare, but the way was upward so why worry. The rim up there would come closer if I didn't look. I declined offers to take the pack. I felt strong enough for anything.

At last I was up there in the vast openness of the treeless summit rocks, and even though the appearance of other hikers, the railroad tracks, the automobiles, and the summit buildings were a letdown after the wilderness of the Great Gulf, I had done it.

Rest in the hotel over lunch. People in clothes that marked them as tourists from the cog railway and automobiles. I looked down my nose contemptuously. Them and their tipped-boiler choo-choo, them and their internal combustion engines, no true knowledge of Washington. Not contempt due them, but pity.

The distances everywhere, and the wind, and clouds over the sun.

Dr. Speight said, "Eat up; if we hurry maybe we'll beat a spell of bad weather."

Jackets out of the pack. I pulled on the big old heavy sweater. Outside I turned up the high collar as the rain came at us in sudden driving sheets. No time to go back and wait it out. Possibly this was not just a shower.

The joy of resisting the elements, leaning into the wind, hurrying down the Carriage Road, face and hair streaming water, but oh, the glory of it! The Wamsutta Trail off the road dropped away over rocks and ledges, more a rocky ditch between drenched slabs than a trail. Rain-swept cairns marked the route, but only once did a break in the clouds show the misty depths into which I scrambled, thighs aching.

Respite from driving wind and rain came soon after the scrub appeared and evergreens began to protect us. The descent lessened, yet sometimes I grabbed branches to keep my feet from sliding me into a sit-down in mud.

Shelter not far. I could smell smoke. Our lone occupance of the shelter was gone, but the family there had started a fire, which they offered along with a pot of hot water while everyone huddled in the overhang and got warm. I was weak from hunger.

Back home by the same trails, same roads, same overnight break at Agassiz Cabin.

My reaction was: MORE. I planned to go again next summer with Claud.

And we did. Ah, the delicious adventure, age 16, and our drivers' licenses, and the Model T. Or sometimes my mother's Model A coupe.

We explored Washington and the Northern Presidentials from a base at Great Gulf Shelter. We learned how rapidly mountain streams rise after a cloudburst. We soon discovered trout in the West Branch of Peabody River right at the shelter.

We had conquered the biggest of the Whites (nobody called them "the Whites" then), and we wanted to graduate from trails to trackless country. By 1931 we figured we were experienced enough to explore the forests of eastern Orford, which joined those of the townships to the east, Wentworth and Dorchester.

The appeal came from views off Smarts Mountain and from Eastman Ledges in Quinttown. The ocean of treetops required a closer acquaintance. It was a call, especially to find some of the ponds appearing there.

The use of a compass could be learned in a class somewhere, presumably, maybe. For us experience was necessary. I had a large brass Army Engineering compass given to me by a friend of the family.

We took notes from a wall map in the attic of my folks' barn. Grafton County, vintage 1860. Very accurate as to town streets and houses, but dreamy as to hinterland. Topographical maps of the area — our wilderness — were just being surveyed. White flags atop hills and mountains, and USGS pickup trucks and survey crews appeared in Quinttown and the other necessary elevations.

In 1931 there remained a dilapidated spruce-pole tower on the east peak of Smarts Mountain. After a death-defying scramble up the tower we took a compass bearing on one of the ponds — blue water set in the green leaves of hardwood trees. We hoped it was the Rocky Pond of the wall map. Our packs contained food and equipment for three days.

We shouldered our loads at the base of the tower and plunged down into the small spruces, trying to keep on our bearing. Before long we walked into open aisles of magnificent leafy trees spreading from massive trunks. They were yellow birch, beech, and maple, with some fine white birch. I estimated the height at 80 feet.

Walking and holding our bearing became easy. Besides, the forest floor slanted steadily downhill. The open glades and the size of the trees gave us an exciting sense of progress. We were not attached to a trail.

This was the freedom of the backpacker with the added thrill of unknown, unmarked, pure vastness ahead! I had read of woods travel such as this and recalled Horace Kephart's accounts in his *Camping and Woodcraft*. In 1931 you could feel that the frontier was not so far back in history. Woodcraft was a recognized set of skills.

Our campfire that night burned clear. Hardwood twigs, dead but on the trees, were everywhere. The flames, almost smokeless, gave us a circle of light down among the great trees.

We had only the vaguest notion of where we were. Freed from our known worlds, we reveled in our independence.

White-footed deer mice crept rustling out of the leaves on the forest floor. Big ears, long hind legs made for leaping. They hopped about in the firelight, investigated the cooking pots full of spring water, and skittered across our blankets, paying us no attention. But they were our companions for the night; keeping them from our grub led us to the decision we should sleep with it in the triangular open-front Forester's tent.

The next morning our compass bearing took us to, instead of a pond, a small hill where we found a climbable pine tree. No pond visible. The position of Mount Cube and Smarts Mountain enabled us to identify a depression in the spread of trees that must be Lamprey Pond. We were on Black Hill.

So we gave up on Rocky Pond and took a bearing on where Lamprey Pond must be. Continued on Black Hill, if it was Black Hill, and entered the hellish logging slash of several years past. Only veneer logs had been taken out, leaving a jungle of tops. Then we fought a spruce swamp.

That night we camped beside an unknown trickle of water in low land surrounded by evergreens. The water was ice-cold and clear.

The next day the trickle seemed more reliable than our compass bearing. We followed it to its junction with the north branch of Jacobs Brook. That last night we spent on Lamprey Pond and planned more excursions into the wilds.

I describe these adventures because their essence was wildness. The White Mountains themselves, not just the southern foothills, partook of this same wildness. Despite the slash and burns in the acquired lands that formed the White Mountain National Forest, or much of it, you felt you were in an unpopulated wilderness. It may have been a state of mind, but you hiked as an explorer, even on the trails. In the thirties you might stay on the trails for a week and see only two or three hikers. Claud and I stayed four days at Isolation Shelter in 1931 and saw only one man, a hiker of the Davis Path, admittedly not a popular path. Remember: no chain saws, no bulldozers, no fast cars and super federal highways. And only about 120 million residents of the United States.

Furthermore, in the White Mountains of New Hampshire — I cannot speak of other areas — hiking was a recreation of the elite during the first three decades of the twentieth century. This began during the era of the grand hotels back in the late nineteenth century. I watched the decline of the railroad visitors, the switch to automobiles, the end of the big hotels whose closing and demolition and fires concluded with the final blow to a hotel way of life — namely World War II. (Some of the hotel fires perhaps came from a phenomenon that Joe Dodge described as spontaneous combustion caused by the friction between mortgages and insurance policies.) Be that as it may, aside from a few outstanding local guides and mountain lovers, the hikers came from the upper social strata, hence the trails were never overcrowded.

Then there were Claud and me, boys from the woods.

The Appalachian Mountain Club was indeed a club. I might say a Boston club. You had to have two sponsors to become a member. More correctly as a club, call it a Beacon Hill club. Harvard graduates seemed to perpetuate it, at least as viewed by a Dartmouth man.

I sometimes think, looking back, that returned GIs began to popularize the mountains in 1946. Claud and I (civilians both), fishing for trout in the Hancock Branch of the Pemigewasset River's East Branch, happened across three of Claud's brothers. They were just helling around the mountains, camping out and fishing in their new freedom.

An elemental disaster before the man-made disaster of World War II, the hurricane of September 1938, put an end for me to the era of the thirties in the White Mountains. Entire mountainsides were laid low. The Forest Service closed areas of excessive damage for a number of years until fire hazard became mitigated by decay.

My first startling sight of damage came as I drove from Laconia to Orford on a visit to my mother. Driving my pickup truck past Lower Baker Pond and up the hill to the west, I saw the slope of Mount Cube come into view. Mostly clad in well-grown trees of spruce and fir, the mountainside looked as though Paul Bunyan had stroked the trees with his comb, flattening them from southeast to northwest.

But to return to that summer of 1929 when Claud and I began camping out. Those adventures led to many more in following summers; memories from these excursions will appear in the story of our last backpack.

The footloose, irresponsible, and lucky years ended in 1934, when we both had summer jobs after our sophomore years in college, Claud at the University of New Hampshire, I at Dartmouth. Claud was hired by Joe Dodge to work as assistant hutman at Galehead Hut. I became a brush cutter for the General Land Office surveying in Wisconsin.

In the 1940s, by coincidence we both were living with our wives and children in or near Laconia, a city close enough to the White Mountains to be a jumping-off place. Our adventures resumed. We had never explored the Mahoosucs, which is why we finally went in 1966.

DAY ONE: AUGUST 31, 1966

THE TAKEOFF

I THOUGHT, "AMONG VARIED BEGINNINGS FOR EXCURSIONS WITH Claud, this of the Mahoosucs must be the most oddly disorganized."

We were faced with an unexpected brick powerhouse. A sign on the wall notified us in threatening letters:

Trespassers Will Be Prosecuted

I am timid when even unknowingly I might trespass, or when I'm in the presence of any authority. Reminded by the stench of rotten eggs in the air that we were downwind from the Berlin paper mills, I assumed the Brown Company meant what their sign predicted. The powerhouse belonged to them, and also its dam across the Androscoggin River, or so I assumed.

I stopped walking along the dirt road. Claud and I had followed it from the railroad bridge over Route 16. He kept on toward a wide door in the powerhouse that was opened to let out a humming roar into the warm breezes of August 31, 1966.

He kept slouching along with his bent-knee stride. He was clumping in his rubber-bottomed, leather-topped hunting boots. They were his preferred footwear for the woods and mountains, winter or summer. I considered calling his attention to the sign. But 46 years of friendship since age six told me he had seen it.

We were both carrying our Duluth packsacks filled with enough food and equipment to live for seven days in the wild, 30-mile Mahoosuc Range, whose unknown peaks rose to the east of us. A Duluth packsack is a canvas bag, 24 inches by 24 inches, with shoulder straps. The flap of a cover continuing the canvas from the shoulder straps could accommodate more than the approximately 60 pounds that the design easily held. Three long straps to buckles secured the flap at various adjustments. Similar packsacks with tumplines for head and neck assistance burdened French-Canadian voyageurs stumbling over portages beyond Lake Superior. I had not dared weigh mine, but estimated it at 40 pounds, which hefted like 60.

Our packs were not part of this excursion's oddity. We had been carrying such packs since our teens, when Sears Roebuck sold them for about $2. Little did we foresee that in 1966 we would be introduced to an entirely different system of packs, food, and equipment for camping out. I suppose we were anachronisms. For instance, I didn't know that our mountains and woods were being called not a known term such as "backwoods" or "timberland" but "the back country." We were not "into" modernized "backpacking gear"; indeed we had a tendency to look down our noses at frames of aluminum piping, if we occasionally noticed them.

Our recent arrival at the parking spot under black girders of a railroad bridge had been by transportation very different from the Model T Ford in which we first traveled to the backwoods of Orford or to the White Mountains. And before this Ford of Claud's father, boots took us camping.

In 1966 we rode in Claud's diesel Mercedes. This vehicle contained Claud at the wheel, his wife, Louise, beside him, and in the back seat with me, their youngest two children (of seven) who were Eddy, 11, and Elly, 8.

As Claud stopped the car, I leaped out. Eddy and Elly had been arguing, fooling, and wrastling all the 80 miles from Laconia as we passed through Meredith, Tamworth, Conway, Pinkham Notch, and Gorham. They popped out the other door. At once they saw the wooden walkway under the bridge and scampered up the ramp leading to this unofficial start of the Mahoosuc Trail.

Louise, calmly as usual, stepped out of the front seat to control them. Claud emerged from behind the wheel. He paid no attention to his wife and kids. They were not to accompany us on the excursion. He leaned into the car for his pipe, then turned to me with a half-smile and said, "Can't put it off any longer." This was his contrary way of expressing eagerness to reach the freedom of the woods.

I started to reply but a pulp truck roared by on the four-lane highway leading to Berlin (pronounced BERlin) and the paper mills. Anyhow, what was to be said? The suddenness of this flight for him from veterinary practice (although the Mahoosucs trip must have been in preparation, ordering food and all, for some time) and sudden for me from writing a history of New Hampshire's Indian Stream Republic, this abruptness, I say, left only my urgent desire to get on with it. He had instigated it; I faced it with serious doubts relating to my physical ability. We had been hiking that summer, ascending some moderately difficult mountains, but my enthusiasm, I realized, far outstripped my physical ability, which two years of late-onset diabetes and diet had reduced. Well, never mind that. For me the Mahoosucs were now or never.

The day before I had found myself quickly involved in this caper. My mind far from any prospect of camping out in the mountains, I arrived home from a visit to my 91-year-old mother at a nursing home in Haverhill, about 70 miles from our cottage in Sanbornton. I stopped my Jeep beside the little white Volvo that Ernestine (hereinafter Ernie) had returned in from her secretarial job at a Laconia law office. She and our older daughter, Ruthie, and husband, Don, were seated in lawn chairs around a table with glasses, sharing a quart of ale. The clearing in the woods, the garden, the happy family scene, the white cottage, were very peaceful.

After greetings and a swallow of ale I learned from Ernie that Claud wanted me to call him. She added, "He's going to the Mahoosuc Range. Where's that? He spoke as though I ought to know so I didn't admit my ignorance."

"Well, it's a remote line of mountains that start north of Mount Washington and stretch over into Maine."

"All new to you both, I gathered."

"Yes."

"He's leaving tomorrow." She smiled. "Guess what? He has enough of what he called grub—"

"I know."

"To last a week for both of you."

"Can I go?"

"Of course you can go."

I began adjusting my plans to my inclinations. Of course I must get on with my book. I had quit work for pay a year ago, but, but...just a week...I could mull over my notes and method of presenting the last half of the manuscript to the editor at Rutgers University Press....

Ruthie picked up her banjo and strummed a tune like Pete Seeger. Don rattled his newspaper. Doans never offered opinions on problems of relatives—well, not often. Recently returned from two years in England, they were looking for a place to live and a teaching job for Don—in English classes. Ruthie was a novelist. She strummed and hummed, "Poor Wayfaring Stranger."

Don said, "Here's an apartment for rent on Gale Avenue. I think the number must be that big white house."

They both had been born and raised in Laconia.

I went into the cottage and took the phone off its hook over the kitchen counter. I listened to 10 or 11 rings before Claud's voice growled, "Herllow!" The tone meant that he'd had enough calls about ailing animals. I also easily deduced that he was primed for release into the wilds. I said, "It's me."

"Oh. I was afraid it was more business. Well, you know I've been thinking lately about age. We aren't getting any younger, and I'm all set for the Mahoosucs. Everything here is buttoned up. I'm leaving tomorrow first thing in the morning. For a week. Louise says she'll take over what's left of the dog and cat boarders, remove the stitches in two, stall off more trouble. You better come along. Real wild country. I've heard of it ever since I worked at Galehead Hut. It'll be a different world from the other mountains."

He began his slow itemizing of the attractions. Five shelters, no need to lug a tent. Probably birds I'd never seen before. Nobody to bother us, off the beaten track of the Presidentials. Probably see a lot of game. Had plenty of lightweight grub. All I needed was my stuff and our cooking kit, the ax....

Came a pause in his steady persuasiveness. I knew that if I declined he would go alone, and I'd never share the adventure.

He said, "First thing tomorrow."

Past experience told me we'd not leave first thing; I didn't say anything except, "All right."

The next morning after Ernie delivered me and my pack to the farmhouse-office-operating room, where Claud and Louise and the kids lived two miles from us, she drove off to her job. There was a delay. We should not have paused to review the grub and divide it. Transportation had been arranged the night before, he to drive up, Ruthie and Don to meet us in Grafton Notch, Maine, on Labor Day, September 5, in the white Volvo.

The delay was a collie who chased cars and had consequently damaged a paw, which Claud splinted and taped. He said to the woman, "When this silly dog is well again, you ought to put a long rope on him, and let him chase and get dumped a few times."

She protested, "I couldn't. That's cruel."

Claud wanted to get away and said only, "I suppose it is."

Then we got away in the Mercedes.

We had a much shorter delay at the parking spot under the bridge and beside Route 16 in Gorham. I noted that we were north of the Presidentials all right. There, looming to the south rose the barren peaks of Mount Madison and Mount Adams.

Claud moved briskly, for him, to the trunk of the car and raised the lid. He extracted our packs and placed them on the ground. This left inside a collection of veterinary instruments of a design to control and doctor horses, cattle, and pigs. Also left were two beat-up leather bags, rubber tubes, canvas slings, gloves, boots, and a set of bottles filled with nasty-looking fluids. One item only interested him at this time—a rectangular cloth bag, which he held up. "How about this reflector oven?"

"I couldn't say. Never saw it before. Where'd you get it?"

"Same place I got the grub. What do you think?"

"The question is, how much does it weigh?"

"Not much. I ought to lug this. You've got the pots and frying pan, and your Hudson Bay ax."

"But you've taken more than your share of the grub. We used to bake frying pan bread."

"Burned on the outside and soggy inside. My gut couldn't stand it now."

He bent to unbuckle the three leather straps on his pack's cover. "I'll tuck it in here. Baking powder biscuits will go damn good. The grub is mostly messes like dried soups and stews, chili, spaghetti and sauce. Could get hellish monotonous in six or seven days."

I said, "Hope you know how to run it."

"Directions in the bag, same with the Chuckwagon grub. Meant for goofers. We'll handle everything easy. Loaf around the shelters after the day's hike and bake biscuits. I aim to enjoy this trip. Also corn bread for your benefit."

He didn't think much of corn bread. I had to say thank you: "Hot biscuits and corn bread. Real luxury."

We shouldered the packs. I noted that a pack always feels heavier at first than it does hefting it. Just need to get used to it.

Louise was watching us. She moved toward the car. "I hope you boys have a fine trip."

Claud kissed her good-bye.

During the two-hour drive north, I had heard them occasionally mention all the responsibilities that Louise was taking over. No evidence of problems; she did it often. She also figured their income tax.

He asked her, "You going to be all right?"

"I'll answer the phone and say, 'Doctor Sharps is on vacation.'" Her soft, low voice added, "It'll be a vacation for me, too. See you next week." She got in the car. Eddy and Elly were arguing about who would sit in the front seat. Louise settled the dispute. "Both of you in back." She drove away. The kids waved from windows.

I said to Claud, "Let's head for the hills. This place depresses me."

"Nothing stopping us now." He turned toward the wooden ramp and walkway under the bridge.

And as I have said, the powerhouse didn't stop him. He continued his steady approach to the brick walls. Beyond this obstacle lay the woods that were his natural habitat. Irrelevantly I thought of the remark made by a man who had for the first time hunted deer with him: "Doc doesn't walk through the woods. He flows."

He flowed into the dark, noisy doorway. I followed him onto the concrete floor. Encased in the silence of absolute noise, we moved past the black humps of dynamos.

An old watchman at a desk turned and regarded us with raised eyebrows. Claud touched a hand to his battered, gray hat. I did the same to my droopy green felt. The watchman nodded to us and grinned. We may have looked to him like woodsmen out of his youth.

The vast room with its monster humming ended at another wide door. We stepped into sunshine. Birds flitted through small birches and poplars. I got a glimpse of yellow feathers—must be myrtle warblers heading south for the winter. Damn silly to call them nowadays "yellow-rumped warblers."

Claud turned left onto the little-used road along the dark water held back by the dam. The emptiness in my ears was at last silence. I began looking for a trail sign. Claud, too, for he stopped and waited before he said, "I'm lost. Ain't no trail here."

I took from my shirt pocket a leaflet of pages 6 inches by 3-1/2 inches. They were #332 to #355 cut from my 1963 *AMC White Mountain Guide*. I had stapled on a cover of white typing paper. This little chore of the previous evening saved the weight of the *Guide* itself in its orange binding. One page folded out into a small map, "#8 Mahoosuc 1963"—bless the AMC.

I thumbed the pages, proud of my only organized addition to this crazy excursion. Claud watched me, then commented, "Good you brought that. The *Guide* I bought at Pinkham an hour ago I left in the car. Too heavy."

"I was never a Boy Scout but I like to be prepared. Let's see…here it is. Ha! Says we should have crossed through the upper level of the powerhouse. No wonder the old guy looked surprised. Well, at the east end of the dam we should follow an old road north 100 yards, then turn right uphill."

Claud looked back. "Are we as far from the powerhouse as my rifle range?"

I visualized the distance from his shooting hut—an old ice-fishing bobhouse trucked up into his pine woods—to the target against a bank. I said, "Nope."

We walked on and soon came to a small white AMC sign on a tree.

Uphill from it was the Mahoosuc Trail, a footpath.

Another sign on a board told us that Trident Shelter had been discontinued "due to lack of proper use."

We had intended to spend the night in Trident Shelter. Counting on Trident and four other open-front shelters, we had no tent. As the optimist, I said, "Maybe tonight will be clear without rain."

"Those clouds coming in from the west look bad." He read the sign again. "'Lack of proper use'!" He shook his head. "What kind of shit is that? I don't know about the AMC nowadays. How do you discontinue a shelter? Burn it down? And why not say so? Sounds like some damned nonsense of the Boston Appies who used to drive Joe Dodge ape. And those bloody clouds over there."

I had always figured that his Welsh father had contributed "bloody" to his vocabulary, or perhaps his London-raised mother, even though his parents never used such words in front of me. I now said, about the "bloody" clouds, "They're fair weather cumulus."

"I hope you're right. We'll find out."

The trail led under a power line as a worn track among raspberry bushes. The tower and cables were to be the last evidence of industrial civilization—well, except for the stench of the mills.

We left behind the power line by climbing up into a growth of young birches and poplars. Because we had not stopped on the road or at the parking spot to eat lunch, hunger now set in. There, south of Berlin's belching mill stacks and rows of little houses built into the sides of the steep valley and hills, where the gorge and the river had provided power to make paper from the spruce forests, we chomped crackers and chocolate which were flavored with the gag-a-maggot breeze from the mills. This atmosphere we would live with for two days. Although we hiked east of Berlin, we were assailed by the smell again as the wind changed to the east from the first day's northwest and brought the foul air up from the polluted Androscoggin at Shelburne and below, or so we guessed. The open sewer for Berlin made a right-angle turn at Gorham. Our wilderness jutted into the bend with Mount Hayes.

Shortly beyond our lunch spot the trail bore left at a fork where a sign pointed ahead toward Mascot Pond. Feeling refreshed and vigorous, we decided to miss nothing on this trip. We left our packs and walked the tenth of a mile to the little pond under cliffs. Beavers had dammed the outlet and flooded woods where trees had died to stubs. We returned to our packs without exploring for the old lead mine reputed to be above the pond. Claud would have, whereas I was getting worried about the two mountains ahead before we could camp at the spring in Trident Col near the discontinued shelter. We would have to miss *some* things.

We passed a young man and a young woman walking up to see the pond and maybe the old lead mine. Sightseeing, I thought, was only one of their incentives. They were the last people that we saw in 14 miles of trail and 48 hours.

My pack felt a bit heavier as I shouldered it. We began following the trail along a little brook cascading over stones. There were frequent crossings, and a steepness on Mount Hayes that explained the cliffs above Mascot Pond. I began to stop frequently and to puff continually. Claud also moved more slowly. We told ourselves that a real rest awaited us up at Popsy Spring, the last water before Trident Col.

By the time we reached the little pool in the woods, and the source of the brook we had been following, we discovered that certain of our careless (confused?) calculations on distance and time were being laid low by simple failure of lungs and legs. Ah yes, packs for seven days make a difference. We shucked them.

Claud sat on a rock and loaded his pipe with Velvet tobacco. I looked at the pages of the *Guide* to learn how far we had come, and read aloud, "'Two-and-a-half miles.'" Claud struck a match with his thumbnail. He waited for the flare to burn into the wood, cupping it in his hands against the breeze. He applied the fire to the tobacco and said out of smoke puffs, "Damned steep little mountain,"

"Let's see," I went on with the calculation of remaining distance. The AMC distances were in a cumulative table after the trail descriptions. "JeeSUSS! We got three-point-nine miles to go to Trident Col." I went back to the text. "Yup, it says we're only two-and-a-half miles from the railroad bridge. It says the summit of Hayes is soon after this spring. I quote: 'The views and blueberries are excellent.' It's two thousand five hundred and sixty-six feet."

"We better get at it."

"Once we're on Mount Hayes the rest ought to be easy. We'll be on top of the ridge."

We got into our packs and trudged on. The evergreens surrounded us. The trail became a corridor leading onto bare ledges. The views were indeed excellent, away to the stark rock triangles of the Presidentials. The blueberries were mostly gone by.

Claud unslung his pack and took out the little camera that Louise had loaned him. He said, "Some lighter than our old Kodak one-six-teens." As boys we had each lugged a Kodak because we could never agree on what pictures to take.

He had me pose with the pack, Mount Washington for background.

Standing there I realized that the sun was lowering into the west. We had spent most of the afternoon—over four hours—to climb about three miles. Never mind, the view was magnificent. The effect was to lift my spirit in the way that requires a weary body for appreciation.

We turned back from the ledges to the trail, ready and eager to hike along this high ridge, up and over the top of Cascade Mountain with ease, and down to the spring near the site of the improperly used shelter. Surely the important—yes, necessary—water would still be there, and we could camp under the trees.

This hopeful dream arose from ignorance and the disorganized take-off of the trip. Neither of us had studied closely the contour lines of the small but accurate AMC map.

Claud led off through the twisted spruces and blueberry bushes. He paused to sample the few remaining berries—he never could resist lingering on a trail to pick a handful. The habit annoyed me. I thought it a waste of hiking time. Now the berries were so shriveled that he didn't stop again.

I followed him. Having surmounted our first challenge, I savored confidence that I'd hike the remaining miles with happy pleasure. The feeling lasted about five minutes.

I noticed the trail becoming indistinct on bedrock. No cairns or paint marks. Little gravelly traces might be paths, although they branched every which way. Claud stopped.

My guess was that he wanted my opinion on where to go. He dreaded making mistakes. I had no opinion, so I took out my *Guide* pages. They told us only that the trail passed over the flat summit of Mount Hayes and descended—yikes!—to the col before Cascade Mountain. I suddenly became terribly weary. A debilitating uncertainty destroyed my recent confidence. I was a pricked balloon.

At times like this I relied on him for help and strength of will. He had followed mountain trails for hundreds of miles. He had made his way through trackless woods for probably more than that distance, mostly alone. Yes, alone, and when he was alone he could decide direction for himself easily enough. Very contradictory reaction. I unfolded the little map and held my compass over it, adjusting the orientation. He waited till I said, "Cascade Mountain looks to me about ten degrees east of north." I didn't mention contour lines that indicated we must descend 600 feet before Cascade...and Trident Col on the far side, down deep.

He stepped closer to study the map and compass. There came with him a faint smell of disinfectant or medicine, of sweaty shirt, of tobacco, and of tiredness. He nodded and strode off in the direction we knew we were agreed upon.

Almost at once we came to a definite path, or trail if it were our route, which began to dip down and down. And then down steeply. And down. Scrub spruces changed to trees of lower elevations—beech, birch, maple, and an undergrowth of moosewood and hobblebush. I looked ahead, and my eyes focused on a solid mass where the trees thinned out. I could see gray ledges through the yellowing birch leaves. A high obstacle. Cascade Mountain. The heart went out of me. Maybe Claud's for him, because I heard him say, "It takes the starch right out of me."

Our careless assumption that a ridge extended from Mount Hayes to Cascade Mountain had caught us in an error we knew enough to avoid. Like many ridges between peaks, this one included a col, otherwise known as a notch, sag, pass, or gap. We were in it, utterly weary, and with darkness coming on. Here must be our camp for the night. We were done in. We realized this mutually without talk, not even about where we'd get our water.

As a campsite, the thick woods and the felled tops of huge yellow birches whose trunks had been hauled out for veneer, offered no inducement to camp. I remembered mention of water in the *Guide* pages. But were we on the trail described? There was a muddy, bulldozed "road," and slash from logging. Evidently by the noise to the north we had descended halfway to Berlin. The roaring mills came as a constant undertone to the stench they made. What a campsite for our first night in the wilds.

Claud dumped his pack and bent over several wedge-shaped gouges in the trail—moose tracks larger than those of a big Holstein cow. We had first known the mountains when moose were animals you might see if you went to Canada. For us their fascination lingered. We recalled seeing our first moose tracks on a huge rotten log beside Sawyer Pond in 1946.

Claud the tracker began now following these along the trail.

I dropped my pack and stepped along after him, enjoying more than anything the delicious lightness without my load. I could step over the moon, if it rose.

The tracks had been impressed into a lush green bed of sphagnum moss. They contained no water, which meant, because such moss is almost always wet, that the moose had recently made them. Claud kept on for the chance of seeing the maker. So did I. As deer hunters we noted that the wind was right—in our faces.

The tracks did not take all my attention as they did Claud's. The lack of water in them might mean that the moss contained none. Supposing we had to rely for water on squeezing sphagnum moss over a pan? Maybe this possible source had dried up. I cared more about water than about seeing the moose. I turned back to my pack for the *Guide* pages and, a requirement in the dim light, my glasses.

Yes. I read the words again, and carefully: "Water will be found on the trail or a few rods to the east."

I pushed off the trail into a tangle of hobblebushes. Shoving free of them, I came to a pool of clear water. I was so relieved and overjoyed that I could pause and admire the red berries of the hobblebushes, which I had been too anxious to notice, and I could recall how lovely in May the flowers, those wide, flat white blossoms, here, high in the north mountains, probably blooming in June....

Now with water for thirst, for cooking, and for tea, we needed only space in the tangle to spread out our sleeping bags. Maybe we could uproot some bushes.

Claud plowed toward me through the waist-high hobblebushes. "That moose must have been just ahead of us. His tracks got water in 'em now."

"And we got water here."

"No place for a fire. I'm not in the mood for pulling bushes."

"Neither am I." Though I could have, I realized, and my shorty air mattress would protect my tricky spine and hip from the hollows and lumps left by uprooting. Claud had not brought one. Anyhow, a hell of a job, plus digging out a fire-clearing in the duff down to mineral soil.

He said, "I've found where the trail comes out of this sag and slash. You may not think much of it but there's clear ground and a rock to build the fire on. Plenty of dry wood, mostly dead maple saplings and moosewood, and some balsam boughs for me to bed down on."

The place turned out to be just right for our camp.

We went about settling for the night easily enough because of long practice together. Water was my job; Claud's, the fire. I walked back to the pool with a cup and the fire-blacked pots. The larger held thirteen cups; the smaller, eight cups. One was a former oyster can, the other a lard pail. The bails were wires twisted together at punched holes, because the original soldered tabs for the bails had melted off. Old and battered cans they were, but lightweight. In addition to these "pots" we had an aluminum coffeepot with regulation bail and folding wire handle opposite the snub-nosed pouring spout. This relic was a hand-me-down from Ernie's Aunt Dot, whose husband had been a camper. Also it resembled the pot that Claud and I had started with, from a kit I bought out of the 1928 catalog of David T. Abercrombie. Galvanizing burned off, it began to produce rusty tea tasting of iron. We called this type of utensil a tea-kettle, as often as coffeepot.

So I was feeling sentimental and very peaceful as I squatted in the moss by the pool and cupped water without disturbing the bottom. A white-throated sparrow gave part of his descending notes, authenticating to me late summer and migration.

Back at our packs, spilling water from trying to carry at once the three pots, I discovered that the woods had become a camp. Beside a flat rock Claud knelt and arranged on it strips of curly birch bark and dead spruce twigs. From a pile of maple limbs chopped and split, and some beech, he selected sticks for a little teepee over the tinder and kindling. A match flared on the rock and fired the birch bark into oily smoke. This soon cleared, the acrid yet pleasant aroma faded, and crackling flames licked up the bundle of spruce twigs. A little breeze urged the fire into the stick teepee. Bright flames began to open the dim glade. It became our home for the night.

Claud set about arranging rocks around the fire to aim the heat toward the reflector oven, which lay flat on its cloth bag with a paper of directions and a diagram for assembly.

In a surprisingly short time these rectangles of aluminum took the shape of a flared bread box without a cover and tipped on its side. I refrained from getting involved. Only once did Claud have to light his pipe and study the diagram.

To be more descriptive of the oven I should say that the sides angled out, the top slanted up, and the bottom down. When the oven rested on its bare legs facing a fire, the shiny surfaces would reflect heat inside to bake the biscuits on a pan supported midway by a rack. Obviously.

Less obvious was the distance required from the fire. We discussed this while Claud mixed water and flour into the biscuit dough, using a package of Chuckwagon ingredients. Quick heat for the rising was the decision. Close to the fire, that is, then move the oven back till the biscuits were slightly browned.

That evening we ate hamburgers—our only fresh meat—with the biscuits and butter from a plastic jar. Macaroni in cheese sauce from another package filled out the meal. We drank tea with powdered milk and sugar—sparingly of sugar for me, two teaspoons for Claud—and smoked our pipes.

Darkness came. Claud laid wood on the coals. I felt stingy about those sticks. I had gathered and chopped them. I planned to save them for morning by covering them with my red rain shirt if we should be rained on. I hate wet wood on a rainy morning. But Claud needed a large fire in the evening or he didn't feel he was camping out.

Never mind the wood. The moon rose behind the trees, yellow and big as a dishpan. No rain due. I gave up worrying about the prodigal use of wood. Come morning he'd bring in more.

All was peaceful. Even the dull roar of the mills faded—if not the stink. Then someone blew a dinner horn, up near the top of Cascade Mountain, like this, OOOOOOWN-AHHHNH, tapering off nasally. No dinner horn up there. This lonely, wild, and haunting sound had to be our moose. Never heard one, but I knew it at once.

The thought of a dinner horn came as the first flash of identification because once upon a time Ernie had sounded one to bring me from the woods for lunch when I was chopping down pines for the frame of our henhouse in Orford. For such a little person she managed a rousing blast. That was in 1937. I wondered if now after 29 years she could raise echoes with the long tin tube. We had both dwindled in strength; I knew that I was incapable of hewing more than one pine log for a timber, let alone 60.

I soon learned that my lung pressure wasn't up to much either. I had to take my time blowing up my hip-length mattress.

I sat on a fallen log and blew out deep breaths into the nozzle. Luckily for me an air mattress is softer if not fully inflated. I laid it beside the log and placed on it my old sleeping bag. In 1947 I had bought the bag from the L.L. Bean catalog for $13. It was a surplus, restored by stitches and patches, an inner bag, duck feathers mostly, mummy shape, with a partial zipper, and an outer cover. Maybe it once flew with the Air Force planes, though I'm not sure why I think so.

I took off my boots and pants before I crawled feet first into the bag. The word "crawled" is inaccurate. First I opened the zipper to its terminus midway down the bag, then slid my feet inside (having changed to clean, dry socks), and then scrunched my butt inside, collapsing on my right side, pulling up the zipper by its thong—a strong old metal zipper with large teeth. Because I felt locked-in with the zipper way up to my chin, I left it partly open, relying on the hood and curved form over my shoulders to keep me warm.

This was real comfort.

I sleep on my right side. I faced the fire, log at my back. I could see Claud drinking his last cup of tea, which he had poured from the pot. It must have been cool, strong and bitter, even with plenty of sugar and dried milk. We talked once more about what had happened to the dried whole milk called Klim when we were boys. This was one of our perennial topics. I felt too tired for speculation.

Before unrolling his sleeping bag Claud had shingled his selected bivouac spot with boughs, both the preferred balsam (soft and aromatic flat-needled fir) and spruce (known as red spruce, and prickly), the stems pushed into the ground, curved side up for resiliency.

He took off his boots and slid into his sleeping bag. The slope at once proved to be steeper than he anticipated, though he lay feet down, and bumpier, for as he squirmed to adjust his hip he cursed freely and feelingly. I heard a swish as he yanked out an offending branch and threw it into the darkness, muttering something about Horace Kephart and skimpy bough beds. His usual system was to chop down a small but luxuriant fir balsam for a plentiful supply of material, which he proceeded to trim on a stump with the ax so as to get a foot of cushioning. No time for that, I thought drowsily, not this camp.

But he began to snore.

I sneezed, not from the cold—only a feather tickling my nose. It must have worked its insidious, stealthy way out of a tear in the fabric of my bag. The cloth around my head, from flydope on my face over the years, had decayed (though the smell of citronella and pine tar lingered—I was scared of the repellents devised during WW II), and stitching to repair the rips didn't help for long, if at all…feathers, like porcupine quills, but working out instead of in…and now without a job I couldn't accumulate money for a new bag…unless my *Forgotten Democracy* manuscript, history of the Indian Stream Republic at the north tip of the state, circa 1830, was accepted by Bill Sloane, whom I'd met at Bread Loaf Writers' Conference in '64…and if enough copies sold…money…if, if…too many ifs….

Maybe I snored, but no, Ernie hadn't complained.

I awoke dreaming of a factory whose machinery roared over my head faster and faster. I lay under the whirling pulleys and looping belts of Department Seven where I started work at Scott and Williams in front of an awesome drill press, December of 1940. The sound faded and came at me again.

My eyes opened. The moonlight was luminous. Not quite daylight, I thought, for it never really is quite as "bright as day." I could see far past the trunks of trees, and up between branches to the sky. The moon, no longer yellow but white, lay meshed in twigs.

I turned my head with chin to chest and there out on the rock some dead embers smoked. The hip and shoulder outline of my old friend stretched in his tapered mummy bag. He snorted, choked, and turned over.

Now that I was awake, I heard the roar distantly, and I realized that not Department Seven but paper mills in Berlin invaded these woods, and...well, not a forest sound, indeed destruction of the forest...the moose had made a forest sound, yes, his urgent call from the mountain belonged in these silver woods...which were wild, apparently remote, yet not...although far from Ernie and our grown, married daughters....

Dozing, I felt comfortably tired, no longer exhausted, and no longer stalking into old age. I was aware, nevertheless, of my life slipping away from me before I could make one last grasp toward the remembered and idealized delights of youth, although obviously they were irrevocably gone. Here I was, lying on an air mattress to protect my old bones from the hard ground, backed against a yellow birch log, when I could be home in bed.

I lay there and dozed or looked at the moon and felt alone. How went that old poem by the well-known Anon..."Christ that I was in my bed again...." Something more...yes the Western wind, small rain...here it is..."Christ, that my love were in my arms/And I in my bed again!" I know flesh stops speaking to flesh. I must resign myself, but later, unless it is quite necessary, quoth Henry from his cabin on Walden Pond of resignation, not love.

Faces and voices talking to me by the log in the moonlight. Love of my life said, "I wish I were young again for you." I said, "No it's all right because I remember. And there was a song that went something about 'They can't take that away, no, no, they can't take that away.'" She said, "I remember, too, yes lovely times, they can't take that away."

But I was alone by the yellow birch log and I said to myself, "Oh yes they can, and will. You must go to sleep for tomorrow. Claud's getting rested."

QUALMS

THE MOON WHEN I AWOKE GLEAMED IN THE WEST LIKE A FROSTED globe for a street light. At first I thought that the day was waiting for the moon to set. When I raised on one elbow and looked behind me, I saw the glow of dawn. This brought a sensation of the world slowly rolling. I seemed to float on my air mattress through the cool air. I felt high up and in the clear although I was surrounded by trees. The leaves of the birches had begun to change from green to yellow. Here at 2,000 feet, autumn was preparing the forest for its long winter sleep.

I unzipped my sleeping bag. Bending knees, required to remove my feet in their woolen socks, protested. I sat up and yawned. I needed more sleep for rest. Never could sleep late in the mornings…"The day shall not be up so soon as I" and so forth…something about fair adventure…I hardly felt like adventure…lie back for a bit….

The next thing I knew, Claud loomed over the fire sucking on his cold pipe. He had touched a match to spruce twigs. I heard the snapping and smelled pitchy smoke. The stones of the fireplace hid the tiny flame. From a bundle of dry branches, probably moosewood and beech and mountain maple, he broke sticks and added them to the spruce tinder. I thought happily and pretentiously, and sleepily, how convenient for us that Mother Nature arranges under spruce boughs the brittle twigs to start our fires, also on birch trees, strips of bark more flammable than paper. Then I realized that "Mother Nature" was a concept of my boyhood, most likely originating with Thornton Burgess's stories of "the Green Forest and the Green Meadows." The illusion might be discredited but it persisted and was comforting, despite my suspicion that ahead of me lay no green meadows or green forest managed by Old Mother Nature.

I unrolled my pillow into pants and pulled on the legs. The next step in dressing was to take from my boots objects that I had not wanted to rest my head on all night: Jackknife, match safe, wallet, and compass went into the pockets of the green pants, which were tough work pants from my recent days as a foreman of the heat treating department. I tucked my glasses case into my shirt pocket. That khaki relic of the same occupation showed evidence of one reason I had quit, namely, several little holes burned by spattering drops of molten cyanide caused by my hurried immersion of a damp steel drum cam in a pot of the stuff, temperature 1,550 degrees Fahrenheit...the assembly line is down for that cam, hurry it up, will you? Can't wait for your man to come in for your second shift...

Pants up to thighs, I put on the boots. Stand up, pull pants to waist and tighten belt. My legs ached.

A breeze rustled the forest.

Smoke swirled toward Claud. He backed away, turning his head to leeward.

Leaves stirred. The breeze, not the dawn, waked the day.

Claud said in his imitation Canuck accent, "Bo-jou, bo-jou, commasava?"

"Tray biann, tsigah."

The reply exaggerated my fitness. And Claud was a long way from a *petit garcon*. I bent to lace my boots. Should have done it on the sleeping bag. The action revealed a crick in my back.

I gathered the pots from their upside-down resting places by the fire. (We always washed supper dishes after the meal.) I walked through the cool woods to the pool. In the silence, a thrush flew from the ground and gave a peevish note. Perhaps he had to miss a bug because of me. Old leaves, disturbed in little clusters, showed that he or she had already been picking them over for insects, larvae, and worms. I thought he was a hermit thrush although the weak light failed to show the rusty tail.

At the pool's squishy edge I squatted and cupped the pots full of clear, cold water. The green moss at the bottom of the pool gave the illusion of green water.

Back at the fire I found that Claud had laid out plastic envelopes containing various possible foods for breakfast. The chili I assumed was a joke.

He motioned at the lot. "You choose."

I decided that dried eggs and ham bits would be good. I mixed them with water according to directions on the envelope. Claud smeared the frying pan with no-stick dope from a little plastic bottle, a modern convenience provided by Chuckwagon.

He said, "This stuff will probably destroy red corpuscles. Hope a hearty breakfast of that desiccated hen fruit and soybean ham will restore them, but I doubt it." He handed me a small spatula. "My wife said I should take this."

"Great."

I used my omelet technique on the mixture in the pan. This consists of lifting the cooked portion from the bottom and letting the uncooked liquid drain sizzling onto the hot aluminum. I said, "No sticking anyhow."

Claud, harking back, made a comment on modern times and so-called improvements. "The old steel frying pans didn't stick."

This was only partially true. I lifted egg-ham with his spatula.

He went on reminiscing more specifically—our usual trend. "Remember that big old steel frying pan we found in Isolation Shelter? Must have been eighteen inches across."

"Remember it well. Summer of thirty-two. Yup, with bacon fat cooking forty short trout from Rocky Branch. You outlaws, you and Joe Bean. Scared me shitless."

"Did you really think a game warden would climb out of Tuckerman Ravine over Boott Spur and down this Davis Path to catch us?"

"He might have walked up the old logging railroad grade from Bartlett."

"Ten miles."

"I worried."

"That six-inch law was stupid. Throw 'em back to die. Anyhow way up there trout never grew over five inches, most of them."

"I caught eighteen one of those days, on a Parmachenee Belle wet fly, following after you and Joe with your worm-baited hooks. All six inches and only two less than my limit."

"Oh, I thought the limit was forty, one panful apiece." Claud snorted and laughed with a crooked expression. "Back in Orford I knew enough to heave 'em into the bushes when Harry Goodwin showed up."

"Yes, after that he also showed up whenever I parked my mother's Model A Ford coupe beside a trout stream."

"I suppose he figured I might be with you. We saw him twice more. Once was that time we were reported lost out back of Mount Cube, nineteen forty-seven, when we met him on Jacobs Brook and we were coming back from Lamprey Pond camping near our fell-in old lean-to."

"In the rain, too. He looked pretty disgusted. I bet he had hoped after we grew up he'd never see us again. Said something like, 'You two again after fifteen years. Lost, hell.'"

I served the omelet in carefully divided pieces, onto aluminum pie plates.

It could not be called good.

It was not totally bad either. The ham bits, if they were ham, needed more "reconstitution," as the label called soaking in water, so the omelet possessed real character and authority. I had mixed too much, or the cold biscuits were too much. The strong tea wouldn't wash down the combination as easily as it should have. We couldn't find the plain powdered milk for the tea so had to put in the chocolate-flavored—and I added three lumps of sugar for energy, hoping rather uselessly that my system might absorb it.

Claud eyed his omelet from under his hat, head sideways, squinting. He shrugged. "Got to get the full food value." He ate the last squalid bits from his plate and spooned half of the remains in the frying pan onto his empty plate. I took the last of the mess. We spooned clumsily because the year before this I had hacksawed off half of the spoons' handles to save weight.

I left part of my omelet. Breakfast had created a bloated feeling. I wondered how Claud's healed ulcer was reacting.

The meal over, I insisted on fetching extra pots of water to douse the fire.

Claud protested from around his pipe-lighting puffs. "On that rock it isn't going anywhere."

"I want to pour extra on the duff around the rock."

Patiently he moved off to look for mushrooms, as I could tell by his slow steps among the trees and his down-searching stance.

At eight o'clock, when we were finally under our packs and setting out he told me, "Found only an *Amanita verna*. The *verna* part of the name doesn't apply to them here in New Hampshire. They come out in late summer, at least that's when I find 'em, not in the spring."

Mushrooms had become his great interest, second only to old rifles. He went on, holding out a small white cone, "This little feller you could write a murder mystery about. Deadly, but the symptoms don't appear for twenty-four hours."

"I tried a mystery once and it didn't come off at all."

He made no comment. We never got into my writing. Although he was in my first novel, he had never mentioned it, nor the second and last, which was set in one of our boyhood haunts, eastern Orford. I never knew if he had read them.

My legs felt cold in shorts. I had changed to them in hopes of easing the leg action for the seven miles to Gentian Pond Shelter. Those seven miles included unknown strains up and down; I dreaded them. There would be enough work for my legs without pants dragging over my knees, left-right or right-left, at each step.

The distance included the mileage we had not made the previous day to Trident Col, necessary to keep us on schedule and to put us under a roof for the night. We couldn't expect another night without rain. I was sure I could make it because I told myself we had plenty of time for seven miles. And after a hundred yards my legs began to function better. I grew optimistic.

The AMC map showed contour lines at 100-foot intervals. The map was only 9 inches by 10 inches, less margins. I became very familiar with it, but this day I had not yet learned to study the contour lines carefully and to count them with a twig as I pored over them through my bifocals. If I had brought a magnifying glass I could have noted the fine detail on the map and made a more realistic assessment of ascents and descents for our second day.

I had learned almost nothing yesterday about the Mahoosucs. Just as well to remain optimistic and cheerful. Still, seven miles with a pack were seven miles. I concentrated on the joy of carrying my necessities on my back—a feeling of freedom, early in the morn.

As we started up Cascade Mountain I made an attempt at humor. "Today will separate the men from the boys."

Claud shifted the bulk of his pack. "I could join the boys without any test."

The trail led up through beech woods. My pack seemed less weighty than the previous afternoon. Against this, my wind was short. I realized that I was hardly moving. But reassurance came when I looked up and saw that Claud, too, climbed slowly. He placed his rubber-bottomed boots steadily but deliberately. The trail's trace steepened in the old leaves and drooping ferns.

Usually in the beginning of a day we walked or "packed"—meaning with loads for more than a lunch—at the same rate. Later in the day I couldn't keep up with him.

Now I concentrated on putting one foot in front of the other. Don't think of the summit. That's the trick. Remember sawing wood when you were a chicken farmer and supplying Ernie's kitchen stove by means of a one-man crosscut saw—you soon knew enough not to anticipate the chunk dropping off the log that lay on the forks of the sawbuck.

I studied the small beech woods and compared them to English beeches that I had walked among the year before outside London. Don had been driving Ernie, Ruthie, and me back from their apartment in Brandon and pulled into a lay-by so I could visit the great trees—many times the size of these. And here no long aisles. All the big yellow birches had been cut for plywood or veneer logs and the tops left behind.

Claud said, "A lot of good firewood going to waste. Yellow birch burns good. I worked up plenty at Pinkham Notch Camp that winter I worked for Joe Dodge."

I thought he might tell about boring with an auger and dynamiting a yellow birch butt's unsplittable twists into matchsticks....

No, I guess he needed his breath.

The trees abruptly became small maples. About six inches through, almost identical, they grew in park-like array from a bed of dead leaves and humus devoid of underbrush. They had the appearance of careful pruning that removed the lower branches and left the trunks smooth for 10 feet. Even the tops might have been trimmed into rounds. I took them to be sugar maples and remarked, "Someone could have a good sap orchard here in time."

He stopped, standing hipshot. "Not Brown Company." And moved on.

The maples ended at a brushy thicket that nearly blocked the trail with wild cherry saplings and weeds. They grew over broken rock tipped into a jumble, surrounded by white birches and a few evergreens. The trees were seeking holds for their roots and barely did so. We clambered among the rocks and pulled ourselves upward by the smaller trees.

The summit of Cascade Mountain appeared as a ledgy curve against the sky. So steep it rose we had to crawl into the open. Claud stood and climbed onward. I paused for breath and looked behind me.

There lay the country we had walked over and through. Far down at the col or sag, treetops hid our campsite. A long wooded shoulder rose beyond to the rocky flats of Mount Hayes. Far beyond them the barren pinnacles of gray slabs above treeline were Mount Madison and Mount Adams. These peaks jabbed into the western sky, which seemed darker than the clarity overhead. Mount Moriah, more directly south, showed its forest as green-black because the precipitous slope rose in shadow below the morning light. Only the crag that formed its summit caught a touch of sun.

The day should have been dewy fresh. Instead, the stink of sewage from the paper mills wafted upward off the polluted Androscoggin River.

I followed Claud to the topmost ledges. He said, "If you stand over on that point of rock I'll take a picture. Gotta have some human interest."

We were above sea level, the map had informed me, by 2,606 feet. Our night's camp had been about a mile west in the col. I felt the elevation as only that, not as an achievement. I stepped out on the point of rock, but not too near the drop-off. My legs were weak. At once I saw a reason for the sensation I was having of a height even greater than we stood upon. Below me the river fog filled the curves and indentations of the valley. Level, soft, white, cottony, it nevertheless might have been solidified foam, or lava, pumice maybe, meerschaum, seafoam. It increased our distance above the everyday world of the highway, Route 2, the polluted river, and the invisible town of Gorham. Not a church spire protruded. I had seen river fog before, somewhere special....

In one of those flashes of memory to which I am subject, for better or worse, I was driving a Model A Ford coupe, yes, my mother's handed down to my sister and me; I was driving from the old white farmhouse on Dame Hill in Orford, down into the fog of the Connecticut River. That was the summer when Ernie and I were first married, and I had a job mopping the porches of Aloha Camp's main lodge before the campers awoke. I drove in clear sunlight, then immersed in a thick cloud....

Never mind that of 1935. Look away to Mount Madison. Its spectacular pyramid rose out of the fog, over 4,000 feet, so I'd heard, abruptly out of the valley for a total of, let's see, 5,367 feet above sea level.

Beyond it and to my left, by a freak of perspective, Mount Washington appeared lower than Madison; 6,288 feet was seemingly lessened by another two or three miles from my pinnacle. The mountain's bulk was there. I gazed into the maw of the largest ravine, the Great Gulf.

Memory and associations again arrived, of sleeping in the log shelter with Claud and other hikers, and next day feeling equal even to the lightning storm on Mount Adams, flashes around us on the bare rocks and a deluge that sloshed over my hair, which had been trying to stand on end. Lightning bolts were not then a fatal danger in our young minds. We were, however, soon wet and cold. The AMC Madison Hut below in a col gave us refuge.

Claud now stood beside me, winding the camera film to another frame. I asked, "When was that storm on Mount Adams?" Of course I knew but I had to talk about it. "Nineteen thirty or thirty-one?"

"I can't say for sure." He thought a moment. "Probably thirty. But I haven't forgotten being hungry as a bear and looking at the food on the shelves at Madison Hut—especially cans of beans, and cans of pears in heavy syrup. We had no money and wouldn't ask the hutmaster for a handout."

"I remember mostly going down into the Great Gulf, by the Buttress Trail, I think, and wading streams. The West Branch was over its banks and we had to find a crossing where an island split it."

"Yeah, waist high and almost too strong."

"That nice family at the shelter treated us like heroes."

"More important they fed us. Bacon and eggs and pancakes and syrup."

I could almost taste that feast, but I shut up about it. This was stupid to dwell on the past so much—an unwise addiction of mine, of ours. I thought how futile it was. The present should be my, our, concern, our interest, and our enjoyment. The present instant is the only reality. Or is it? Memories are reality, too, which draws us back with an irresistible compulsion.

Never mind all that now. We have six more miles to lug our packs, and we're not 16 but 52 years of age.

I wanted to get at it. I stepped out while Claud shifted the reflector oven in his pack.

The trail, so called, consisted of an unmarked path of dark or gravelly soil or bare rock, through patches of blueberry bushes, low spruces, firs, and bracken ferns. The trees soon began to reach over our heads. The path became a trail and an aisle with green walls. We came to damp sphagnum moss, then sheep laurel growing knee-high below taller withe rod on which clung clusters of dark blue berries.

Again bare ledge. Stumps bordered our way. Black from an old forest fire, they explained the bare ledges.

Cascade Mountain fell away from the trail. We stood on an east-facing cliff. A zigzag of sheer or shelved rock formed a possible descent. The treetops far below grew in Trident Col. Those pointed evergreens hid the spring somewhere below. Ha-ha for our objective of last night.

I could see beyond to three little summits of pointed rocks to match the trees. They must be the Trident. At a farther distance, forests of leafy trees as well as conifers clung to endless ridges, steep slopes, declivities, rock faces, ravines, and jagged peaks. Aghast, I reached for a tree to steady me. I did not like anything I saw. What in hell had I gotten myself into?

Claud started down. He had several choices of routes. They all dropped enough to hook my pack if I sat down and dangled my shorter legs toward a foothold on a projecting rock. Claud seemed to be employing a technique that relied on clinging to spruces overhanging the ledges. I discarded the notion of backing down. My pack would certainly flip me into a reverse somersault.

I kept recalling how we had planned to reach Trident Col in an afternoon. Fools we. Fools rush in where, et cetera. The spirit is willing but the flesh, et cetera. I should have stayed at home with my dear wife of 31 years and worked on my manuscript. I dared not call it my book because that hubris was bad luck. What business had I here?

I crept down carefully. The pack pushed me toward empty space. I grabbed bushes and small trees, first making sure none of them were rotten, loose, or scarcely attached to the earth. I knew enough to place each boot without weight as I felt for security before stepping down.

We lowered ourselves the last few yards to level ground under evergreens. A sign in one tree assured us we had achieved Trident Col. Red paint of another sign told us once more that the shelter had been discontinued for lack of proper use. I remembered that the *Guide* pages mentioned an unofficial trail leading down to a field above Berlin. I told Claud about it and added, "Probably Berlin guys used it for drinking parties."

He leered. "You mean with Loose Wimmin?" He peeled off a shoulder strap. "I'm going to see how the Appies discontinued it."

We left our packs and walked along the spur trail through dense spruce and fir. Faced by a scramble up a ledge, I stopped. A failure of energy overwhelmed me. I told him, "Go ahead. I'll save my strength."

What strength? I stretched out on a hummock of dry balsam needles and hair-cap moss. Blessed rest. I couldn't doze, however, because in my mind's eye lay that view of the rugged country ahead.

Claud came back whistling "My Old Kentucky Home."

He made no comment on my collapse but described the remains of the shelter. "The roof's flatter'n a pancake. Looks as though the walls had been cut apart with a chain saw to break up the logs and let down the roof. No beer cans or liquor bottles or used safes. Guess the Appies cleaned up the mess. Great view west from an opening in the trees. Stench from the mills worse than here. Maybe someday it'll blow up."

"We can hope so." I knew by his long speech that he was worried about me. I got to my feet. "Time to separate the men from the boys."

"I've wanted to see Gentian Pond ever since I heard of it from AT hikers at Galehead."

"It'll be a new one for our collection. Also Page Pond, Moss Pond, and Dream Lake. I guess Dream Lake comes after Page Pond.

At the junction with the Mahoosuc Trail we shouldered packs and turned left into the wilderness that we had looked across from the cliff above. I paused and breathed to gather myself for the effort required by Trident Peaks. Then after a few yards, lo and behold! (a phrase of my mother's) our luck changed. The trail skirted the peaks to the south, level, and even downhill a bit. We moved from the gloomy spruce and fir into open hardwoods. Claud stopped to load his pipe.

I took the lead, striding along, swinging over the easy trail past fine beeches and maples. Optimism flooded through me. Five miles of this would be "a pure damn"—to borrow an expression from my old boss in the hardening rooms, Carl Booth, foreman of that Department 14 before me, glorious old guy suddenly gone 10 years ago. My optimism could accept that bereavement on this beautiful day. Yes, the splendid sunshine on the green leaves seemed only to emphasize this warmth of late-late summer. My legs felt warm and strong, and all the free days beckoned ahead in this perfect season for hiking.

I knew I was walking alone because Claud made a slow ritual of lighting his pipe. I could go through it with him back there. First take from his hip pocket the can of Velvet, open the lid. He would think, I knew from many comments, that the present top, which snapped in place, unlike the old one that fitted down around the edge, might be change but it ain't progress. His next unfolding of the inside paper differed from my impatient tearing it away from a new can of my Union Leader or Revelation; he always kept the folds to preserve the correct moistness of the tobacco. Nor did he, as I did, tip the tobacco directly into the pipe and tamp it unevenly with an index finger. He shook a load into his left palm, slipped the open can under his left elbow while he inserted layers of tobacco into the bowl. This care insured a steady-drawing, long smoke. Next he folded the paper—no, he first put back extra tobacco, even two crumbs, into the can—and closed the lid.

The lighting would cause a comment about the "new" matches—shorter, with smaller heads, and with flames more inclined to blow out in a breeze. Had they arrived during the war, like so many economies? I couldn't recall, and the passage of time began to weigh me down more than my pack, because I could see him establishing the pipe ritual ever since we were 15, and earlier. I used to remonstrate with him about flicking a match alight with his thumbnail. Waste of my breath.

He had probably done it again just now, and cupped the flame in both hands till it burned clear of sulphur fumes. He would draw in gently so as not to scorch the tobacco, then blow out the match with a jet of smoke, snap it in two, kick a hole with his heel in the duff, drop in the match and scuff it over.

Yes, I could almost see all this. Our days together were both a burden out of the past due to advancing years, and a comfort at the moment because I suddenly realized I was straining up a little rise. My God, I must be weak for no reason. I looked ahead to a steep pitch topped by a little cliff.

This wasn't right, here in the lovely forest of beeches with their smooth gray bark, and the white columns of birches. A ledge to scramble up was too much. My legs wanted to fold. I told myself that the abrupt depletion of energy was caused by hunger. Despite my diet I must take on more calories to replace those I burned up so much faster lugging this pack over Cascade Mountain. To hell with my doctor. What did he know about a diabetic climbing mountains? I had lost 12 pounds, down to 154 in two years—close to my weight at age 22. Well, maybe I had been a trifle overweight, but what low limit had he set, or did he know the correct one?

Whatever the answer, my damned pancreas would have to rally for this trek. I told it, "Pancreas, get off your ass and make energy out of this food I'm about to eat."

Beside the trail a seep of water trickled into a little pool before it crossed the woods on my right. I slipped off the pack and unstrapped it for crackers, washed down with water. I was munching and gulping when Claud came along.

He nodded and dropped one shoulder to release his pack and slide it to the ground. Mutual agreement on lunches required no talk.

I offered him my pocket cup, an aluminum-foil envelope that had once contained dried pea soup. Its use as a drinking cup was a hiking kink passed on to me by Rodney, the husband of my younger daughter, Penny. He'd got it from his Boy Scouting in and around Laconia, I supposed…had he been a Scout or too busy with a paper route? I drank three envelopes of water. Ruthie's husband remembered as a Scout nearly freezing to death on Mount Belknap…my mind was wandering. I concentrated on watching Claud unstrap his pack-cover.

He straightened up and showed me a larger foil envelope. A questioning look, and he asked, "Strawberry milkshake?"

"Good," I said.

"There's a little problem. It's for eight men. Chuckwagon food packages are for eight men."

"I remember you said something like that."

He was studying the label. "Umm, this makes two quarts. I can guess at half of it. Can we drink a quart?"

"If we put our minds to it."

While he was figuring measurements, I lay back on dry leaves and ancient humus. Weariness of spirit and worry of mind arrived together. I visualized the foodless mountains ahead. The weight of my pack shucked beside me might have reassured me. It didn't. I began counting off the packages that I recollected spread on the big kitchen table at Claud's house.

He had told me during the fuss of departure how he ordered Chuckwagon supplies. "All their grub was in eight-man rations. I got 'em for one day. Two into eight, see? But we might be out a week, so I ordered another day's meals. Pretty poor stuff. I showed it to my wife."

Louise had been standing right beside us. She stepped to the table. It was long enough to seat their family of nine, had they all assembled. She began arranging packages while she admonished us. The old wall clock ticked inexorably.

"Come on now," Louise said. "If you two slowpokes don't get moving, there'll be another customer. Claud's trying to tell you, Dan, that I drove to the IGA in Laconia for some real food. Chuckwagon is low on protein, even if you two can bring yourselves to eat the dried eggs."

The low-ceilinged kitchen was warm from the wood range. I sat down on the bench that backed up to the original brick chimney, just as a streak of kids, Elly chasing Eddy, circled the chimney and banged out the back door shouting, "Let's go, let's go!"

Louise began setting out from a carton and from the refrigerator her supermarket food and some homemade.

"I bought two pounds of rat-trap cheese, and a pound of hamburg for your first supper. Mashed potato flakes, biscuit mix. Forty-eight teabags, dried milk, sugar. Pilot crackers and zwieback. Now from here, a slab of our bacon, half a pound of butter in a plastic jar, and today's sandwiches for all of us. There."

Claud asked me, "Think that's enough?"

"Plenty—if we can lug it all. I'll pay my half."

Louise shook her head. "Later. Now for God's sake let me divide it or we'll never get out of the dooryard, you two each aiming to take your full share. Claud's so slow he drives me wild."

Claud told her, "Dan's slower than I am."

That wasn't entirely true.

The division of the packages may have diverted him from a previous intention to bring a little medicine bottle of Myers rum out of the fifth that lasted him a year. He forgot because the urgency to escape seized both of us. I was supposed to be off booze entirely.

And now about 24 hours later, there below Trident Peaks, I dozed in the assurance that we had enough grub.

Vaguely high up among the ledges and out of sight, I could hear ravens cackling hoarsely and then barking. To me they were still fascinating new arrivals in the mountains, new from Canada since we were boys, exciting wildness added to the woods. My first sighting had been only five years before at the guts of a deer Claud had shot near his camp on Crystal Mountain south of the Connecticut Lakes.

The strange black birds, heavy of body and beak, not given to flocking like crows, were alien compared to their relatives we had hunted with dedication in Orford 35 years before. I could see the head of a crow—

one desperately wanted—over the sights of the .22 rifle. I could hear the sharp crack which seemed miraculously to drop a mass of feathers and wings from an elm in my Aunt Jane's pasture.

Ravens, however, were mysterious birds of folklore and ill-omen. The image of Poe's "Nevermore" persisted. Yet I had seen them high in the sky as they tumbled together, cavorting, surely for fun. All the same, a grotesque fantasy glided darkly into my consciousness.

I was lying near their home on Trident Peaks, and if I were alone and died, they would fly down and peck out my eyes.

I opened those eyes.

The trees rose far overhead, harmless and sheltering. Was this the wilderness I'd looked across from the cliff? Greenery spread calmly below sunshine, which the leaves filtered into green shade…"Annihilating all that's made/To a green thought in a green shade." And, and…"Casting the body's vest aside,/My soul into the boughs does glide."

How about Marvel's complaint to his coy mistress…"The grave's a fine and private place,/But none, I think, do there embrace."

Quotations are the plague of educated men. Or a delight? Both.

I wondered where the blackflies and mosquitoes and no-see-ums had gone, to leave me unharried. Of course they were gone for the season mostly; this was the first day of September. And I wondered why I was so pooped. We had walked only about three miles, probably less. Three miles used to be a warm-up.

I turned over and felt the water in my stomach slopping about. To stop that I ate more pilot crackers and two slices of cheese. The paper around the chunk was oily. I thought of a plastic bag, yet didn't care enough about the possible mess in my pack to look for one. I lay back.

Claud was whittling a little paddle from a stick. He began stirring the strawberry milkshake in the teapot. I realized that the truncated spoons and forks were too short to mix a quart of water, strawberry-flavored dried milk, and sugar. He made no comment on my weight-saving foolishness—foolish to him because he could carry a loaded pack using the muscles developed in the thirties from packboards of supplies for Galehead Hut.

I saw him pouring out two cups from the spout of that coffee-teapot.

We drank the entire quart.

This ersatz milkshake derived its pink color and strawberry flavor from chemicals. The taste and smell were just near enough to those of the berry for a suggestion of the shortcake that Ernie had not made for me this year because of my diet, indeed not since 1964, although that summer she did and I ate it because the physical exam and discovery of high blood sugar came after the shortcake season.

But now I was in need of those calories and I welcomed the sustenance in the milkshake, however disgusting. For more insurance that I'd make Gentian Pond Shelter, I broke off a chunk of semi-sweet chocolate, figuring that maybe the oil and other food values would soak into my blood stream somehow. Pancreas and guts, do your stuff. I did chew it into a paste.

This was about noon. I told myself, "See here, don't worry. Hellfire, we could be at Gentian Pond by five o'clock if we averaged only a mile an hour. We could take frequent rests. After this next rise the trail must be mostly level. The map showed something called Wocket Ledge, which couldn't be serious like a real peak. If we did it a little at a time...."

I began to think of an associate at Scott and Williams. Roy Bagley was a foreman of the bar machine department and a very nice guy. He and I had become acquainted back when I was taking time studies of his men operating the big automatic lathes. I had learned that after his daughter got married, he and his son-in-law had built a house for the newlyweds. I had wanted to manage an escape for Ernie, Ruthie, Penny, and myself from the cramped, half-house we then had rented for 10 years, including the war years. Could I build a house with the help of a carpenter I knew? But how find the time and the energy and know-how? The project loomed like a monstrous undertaking.

I asked Roy about it. He was a large, quiet man at his desk. I had to lean over and speak low near his ear to be audible under the throbbing, banging crescendo of steel bars feeding into lathes as the bars whirled, as tools shrieked into steel, as the driving hum of motors took over the air. "Roy, how did you and your son-in-law build him and your daughter a house spare-time, when we were working those long hours during the push to make five hundred knitting machines a month to cover women's legs with nylon?"

Roy smiled at the suggestion of the ultimate end of our endeavors for the company. He smiled especially with his eyes. "That house? The answer's easy. First we put on one board and then we put on another."

I began to think of a boardwalk stretching to Gentian Pond. It came to me plain and easy, if we just first put on one board, and then we put on another, not boards, but short distances, say from here to the top of the little ledge, and then on to perhaps a giant yellow birch, and then Page Pond…I told Claud about my concept and about Roy's explanation.

Claud said, "I should think he had to look ahead some, or he'd have ended with a ramshackle contraption."

"It's a fine house. Up on Mile Hill."

"I know Roy's brother, the hunter and fisherman. Well, I get the idea." He shouldered his pack. "All right, let's nail on another board."

He was gone up the slope, knees bent as usual in his woodsman's walk, boots slowly driving, with the push from the inside of his heels—the reason for the Bean boots, he claimed, because leather wore sideways right into the counter. He once had explained, "I used to wear leather boots with edge nails and hobs when I packed into Galehead, but even so I ruined two pairs a summer. And you can't get edge nails now. Anyhow these Bean boots are lighter." Yes, they carried him all right.

I managed to stand up. Under my pack and moving finally upward, I thought of learning about this trip from Ernie while Ruthie played "Poor Wayfaring Stranger" on her banjo. The incident seemed an age ago. I noticed beside the steep trail the tangled branches of hobblebush, the broad leaves turning their delicious maroon, and the flat cluster of red berries, which began as the startling white blossoms against greenery in June. I seemed to recall that the shrub had a nickname, Wayfaring Tree, or was it bush. I felt too winded to care. I had to climb by handholds and footholds.

Claud was waiting for me at the top of the ledge.

Alone, I never could have continued into wilderness. This was the point of no return. He moved on and I followed, while I tried to formulate words of protest: "This is crazy. I can't go on."

Maybe not. Then I thought, "You can't face the obdurate lack of sympathy, which you know well. You'll turn back alone and die struggling up Cascade Mountain and over Mount Hayes."

Yet soon one boot will not follow the other.

Now wait!

There's a bulldozed road stretching ahead. It's wide and clear.

Christ, I hope it goes all the way to Gentian Pond.

I had dropped behind. Claud turned and looked me over.

He told me, "Easy going now." He pointed to the dirt and gravel boulevard. Uprooted stumps grotesquely lined the edges, interspersed with massive rocks and forest duff heaped up from skinning the centuries of organic matter down to mineral earth. This formed a seed bed for raspberry bushes and maple sprouts. He said more emphatically, "Good walking."

"I need it."

He said, "Looks like an easy board to put on. We'll move right along to Gentian Pond. Funny thing, my wife would like to see it. The name, I guess, as if the shore was lined with gentians. She says one kind is rare."

"Fringed," I told him. "If we find any gentians, they'll be the common bottle ones—closed."

"Well, I've wanted to see the pond and shelter ever since a white-haired hiker at Galehead told me the place was the best in the mountains. We'll build a fire and sit back with a pot of tea. I've heard the shelter faces away across the valley to Carter Dome. Nobody to bother us. Time to bake biscuits. Real old-fashioned camping out."

I felt enchanted. I set out with a stride I hoped was jaunty. The level road urged me to enjoy it. The hell with wilderness. Ah, beautiful modern innovation, the bulldozer, easing my way, resting my legs. How could I ever have hated bulldozers and roads in wilderness?

I stepped out in a state of euphoria, so contentedly that I almost passed a rock on which some idiot had painted a blue arrow pointing to the left. The road continued invitingly. I took another step and saw a trail sign on a tree above the rock. The path there entered rough brushland.

Disappointment emptied me of strength and confidence. Had not the simple life been a dream and the seeking of it a powerful compulsion 30 years before, when nothing was modern by the standards of 1966? An aeon ago I had longed for woods and a life in that pressure-free remoteness. This Mahoosuc Trail again leading into secret places once would have enticed me. Seduced by the results of a snorting bulldozer. No philosophy from my years of innocence came to my help.

Pessimism is perhaps the bulwark against disappointment. Claud said, "I knew it was too good to last."

With an automatic response I countered by refusing pessimism, "Well, someone has brushed out the trail. Looks like they used a bush scythe and a machete. It must lead to Page Pond. Another one for our collection."

After a few yards I realized that I could have no real complaint about leaving that scar of so-called civilization, the bulldozed road. The trail wound through interesting cutover land, which had begun to recover. We climbed gradually among small trees and through growths of crowded, head-high saplings. I guessed the logging to have taken place five years before. Stumps of maple and birch had sprouted into multiple buggy-whips. The rocks in the trail looked raw and recently exposed.

Soon many sharp stubs protruded dangerously with the nasty points that I remembered from my summer on a surveying crew for the General Land Office. As a brush cutter with a machete I had left many of them on survey lines of a National Forest created out of logged, burned land near Washburn, Wisconsin. A slash with a machete would do it, and you wanted the blade's tip dulled so you'd save your toes and shins.

Evidently here the felling of bigger trees had blocked the trail, which a crew for the AMC had opened hastily. The way became narrow and rough. In the rapid changes of moods that were gripping me, I suddenly hated this difficult reentrance into the mountain fastness, as I now saw it, having been spoiled for it by the bulldozed road. I dreaded walking away from civilization. And I regretted my lost youth because I remembered wandering with Claud during our teen years unconcerned, relishing the wildness, exploring the almost trackless forests that stretched east of Orford into Wentworth and Dorchester. I blamed my present anxiety at losing the bulldozed road, my lack of strength and courage, on my 25 years of working in the artificial environment of industry.

Not that simple, so forget the past. Think of Page Pond. Pay attention to each step. Walk between the raspberry bushes and the rocks...if we had been a month earlier we'd be feasting on the red delicacies. Choose good footing. Try that patch of grass with your right foot, then that stone for your left. Step past the stump, over the log, past the sawed butt of a white birch, whose bark shows like unprinted newspaper in sunlight, mottled by the shadows of bracken fronds. The sun beat down on us.

We moved on, east and north, our direction, our bearing, although the trail kept winding south at times, correcting itself. Then it led up and then down, and my brown boots reached ahead, left and right, not left-right, left-right, too rough for marching, which fate spared me, praise be. But the boots were military in shape, the old Munson Army last adapted by L.L. Bean, the most comfortable shape for my feet, and hard to find in a civilian boot; does the military still use this last? Seems as though Dan Beard in his book on camping advised Munson Army last…or was it Horace Kephart…not Ernest Thomson Seton, seems as though…boyhood reading matter.

Called the "Maine Engineering Shoe" by L.L. Bean, my boots were the worst to break in I ever wore. They even resisted the old trick of wading them wet in a brook and walking them dry, though the treatment helped—grin-and-bear-it breaking in. They were comfortable now, the brown toecaps and wide flare toward my little toes preceding me. The composition soles gave a protected grip on sharp rocks. Eyelets and hooks laced snugly. Boots become friends if you walk far enough in them.

Page Pond first appeared, not at all liquid, as an opening in the woods. Had we not known from the map and *Guide* pages, we might have taken it for a swale as we approached up a slight incline through tall grass. A spruce-grown ridge rose beyond, up and up to blue sky. We came to the small saucer of water. A cold breeze raised little waves.

I thought to myself, "We've nailed on one board." Claud spoke the thought, "Another board." We stopped to admire.

Beavers had blocked the outlet with peeled poplar logs, twigs, rocks, and mud. The pale wood of the logs and poles showed the scaling gouges of buck teeth making meals of bark. The beavers had dragged their leftovers lengthways into the outlet. This construction was the opposite of the method that Claud and I used as boys. It proved the superior intelligence of the beavers. They accepted water's fluid persistence toward lower levels, and yet they held back the bulk of the flow. There was no spillway to wash out. The excess trickled between the logs and poles below the dabs of mud and stones that formed the top of the dam. I wondered how the beavers carried these materials, an old curiosity, if only back to the time in 1949 when I first noted the feat on the dams along the Bog Brook Trail to Perkins Notch, beavers having returned to New Hampshire. How glad I was for the trout in beaver ponds.

The dam blocked the trail. We stepped gingerly across the slippery poles and squished in the mud that topped them. Balancing on a beaver dam with only a trout rod and creel is fairly easy. With a Duluth pack it's tricky. We steadied into grass on the far side. It was waving in the breeze around the sturdier stems and blue flowers of closed gentians. The pointed capsules that are the flowers, big as my thumbs, varied in color from dark blue to a shade like that of an often-washed work shirt. I think of closed gentians as growing in the ditches of old dirt roads, doubtless because I first found them thus in Orford, so here in the wilderness they seemed a small miracle and delighted me.

Before us rose the steep slope of a high ridge. Page Pond's shore became a rest place. We dumped our packs on the first dry ground. Claud walked back to look at the water. I felt no desire to study it. The possibility of trout in Page Pond seemed unimportant compared to finishing our day's journey. Would I want to return someday and fish it? No, too far to walk. Yet I knew that once I might have walked here for trout.

Besides, I had a personal need. I pushed into the bushes with toilet paper from my pack. Sometimes at the time of this necessity in the woods I think of anarchists. This bizarre association comes from reading *For Whom the Bell Tolls.* In it Hemingway has Robert Jordan comment to himself that cats are better anarchists than some in the Loyalist army who left uncovered turds near a fortified position.

I had followed cat behavior for a long time. From habit I kicked clear a space and with the heel of my boot dug away fallen leaves and surface dirt. After defecating I used the toe of my boot to shove back the material from the small excavation, and added a rotting stump.

Returning to my pack, I noticed in the trail an example of a cat that didn't bury its scat. Bobcats choose not to bury, indeed search out a prominent location. On a flat stone a few yards from our packs lay a small cylinder of dried white fur. In wintertime a bobcat had eaten a white snowshoe hare and deposited the resultant waste on the stone. Hare to hair, I thought, and wondered why I had never seen bobcat scat of brown hair. Certainly bobcats continued to prey on hares in the summer.

Claud came back from the pond. "Mighty shallow. It could freeze solid in winter."

"I didn't want to take time to fish it anyhow."

"Yes, time marches on. What's the guidebook say is next?"

I took the pages from my shirt pocket and read, "'The trail passes the south end of the pond and climbs gradually, then steeply to the summit of Wocket Ledge, a spur of Baldcap Dome.'"

"What else?"

"'The fine view from the ledges fifty yards to the northwest, reached by a side trail, should not be missed.'"

"Do we go over the Dome? Whatever that is?"

"Nope...descend to Dream Lake."

"Good," he said.

"The AT comes in there."

He squinted along the trail and upward. "Wocket Ledge must be that ridge. Looks like it'll separate the men from the boys. We better get at it."

A spruce-fir forest makes soft walking on the fallen brown needles. This carpet unrolled before us under dark branches supported by the straight trunks. The earth cushioned my boots as with a million little springs, giving new life to my dying legs.

Or the illusion of new life, until it was revealed as such by an abrupt upward tilt, which raised the brown carpet to the level of my eyes. I looked up at the rubber soles of L.L. Bean's Maine Hunting Shoes. We had reached the guidebook's "then steeply." This, from my point of view, meant straight up, meant grabbing roots and sharp corners of rocks, and prickly spruce branches.

Above me the Bean boots vanished. I crawled. Spruces grew out of the wall on which I was a human fly. Or spider. There seemed endless effort of arms and legs. Empty lungs and flabby muscles forced me to rest several times before I finally noted that the wall in front of me was a floor under me, but the same brown needles. I got to my feet. A little sign on a spruce, visible through a sweaty haze, stated "Wocket Ledge."

An opening to the left ended in sunlight. Claud stood there on a jutting ledge. His back was toward me. His attention must be on the view, unless he had caught sight of a moose, deer, or bear. He was that absorbed. I walked toward him, in no condition to question the "50 yards" although I swore to myself that it was as long as his rifle range up in the woods.

I said to him, "Here's the boy."

"I've only been here a couple of minutes."

The view indeed was not to be missed.

It hit me so hard I could only manage, "Jeesus! What a stretch of country. Talk about panoramas."

"I wish we had one of those old panorama cameras. I'd frame the picture for the living-room wall. Or if my wife objected I'd hang it in my hideout room with my reloading tools and all."

He could stand up to the view. I felt overwhelmed. The view pushed me. I sank down on a rock and tried to sort out some detail from the total wildness. The silent splendor was too simple for the word, just trees really, but it brought me a shiver.

Looking back along the way we had come I could hardly believe the extent of the mountains and valleys we had traversed. I was adrift from the Real World, yes I was, and I missed it, damned if I didn't. And how could I get back?

Facing about I saw immensity ahead in the waves of forest. They daunted me even without my thinking of what was beyond the range of my eyes.

I said to myself, "Now wait, and remember that naming anything gives you power over it. If you know what you're looking at you'll feel better."

Obvious enough were two mountains west of us. We had climbed over them to get here—Cascade, nearer, then Hayes. Distant rock peaks were too far away to appear familiar although they had to be the Presidentials in order of succession from us—Madison, Adams, Jefferson, and Washington.

Claud sat down and lit his pipe. I groped in my pack for a hunk of chocolate and a pilot cracker. The map seemed the best means of finding myself. I had sweated it in my shirt pocket and had to unfold it carefully. I held my compass over the map and moved the paper till it headed approximately north. I needed my glasses, and put them on.

The study gave me more questions than answers. Was that peak the Baldcap Dome on the map? The dark green triangle beyond, with a suggestion of summit rocks, could be Mount Success. The map showed the trail heading northeast from Dream Lake past Gentian Pond to Mount Success. Could I climb over that tomorrow, if I got that far? I had to get that far, and much more.

I turned to look southward. A triangular peak wooded to a crag must be Mount Moriah. The map was no help because it did not include much of the area beyond the Androscoggin valley, over Route 2 and Shelburne, which was a scattered village invisible to me in the depths. To the east a long ridge of folded bedrock might be Shelburne Moriah.

Claud came over and we arranged more accurately the map and compass on a lightning-blasted slab of spruce.

He pointed at the map with his wet pipe stem, then wiped it on his shirt and pointed again. "We haven't allowed for the sixteen degrees deflection, donchaknow."

"No, especially not when just trying to draw a bead on that mountain off northeast of us. Suppose it's Success?"

I didn't adjust the map 16 degrees. He had not expected me to. We never bothered with it in our woods travel.

He said, "On the map there's a bend of trail toward Mount Success at Dream Lake, so sure, that's probably our next mountain."

"Damn glad it's after Gentian Pond."

"Shall we go? After you, my dear Alphonse."

I had been about to take a sight on the far mountain through the cover of my old brass compass. I was torn between wanting to study the territory more and an urgent need to get through the distance to the shelter and rest, which won out easily. "Indeed, yes, my dear Gaston. Let us proceed at once."

The silly exchange from boyhood—had the Frenchmen been characters of a comic strip?—was a measure of our constant turning back for some touch of youth out of our past.

I walked back into the woods. Neither of us thought to take a picture. We hoisted the packs and started east from Wocket Ledge. I knew the feeling that I might never be there again. Claud, too, for he commented, "So we've seen Wocket Ledge, in case anyone should ask."

"A rare place."

"Yaas indeed."

We were silent; I stayed in the lead. I felt unrefreshed but breathed without strain on the down slant. No headache yet. Maybe the heartbeat remained a little rapid despite the rest.

I never knew whether Claud thought of his heartbeat. Probably not much. Eight years had passed since his heart attack in 1958. He never admitted it was one, or wouldn't to others. Typical comment: "Damn fool doctor, just my liver acting up, or a freak pain from my ulcer. Most likely it was from all that ether I breathe in." For reasons adequate to him he declined to use other anesthetics.

That September, after he had recovered from the heart attack, we camped out in Greeley Pond Shelter near the head of Waterville Valley. An easy hike, and we did it slowly. I fished for trout in the pond, casting off the little beach behind the shelter, letting the bucktail sink and then twitching it along the bottom. The technique resembled worm fishing, illegal for trout after Labor Day.

Claud loafed around the shelter, worked up wood to keep the fire going in front, and smoked his pipe. We talked some of the May weekend there in 1947, one of our more notable excursions after the war. Snow and cold had failed to stop the trout biting. We fried and ate many.

The 1958 trip included a visit from our boyhood game warden, Harry Goodwin. While I was fishing, I saw a man easing through the woods to my left in the direction of the Greeley Ponds Trail and thought he was probably a hiker. I raised the line for the back-cast and then shot the line forward again. Waiting for the bucktail to sink I heard a voice close in back of me command sternly, "I'll just take a look at that fly you got on." Harry was a small man but hardy, and somehow I knew him at once.

The "brown and white bucktail," as it was called by its creator, Ralph Lee of Laconia, and to others known as the "Lee Special," satisfied Harry. He gave me a closer appraisal as Claud came around the shelter and leaned against the logs.

Said Harry, "Oh, it's you two again."

I made some inane remark about "Been a long time." Yet only 10 years had elapsed since he had met us as lost persons.

After Harry saw my license, and Claud's, he took off on his patrol.

Claud remarked, "I wanted to ask him if he'd met up lately with two kids and a dead skunk out of season."

"What stopped you?"

"My better nature."

"He might have asked if those pheasant feathers there by the Connecticut River really had been spread by a hawk."

"That was another time."

"I remember."

"The pheasant was awful good eating. Didn't go far, not for all of us. Hellfire, they didn't winter over in Orford unless someone fed 'em. Stupid Fish and Game Department. You know, Verne Snow I think sicked him onto us about pheasants. It was his farm. Remember those two ducks we shot that spring in the flood-water pool and we had to give them to Clyde Spooner because he saw us?"

"Your criminal mind figured that would shut him up."

He smirked.

In 1958, the year of Harry at Greeley Pond, I didn't tell Claud how Dr. John Miller, with whom we were both consulting, not only a GP but a heart specialist, had said to me, "Your friend the veterinarian will have to stop wrestling cows and other large animals."

So on the Mahoosuc Trail in 1966 we were two old crocks heading for Dream Lake, and both of us in our different ways dreaming of younger days.

The trail descended from Wocket Ledge's summit spruces to a little brook no bigger than an elongated spring trickling across the trail like the one at Trident Col. Probably it was the "branch of Peabody Brook" mentioned in the *Guide* pages. We stopped to drink from the aluminum-foil envelope.

To me the envelope still smell-tasted of pea soup. This seemed unlikely. I ought to tell Claud about the envelope. Two weeks before I had eaten the soup with Penny's husband, Rodney, at the Perkins Notch Shelter near the bogland that held the sources of the Wild River. Carter

Dome loomed to the north. Rodney and I spent the morning fishing the beaver ponds and the dark channel of water in the western bog's floating vegetation. I wanted to tell Claud about it. When we fished it 10 years before, I had caught 30 trout in a hundred yards and released half of them. A nice trout on almost every cast of the Royal Coachman fly.

Rodney and I caught none. We hadn't even seen a rise. I blamed myself for our arriving too late at the bog. The sun was casting bright rays over the pointed spruces and on the channel. Carter Dome's unbroken forest glistened in warm sunlight. I had forgotten that dawn was the time to catch trout in the bog.

Claud and I finished drinking from Rod's cup. I led off on the trail, saying over my shoulder, "Rodney and I caught only four trout in Wild River. Tried all one evening and the next morning. Reminded me of the time you and I caught barely enough to eat. The time we met old Fernald at the log cabin in, oh, nineteen fifty-two maybe."

"Nineteen fifty. He was so disgusted with the fishing he headed home to Jackson."

"Said he couldn't believe he'd walked all that way in for nothing." I tried to imitate the gruff old man's voice. "Why, you younguns don't know how 'twas years back at this camp. I came one day and while I was riggin' up my rod and reel I drank a teacup of rum—I was still taking spirits then. I walked up to the bog on the old trail. Stood right there on a spruce stump and filled my basket with trout before I felt the rum. I'm getting out. Good day to you."

After a few yards of trail had passed under our boots Claud said, "That evening we caught plenty in No-Ketchum Pond."

"I remember we each brought thirty home—two days' limit. Fernald should have stayed. I can still see him heading out, annoyed, long woodsman stride, and the beat-up little knapsack."

Claud put in his memory. "How about the time he came on us frying trout, a year or so later, on the East Branch of the Saco? He made believe he was a warden catching us with short trout, then spoiled it by smiling. Said he was celebrating his seventieth birthday."

"All by himself." I thought of the old man, active and independent at that advanced age, and wondered how he managed it. I wouldn't, not the way I felt at 52.

Claud moved past me, saying, "With his thirty-eight pistol on his hip. Seems as though I heard he'd been chewed by a bear once."

We walked on silently until Claud stopped and pointed at the trail. "Here's our moose again."

Fallen yellow leaves lay lightly near the deep impression of a cloven hoof. We came to another track, and another and another. They had been regularly imprinted in the moist duff by the lumbering stride, which I could imagine although I had never seen a moose. Neither of us had seen one. The big tracks indicated an antlered bull, large as a work horse.

I said, "Fresh."

Claud whispered, "Don't talk. He must be up ahead."

The breeze was in our faces. We sneaked along slowly, staring ahead.

Like many real hunts, this unarmed one petered out. The imagined patch of brown, the turning of massive head and antlers, all in our minds, faded for us. The moose could be miles away. Perhaps he had made the tracks early last night. We lost patience and stepped along faster without pausing to scan the woods.

Climbing up a ridge I began to puff and drag. Claud waited for me where a gleam of light came through the yellowing leaves, not high up but down below us. He said, "Must be a pond."

"Reflecting the light, sure. It could be Dream Lake."

We came to a sign for the Peabody Brook Trail, leading south. After this we'd be on the Appalachian Trail, of which Peabody Brook Trail and Mahoosuc Trail were links. I felt a little twinge of pleasure and regret; as boys we had intended to walk it, Georgia to Maine.

From reading ahead in the *Guide* pages I knew that this junction of trails was at Dream Lake. The shallows might offer food to a moose. I said, "Maybe our moose is in the pond eating water-lily roots. I've heard they do."

Claud made no comment nor did he move to Dream Lake. This meant he was too tired for extra walking along the side trail to the water, not even to see a moose and a new pond for our list. Then I realized that I too was more concerned with mileage ahead and conservation of strength to take me over that distance. I was glad when he started off past the first AT blaze—a white stripe of paint about six inches long and two wide.

Approaching the east end of Dream Lake, after less than a quarter-mile during which the water was mostly hidden by evergreens, we came to a fir tree and an attached wooden box containing a glass jar. Under its screw top Claud discovered that the paper it contained was an AMC register. He passed it to me. "You're the writer."

I signed with the date, the place of starting, Gorham, and the destination, Grafton Notch. I stared at the blank under "Remarks" and passed it back to Claud. "I can't think what to write. Always a problem for a writer."

He placed it against the box and went to work with the stub pencil. At once he stopped to take out his jackknife and sharpen the pencil. My attention turned to chickadees looking us over and talking about us in the fir branches. At this season the flock was composed of parents and offspring, I guessed, maybe two families. They were black-capped, although I thought I heard the deeper notes of a boreal chickadee, their brown-capped cousin. We were high enough for boreals.

Claud put back the jar and closed the door of the box. I wondered what rare bit of wit he might have written under "Remarks." I had in mind our earlier days together when there was no telling what he'd write in a trail register at summits we climbed or shelters we stayed in—notably registers in cabins of the Dartmouth Outing Club, say, on Smarts Mountain, when we had no right there, although the more primitive cabins were not locked.

Well, come to think of it I quite often wanted to disassociate myself from his particular brand of humor, wild schemes, violations of rules, regulations, laws, and authority in general. I was timid enough to respect all such restrictions on individual freedom—or at least to observe them. Nowadays I was more tolerant of his shenanigans, and of course his violations were more rare.

I asked, half joking, "What shit did you write for remarks? Something about demolishing Trident Shelter?" I added, "In some of your well-chosen words? Such as fucking fools."

He looked at me seriously under the brim of his hat. "I wouldn't do that. Not in an AMC register."

Revealed were two characteristics that had never occurred to me. 1) He had mellowed. 2) He had pride in his association with the AMC.

Although he joked about the members—Appies, as he called them—and their highfalutin ways, and their fetishes, such as making record climbs then boasting about summits conquered, he honored their organization without being a member. His part in it as a hutman during his college years meant more to him in a nearly reverent way than I had guessed.

I had long understood his respect for his profane, great boss, Joe Dodge. Unlike the Appies, Claud was primarily a woodsman. He lived up to Joe's name for him, Huck, by exploring the Pemigewasset Wilderness in his days off from Galehead Hut, bushwhacking alone down Twin Brook, camping out and feasting on trout from the pool at Thirteen Falls, and climbing trailless Owl's Head. Yet, too, he had tried an Appie stunt, visiting all the huts in 24 hours, and had consequently spent part of a night under a rock slab by the Gulfside Trail near Mount Jefferson when his flashlight burned out. He had told me, "Lucky I had my packboard. I lay on it till daylight. Shouldn't have started at Lonesome Lake. That's the wrong way to do it."

Now on the Mahoosuc Trail he said of the notes he'd seen in the register, "Not much traffic. Three days ago a man and his dog, a Dalmatian. Yesterday a man and his daughter signed. Last week eight hikers from a boys' camp. Early August a party wrote that they hated the trail and had seen a bear."

During this stop we did not take off our packs, and so walked on. Soon we came to another white-painted sign with black lettering, typical of AMC boards, about 12 inches by 8 inches. It identified the Dryad Falls Trail on our right. I wanted to rest and figure mileage. This seemed important because I was suddenly tired again and I had to know how far to Gentian Pond Shelter. Maybe if I knew far, then I could make it. Or maybe the mileage would fold me right here. Still, I had to know, and I dumped my pack. Claud nodded and did likewise.

For me there was an extra attraction in my present mood and condition—evidence of civilization. A bulldozed road headed south in conjunction with the Dryads Falls Trail. This seemed strange because I saw no stumps or treetops left from logging. The trickling inlet to Dream Lake issued from a boggy area eastward. The Mahoosuc Trail disappeared into the bog.

On the tree with the AMC sign, nails held on the logogram for the

Appalachian Trail, the "A" crossed by the "T" as of yore. Unlike this wooden identification, however, the insignia in the early 1930s had been little tin squares tacked to trees with corners vertical and horizontal, forming a square diamond. I thought, "Unbelievable—thirty-odd years ago." The tin square then was exciting on the Smarts Mountain Trail next to the Dartmouth Outing Club's painted red and white blazes. (I forget when they changed to orange and black. Never knew why.)

I wished I had the strength of that time. I hadn't yet learned from Isak Dinesen's old-age attitude that I should be glad I had once possessed more strength than I needed.

At the Dryad Falls Trail my mind was truly wandering.

By some unlikely association, memory presented me with my Aunt Jane's little white cottage next to my grandmother's larger cottage in Orford. But then at once I was inside, sitting by the fireplace and its glowing logs. My middle older sister, Isabel, known as Ib, sat hooking a rug. Her husband, Lou Crone, slumped with his nose in a book, a common occupation. They were renting the cottage that winter of 1933 and '34. A car stopped in the driveway.

Ib said, keeping on with her hook and strips of cloth, "That'll be Ernie."

I knew she meant Lou's sister, Ernestine, who must have driven up from Lexington, where she lived with her parents and worked at Harvard for a sociology professor. I was about to tell Ib that I should have called from Hanover on the pay phone in my dormitory before hitchhiking up for the weekend. No words came because Ernie walked through the door in a green knitted dress. I stood up.

She glanced around and gave us a general "Hi."

Her eyes swung back to me, then quickly to Ib. "Like my new dress? I finished knitting it yesterday."

It fitted her nicely....

I now focused from Ernie in her green dress to the *Guide* pages. Mileage listed was cumulative, so while Claud loaded his pipe I subtracted. There were tenths to deal with. The inlet of Dream Lake was 9.25, whose two decimal places were silly and I called it 9.3. Gentian Pond Shelter was 11.4 miles.

I turned to announce happily, "Only two more miles." The extra tenth was unimportant, or so I thought.

He sat quietly smoking his pipe and only nodded. He must be very tired, too, not to be exploring along the Dryad Falls Trail. Then I recalled he'd acted the same way at the Peabody Brook Trail, so I read to him from the *Guide* pages about a place to check on. "'The Dryad Falls Trail, here a lumber road, leaves to a point affording a beautiful view of Mount Washington across the lake.'"

He just held up his pipe to show he was resting.

The smell of the burley tobacco he liked, trade name Velvet, made me want my pipe. I smoked a mixture called Revelation, a brand I had learned of from Ernie's brother. Although Lou was four years ahead of me in college, his tastes and philosophy and some bad habits worked on me, their effects lingering on and on.

My Revelation contained perique and latakia, among other ingredients that hooked me. Still I had cut down on smoking lately. It sometimes made me feel woozy. Now I decided I needed not a smoke but food. I was hungry, plain and simple. I went into my pack again for crackers and cheese.

Claud stood up and said, "I'm going to get a picture of Washington." He took the little camera from his pack, adding, "I can manage an extra hundred yards and back."

We started off together on the "lumber road," a term that always made me think of a sawmill, not a woods road. I munched my pilot cracker and cheese, first a bite of cheese from one hand, then a bite of cracker from the other. I had learned to bite all across the wide cracker to avoid losing crumbs.

A gravelly overlook opened before us. We stared down the length of the still water. Westward, the distant triangle of Mount Washington had been pasted on the horizon. The mid-afternoon sun blazed above the silhouette. I thought, "Not the best light for a picture."

Then I noticed upturned roots of a tree far along the shore. It wasn't right for a windfallen tangle of roots and dirt. It had to be a moose.

At the same instant Claud mumbled, "That's no stump."

"Damnation," I whispered, so excited I had the silly fear I might scare the moose with loud words. "If we'd only gone down that trail near the end there."

I felt a terrible regret. I tried some lines of the poem by E.A. Robinson: "Futile as regret." They didn't help much.

Claud silently unbuckled the strap on the cover of the Kodak Pony camera. I was trembling. The moose would plow water to the bank and vanish. I couldn't see details at that distance and felt robbed of a fair sighting of my first moose.

The spreading, palmated horns—antlers—appeared only when he moved his head and confirmed our identification. He appeared to be raising his head out of the water. Then the antlers showed clearly. I longed for my binoculars. Feeding belly deep, he looked shorter than in pictures of the body on long legs. The height at the shoulder seemed less than I expected.

I held my breath waiting for Claud to take the picture. This priceless chance could be gone in seconds. The fantastic scene of a moose in Dream Lake against a backdrop of Mount Washington might be lost forever. I thought of an enlarged, framed picture we'd each hang in our living rooms as mementos. I'd use one to illustrate an article about our trip, maybe in *New Hampshire Profiles* magazine....

Claud kept examining the camera. I wanted to snatch it from him. The first excruciating minute passed, and the second.

He said, "Let's see. I've taken two or three pictures, and my wife took a few at home...." He seldom, when not speaking to her, called her Louise. This was from talking to clients, I figured, but after all, I'd known for 25 years or so that she was his wife. He went on, "Now maybe there's only one left. I have a new film in my pack. Eight pictures to a roll...."

"For Christ's sake get a shot of that moose!"

"Had I better set it for infinity?"

I tried to speak calmly. "That's what I'd do."

"How about the aperture? You know these new cameras better than I do."

"There's a red dot, isn't there? This Pony is different from my Bolsey, which I wish to hell I'd brought along and damn the weight. For God's sake hurry up."

"Aw, he can't see us, and we're whispering, if you didn't notice." He stared down at the camera. "Now this is important. Too much light will ruin the picture, and the sun is over that way. My wife said something about backlighting."

"Didn't Louise show you how to run the camera?"

While I waited for him to answer I realized that his use of "my wife" was an idiosyncrasy which somehow went deeper than professional habit, in a way that I could not correlate with Ernie and me. Maybe after seven kids....

"She said if I couldn't remember, to ask you."

"Well, Ernie and I gave one of those cameras to Penny for high-school graduation, but that's seven years ago."

"Anyhow," he said, "the moose is too far away."

We began a disjointed conference on that problem: How about if we walk back to the far end by the trail? Then sneak to the water's edge. No, I don't think my legs afterward would get me to Gentian Pond Shelter. The light will be better, sun behind us. Yes, but we'd probably scare him.

There were too many problems.

Discouraged, I suddenly didn't care a damn for the moose. I looked at my wrist watch. Three in the afternoon. I was tired enough to camp right here. But I had to think of our schedule. We must be at Grafton Notch in time to meet Don and Ruthie. The allowance of one extra day, with them camping in the notch if we didn't show up on Labor Day, the 5th, as planned, might not be time enough. Then there'd be search parties, agony for our wives, and failure for us. I needed not only more strength but also more time. I felt depressed that the freedom of the wild forest and the joy of being in the mountains were no more. The carefree days, I said to myself, are gone forever. Shit.

Claud's low voice interrupted. "Tell me what exposure."

"Use a figure from the list on the camera. Lemme see. Well, looks like f-eleven at a fiftieth. Better open up to f-eight for backlight—oh goddamn, take it—no, I'll shade the lens with my hat."

"Wait till his head is up." Claud pressed the camera against his face. "Hell, I can't see anything in the finder like a moose—just a brown dot. Tell me when his head is up."

I held my green hat above the lens. The felt was so weatherbeaten that the brim had stretched downward the way those roll-up hats do. It was a dunce cap, very suitable. I watched the moose. The massive head and antlers rose from the water.

"Now!"

The camera clicked.

In the relief of having the moose on film, neither of us cared enough to attempt another shot at another aperture. The sun was wrong. The moose was too far away. Mount Washington had no definition. That faint triangle wouldn't show, nor would the moose.

We walked back to our packs and shouldered them.

Heading east we found that the bulldozed road ended almost at once. Claud sloshed into a bog where the inlet to Dream Lake meandered among black spruces and through a muskeg of sphagnum moss and leatherleaf bushes. The water would fill his boots and not drain out on dry ground as it would from my leather boots. But his laced leather tops protected his legs from the black ooze, whereas I felt not only icy water but also organic mud seeping down my socks into my boots.

When Cree Indians used their pronunciation of the word "muskeg" what did they say about the muck in their moccasins? And where had I first encountered muskeg and muck in moccasins? I wore moccasins in my woodcrafty youth, ah, where else but the source of Jacob's Brook in Orford, the Meadows, now flooded by the returned beavers. Camping on a nearby knoll with Claud, sick on bog water, next year exploring more of the wildwood between Mount Cube and Smarts Mountain, to the real source of Jacob's Brook, the North Branch, at the inlet to Lamprey Pond, where we half-finished a log shelter and fireplace....

What country for moose! If we were now 17 and camping there, with moose returned like the beavers, we might see moose feeding in Lamprey Pond. Supposing we were hunting deer and had our rifles?

Sloshing through the so-called Mahoosuc Trail following my friend the hunter, I realized he had said nothing about shooting the moose in Dream Lake. Among our varied avocations, his was that of the genuine hunter. I classed myself as a rank amateur.

Ahead of me his wading stopped. He looked back at me, his left hand on his chin.

He asked, "Do you think that moose was as far away as the length of Hogs Heaven?"

Instantaneous came the sighting down that narrow sward, enclosed by woods, and far distant an old pine stump with a dot of white tacked to it. Our youthful target range in an abandoned (we thought) pasture turned out to be a possible testing ground for my new deer rifle. How could I forget the slow squeeze of my trigger finger as the square of white paper blurred black and then a tripling of the white as a Holstein walked in front of the pine stump?

Claud repeated his question. "Think the moose was that far?"

"Umm, yes," I said. "We measured it with fifty feet of clothesline."

"Eighteen times fifty. I've always wondered if your forty-five-seventy would have dropped that cow."

"If it had, I'd have scorched my drawers. I raised the rifle just as it went off. Good thing we hadn't been trying to hit our moving deer target along the edge of the woods there."

"Hell, the one running with the cord to the deer would have seen the cows and hollered."

I said, "Just to change the subject, how come those pig skeletons in the east corner?"

"Before our time. Possibly hog cholera."

We sloshed onward, while I considered the woods that had grown up in Hogs Heaven so thick they lined the road to Orfordville, now Route 25A, when it was cut through our old target range.

Claud's ruminations came out as he stopped again and said, "I think I could have hit that moose with my 'scoped three hundred Magnum."

I knew he was about to conjure up a dream-game from our teen fantasies.

"All that meat. We could live through the winter on it if we waited till late fall and shot him. What do you say? Pack in enough tools and grub to build a cabin. Then go out for a load of books we've never read and spend the winter just hunting and trapping and improving our minds?"

Dream Lake seemed the perfect place. But at 3:30 in the afternoon of September 1, 1966, pretend-we-can-escape no longer worked. Our game of the simple life had become ritual only, yet I said, "Sure thing."

He failed to elaborate on the boyhood theme. Maybe no good, also, for him. He pushed on against the ankle-deep, dark water.

We stopped talking.

The trail emerged as a footpath. It was a wonder we hadn't angled off it into the bog. I realized that the water was clear instead of brown. I could see the forest floor through the shallows. We walked up, squishing in our boots. Mine, as I knew they would, leaked out water, and the wool socks formed a wet cushion. Claud's rubbers contained the water. He declined to stop and empty them. He clumped wetly on up the ridge of maples, birches, and beeches.

Beyond the low crest we descended into evergreens, which contrasted in their location below us, for usually we ascended into the spruce-fir growths. Maybe another swamp lay ahead. Odd that the trees could adapt to swamps as well as to crags.

Most of our rabbit hunting had been done, was done, in evergreen swamps. Not rabbits now, cottontails had disappeared, so hares only. Years ago there had been that day of "jackrabbits" as we called them, scooting like white ghosts through the spruce cap of Cottonstone Hill in Orford. Don't mention it. The relics of the past, about the targets in Hogs Heaven and the near disaster to the cow, had been more than enough, and the hounds, that day of leaping hares, were Bean hounds, which would remind Claud of our friend Malcolm who had hanged himself.

A bank of moss flourished as unobtrusively as moss does, around a trickle and a pool. We stopped to drink from the envelope. The pause stretched into a stop after I pointed out a burl on a spruce near the pool. It was that unusual for a spruce, although we were almost past commenting much on anything. We dropped our packs and examined the burl. Ballooning out from the trunk about four or five inches, the excrescence was a good six inches across and curved inward to its attachment, blending with the bark of the main tree.

We sat down to take off our boots and wring out our socks. I had short lacings on my boots. Claud's 10-inch leather uppers kept him busy longer. I rolled over and pushed onto my feet. I wanted to make sure the burl tree was a spruce.

Yes, it was a red spruce. I said, "Never saw one on a spruce before, always a hardwood—maples, mostly."

"If I had the strength I'd borrow your ax and chop it out and take it back to Louise for her to carve." The personal name meant he had left behind his profession.

Louise carved bas-reliefs and figures with a set of chisels and gouges.

How she found time with seven kids, a big garden, bookkeeping, income-tax records and accounting, knitting, sewing, milking the cow twice a day, feeding chickens and pigs, acting as Claud's assistant during operations, canning fruits and vegetables, freezing them, too, cooking—these activities and duties made wood carving seem impossible.

His attention to the burl shifted, perhaps at first because of the effort involved in bringing it back to Louise, more likely because that summer his eyes had acquired mushroom-awareness. He tied his second lacing, having tucked in his pants. He pulled himself up by the spruce and went a few steps to the mushroom.

I heard a blackpoll warbler overhead. While Claud examined the mushroom I examined the little resident of mountainous spruce-fir forests. I had learned as a boy some warblers from my narrow birdbook, Reed's *Birds of Eastern North America*...why were modern field guides not made to fit into a pocket?

Claud showed me the mushroom's yellow-orange cap, saying, "Fly mushroom, *Amanita muscaria*. It wouldn't kill you. Just make you damned sick."

"Red squirrels eat them."

"I guess red squirrels can stand alkaloids. Tough little bastards. Remember how we used to hunt them in that hemlock woods east of the Ledges, and we didn't know that the Wheelers owned the land till their hired man came to our shack and told us he had orders to tear it down?"

"I remember. Let's go."

"All right. Can't put it off any longer. I feel like the man who said, 'I'm gonna get drunk and how I dread it.'"

I began walking, but soon I sensed that he wasn't behind me. I stopped and turned.

He was kneeling, pack on his back, beside a spectacular fungus large as a ceremonial chalice except that it opened out to ruffles. Its orange color glowed, in spite of shading boughs above it.

He said, "Probably not enough light for a picture. At home, if I had a picture I could identify it."

"We could dig it up and take it to some sunlight."

He sat back on his heels and rubbed his hands together thoughtfully. "So rare and all, I hate to disturb it." He grasped a nearby tree and came slowly to his feet. "I suppose it's poisonous. There's a smaller one that people get mixed with chanterelles. Makes them sick."

"Then this one must be a regular killer."

"I'll find out the name someday. I was going to buy a big book to use at home instead of a pocket guide that one of my boys had. Cost too much. They wanted twenty-seven dollars for it."

"Sure," I said, "too much for a book. You've located another antique rifle for your collection."

He smiled crookedly. "Well, there is a rolling-block Ballard."

I suspected that Louise would give him the mushroom book. (She did.)

Proceeding again, we picked our way down a steep hillside among evergreens that had managed to thrive despite rocks that required the trail to twist through their scattered pattern. Beyond a jagged heap we stepped out on the shore of a little jewel of a pond. A stiff breeze ruffled the water. Wavelets glistened in the western sunlight. Moss Pond, so I remembered from the *Guide* pages, had once been called Upper Gentian Pond.

This gave me a vast lift; if it was "upper" we had just a descent to the end of our day's journey. We stood on the only strand, for all around the water the evergreens cupped it, and no vista rose above their pointed tips, so the pond appeared brimful, deep, and likely to have trout in it.

A mood of optimism made me ask, "Shall we try for 'em?"

Claud nodded and began kicking open a rotten stump and pawing in the bits of punk for grubs. We had lines and hooks as part of our woods equipment. I took off my hat and looked at the flies in the band. We hadn't dropped our packs. I reached for my jackknife to cut a rod from a clump of alder. But suddenly, hand in hip pocket, I had not the energy to bother with trout.

Claud said, "No grubs."

"And I can't cast a fly with an alder pole."

"I keep thinking of that shelter and a good fire blazing."

"Me too."

He paused, staring at the pond. "There was a time when I would have fished here till dark for a mess of trout. Even without bait they might come after a twist of birch bark on a hook, like they did in the Great Gulf when we were sixteen."

"Catch one and cut off his belly fin for a lure. Said to be the inspiration for the Parmachenee Belle."

"Come on. There's only one more board to put on today."

I had supposed he'd forgotten my little story about Roy Bagley and his son-in-law.

The trail turned left into thick trees. It was rough and hummocky a few yards from the water, mostly dark and gloomy along the north shore. We stopped at the east end of the green-glinting ripples, which I realized reflected the setting of green boughs. An evening sound came from across the pond. A hermit thrush tried an improvisation of flute notes. Maybe he was an immature male testing his instrument.

I couldn't stop thinking of trout. I said, "We've fished till dark and after, a number of times when we had made camp. On Whiteface Brook below Mount Carrigain."

"That was twenty years ago."

"Twenty-one. We had to use your gas coupons to get there."

"I'd never climbed Carrigain."

This said nothing about our previous four years in Laconia while the war went on, nor about the longing for the mountains, nor about our luck in not being shot at. Those four years had increased the trout in Whiteface Brook, a terrible way to improve the fishing.

We paused once more, for we were at the outlet of Moss Pond, and we saw the reason for the brimming shores. Fresh beaver-chewings of poplars and alders on sticks floating nearby led our eyes to the dam of poles and mud. It plugged a narrow gully and prevented at least two feet of pond water from pouring out of the little basin down the mountainside. A civil engineer might figure the pounds per square foot on the dam and disbelieve that animals other than men could build that junk—mostly from past meals—to hold such pressure. And how from men's meals? Not from spaghetti, shredded wheat, and bananas...I must be getting hungry again. My mind boggled.

Our trail, like the outlet brook, fell away steeply then swung left under the gray cliffs appearing through yellow birch leaves. Great slabs of rock lay about among the white trunks. The obscure path wound between the rocks and trees as in a maze, but steadily downwards. The final abrupt descent delivered us suddenly toward shimmering silver patches. We stepped onto the northern shore of Gentian Pond. I thought, "At last, at last, and why all my concern, nothing to it, here we are!"

Relief made me want to laugh.

A few dead stubs in marsh grass showed that beavers had once dammed the pond to a higher level of water. The trail turned to the right among thickets of brush and mountain holly before it led to a high, smooth ledge. We climbed and peered down. A gap in the natural dike contained the remains of the dam, a mere jumble of sticks in the outlet. Beyond the gap an equally smooth, sheer ledge rose to spruces and the small shelter of logs. It faced over the valley from a perch of flat ground.

The shelter! So near and yet so far!

Our haven and blessed rest were only a stone's throw away from my aching legs, creaking knees, and sore feet. I saw no way to reach the comfort of the bunk inside those old log walls. I started cursing, which availed nothing, nor did it relieve my feelings. I stared down at the impervious rock. Green leaves and tiny red berries of a vine grew from a crevice. Mountain cranberries thrive on cracked ledges, and always high up. We must have climbed to their territory. I felt better.

Next I realized that Claud was backing down over the edge, following the extension of the crack.

I said, "You better take off your pack and let me lower it to you."

No reply.

I admonished him, "You'll break your goddamned neck!"

"Who cares?"

The bulky pack and powerful shoulders and arms and fingers moved down the rock. The protruding pipe grated. His free hand removed it to a shirt pocket. I hoped to hell he didn't break it. The torn gray hat disappeared.

By the time I had explored out a less dangerous and inevitably longer route through the brush and scrub evergreens and had pulled myself up the opposite ledge, Claud was snooping about the shelter. And smoking his pipe.

This exploratory routine, nothing new, dated back to excursions when we sometimes ran low on food because we had underestimated our appetites. Now he examined a jar of rice, a box of pepper, and a pair of tattered sneakers. He began to read the register. I ducked under the overhang and dumped my pack on the bunk.

Ah, that lightness, that release, that freedom! These emotions and sensations eased the agonies in every muscle and joint, even in the headache that was beginning to tap with a little hammer. I started to step outside, remembering, luckily for my head, to stoop under the overhang of the log supporting the partial front roof.

Distance opened before me. I stared away downhill into the valley of the Androscoggin River at Shelburne and the highway, Route 2. Farther away rose the summits of the Carter-Moriah Range. I felt I could sail off this aerie like a hawk and dive down with wings folded to inspect houses and fields before I zoomed up to a crag far away against the sky. My thoughts, such as they were, slowly numbed into a pleasant daze through which ran the words, "You made it. Yes, you made it." I went inside and stretched out on the bunk's balsam boughs.

I was awakened by Claud's stirring a stick out in the fireplace and rattling tin cans. I sat up. The half-circle of blackened rocks rested on a foundation of larger rocks. I slid my boots over the end of the bunk and sat there to watch him pull out the last of the cans. His comment reached me easily, though to himself. "Bloody goofers, leaving a mess like this." He winged a can into the vastness below us. One after another the burned cans sailed into the distance. From the treetops down there two red squirrels scolded Claud's disposal system. I thought, "Quick and effective, if not ecologically sound," and felt young again. Great little nap.

Claud turned about and surveyed the shelter before he said, "Best shelter in the mountains."

"Don't forget Isolation. Never any smoke inside."

"Wonder if it's still there. We'll have to go see it sometime."

"Sure."

I had to look again at our view, which required another hunched exit. Staring into the valley I could make out sunlight on a black ribbon beyond the river. Creeping bugs moved along it as if under a microscope. Cars on Route 2. The effect, framed in the peripheral distances of the mountains and sky, suggested some cosmic insignificance for mankind, if I could just grasp it.

I couldn't. And Claud was breaking twigs from the bunk's useless dead branches. I gathered the tin pails and coffeepot. This required opening my pack, which also held the ax. Habit was taking over be-

cause water was my job, just as the fire belonged to Claud. He'd need
the ax. The handle protruded, being almost two feet long. I took off
the leather sheath. The head was shaped like an Indian tomahawk to
save weight. I had bought it as a then-unusual shape from the catalog of
David T. Abercrombie. So it had been with us for all of our camping
since 1929.

Claud accepted it without comment. We both knew I had to take it
from my pack, not him. Packs were private.

I found a smaller pail hanging from a nail and added it to the collection. The walls, ancient spruce, were caulked with oakum, which the
years had dried to wisps.

I told Claud I'd look for the spring. "I don't dare drink the water
from the pond."

"Well, I haven't noticed any *kalmia* growing along the shore."

"All the same, I'm leery of pond water. For the shelter there must be
a spring."

I picked up our kettles by the bails, then remembered I might need a
cup, so had to reorganize by putting down the three in one hand and
dropping a tin cup inside a tin pail before starting off again.

Where was the pond's inlet? That could be the "spring" I hoped to
find.

I spotted on a small fir an arrow-sign marked: "Water 200 yards." It
pointed into the east woods. Some wag had penciled in another zero. He
was wrong by another zero or two. The distance up and down through
the forest to a tiny inlet proved to be longer than I liked, but it was worth
the effort.

The water trickled from a growth of waterbrush and sphagnum
moss. I saw no sheep laurel. The pool was icy cold. I had to sip from the
cup. I began ladling the water carefully so as to leave the green moss and
wet yellow leaves undisturbed by filling the pails. I could see out across
the darkening pond to the wooded half-bowl that contained it on the
mountainside. The sun had disappeared behind the western wall. There
wasn't a sound. I squatted in shadow. If I paid no attention to my throbbing forehead I was very happy.

The pails were full yet I lingered till my duty as Gunga Din took
over.

I trudged tediously back through the woods. Alternating patches of light and dark spread before me so that I moved among the tree trunks from a brilliant stage into the shadowy wings and back out again. Dead branches of the many small evergreens tipped the pails and sloshed my pants. I had a vague thought about the natural thinning of a young forest that produced so much good firewood—well, as good as spruce and fir could be if not compared to dead maple or beech. I wondered that I saw no chopped stumps. Lack of campers at the shelter probably.

The log walls finally appeared. Peeled spruce lasts a long time. Maybe 30 years had passed to make the back of the shelter look decayed. The notches at the corner, although fitted by neat ax work from the underside so as not to collect water, had begun to rot. The walls could have been laid up while Claud and I were in college. The AMC must have kept a good roof over them. Yes, tar paper in fair condition.

Claud had started a fire. The shelter would not fill with smoke. It blew away toward the distant valley and the far mountains. I felt the fire reviving me. The wild surroundings took on a homey familiarity. Claud was unfolding the hinged reflector oven and locking in place the sides and angular top. He said, "Take a look at that bundle of grub hanging in the shelter."

His investigations had revealed a bulky plastic bag suspended from a nail driven into a log rafter. Attached to it a piece of paper displayed careful writing. I read, "Please do not use except in dire necessity. Will return and eat them ourselves tomorrow."

From the shelter's register, a cardboard-covered account book, I learned that in the morning a father and daughter had gone on over Mount Success to Carlo Col Shelter, and would come back tomorrow. I recognized a little twinge of nostalgia from memories of camping with Ruthie and Penny. Those unlikely outings seemed long ago. I was now a grandfather to Penny's daughter, Thane, and father of a novelist just returned from England.

I said, "Probably we'll run into 'em tomorrow."

He commented, "Unless they're traveling too light and have died of inanition. I like to have all my grub with me."

Mixing biscuit dough from Louise's packages, he stirred it in a saucepan he had found hanging on a log wall. Otherwise the pan for the oven would have had to serve. This might be a problem later. I saw that he had whittled out a crude paddle.

He had also laid out an envelope of hamburg-macaroni mix. I asked, "Want me to add the water?" He nodded.

I hesitated over the pails. The envelope called for three cups of water. I poured some from a pail into the frying pan till I guessed three cups were left. I stirred the mess with a twig, it being too deep for my short-handled spoon.

Claud was feeding the fire with sticks of dry maple he had found somewhere while I was getting water. And he had rearranged the stones of the fireplace to support the oven and to reflect heat from the hot flames and coals. He found a place for the pot of hamburg-macaroni in a corner of his fire's coals. Twigs around it caught the flames at once.

The biscuit dough had to be reshaped into a rectangle to fit the pan of the oven. His floury hands poked at the white mass to spread it into corners. He slid the pan into the oven. Because the fireplace was raised on its foundation there was no need for a tired cook to assume the position of a catcher in a baseball game.

I saw that he had laid out on the bunk log another envelope labeled "Apple Pudding. Mix with two cups of water."

We had an aluminum bowl that would hold the mix. When I stirred the pink powder with the water, there arose a smell suggestive of apples left too long under a tree in October. The fragrant sauce began to thicken almost at once, doubtless due to some deleterious chemical, but never mind; what processed foods now were truly "natural"?—a term that was beginning to be a great selling come-on.

Claud had been too busy to gather and chop sufficient wood. I dragged up several dead spruces the diameter of broomsticks and chopped them to length with the ax. A little gnome in my head belted me with a mallet at each stroke of my ax. I ducked into the shelter and blew up my air mattress. The bunk, deep in dried balsam needles, occupied the entire inside except the area of bare ground under the front overhang. I laid out the mattress and sleeping bag next to the west wall and about the distance of four sleeping spaces from Claud's pack and mummy bag next to the east wall. I'd sleep on my right side, hood over my head, back to his noise. I ought to be tired enough to sleep through doom cracking.

Claud came back from the pond wiping his hands on his shirttail. He ducked in and surveyed the layout of both bags. His fingers probed the depth of the fir needles on the bunk. "Ah yes, good old balsam. Better than the goddamned wire mesh used now in some shelters. Wire mesh or bare boards. The Forest Service and the AMC are improving shelters into torture chambers."

"Young people sleep on those styrofoam pads or whatever they're made of."

"You gotta lug 'em and anyhow camping out you should sleep on balsam boughs." He returned to the fire, where he lifted away the oven on a pair of sticks.

I said, "It's a bureaucratic solution to stripping fir trees of boughs."

"And the same bloody bureaucrats let the lumber companies cut down thousands of acres in the National Forest."

"You've heard of multiple use."

"Multiple shit. Congress was bought out by the big Western loggers." He withdrew a splinter from the biscuit-bread. "Done to a turn. Guess we can eat." He filled our aluminum plates with squares of biscuit and heaped hamburg-macaroni mess.

We sat on the log that formed the front of the bunk. Evening lay in the valley below us. Our fire burned smokily in the daylight. New wood had not yet caught flame. A cool breeze slid past us from the mountain.

Partial walls closed in the front for about three feet on either side of the opening. I was interested in the construction because log walls usually require notched joints at the ends. These walls ended at the open entrance against split posts through which spikes were driven. I chewed and thought, "All right, nothing new, but neat job. No chain saws for the builder of this shelter. You remember working on parts for newly-invented chain saws to be used on the Alcan Highway clearing—pneumatic saws. These posts were probably halved by hewing with an ax."

The hamburg-macaroni mess was hearty. It had only a slight and indescribable taint of the dehydration method, or of storage, which resembled nothing except a suggestion of mold. Claud had brought his double-ended shaker of salt and pepper. We applied both liberally. The biscuit, or more accurately shortbread, soaked up butter from the jar and gave off an aroma of the dough, crisp crust, and melted butter. I spread some of the apple pudding, so called, on my second chunk of biscuit for instant apple pandowdy.

I told Claud, "This is better biscuit than I ever baked in a frypan."

"That bread you called doughgod, with chopped bacon and shortening of bacon grease, was good. I never thought much of your corn bread except when we ran out of anything else to eat."

"It went good with the rabbit stew at Isolation Shelter."

"We were starving on those trout."

Our tea from the coffeepot looked too strong for me. I diluted mine with water. We drank from two battered nesting cups, which had been part of the first cook kit by David T. Abercrombie and my savings account via school banking. (Ernie, the mystery reader, once told me the kid-hustler had been Rex Stout, creator of school banking as well as of Nero Wolfe.)

Because there was extra food we didn't clean the pots by going down to the pond outlet in the gathering darkness. I arranged the pots and covers—biscuit and mess—in a corner near my sleeping bag, saying, "I'll keep the ax handy in case a hedgehog tries to get at the food."

"No signs of hedgehogs."

"Scarce since fisher-cats came back."

Claud offered me more tea from the coffeepot. I was afraid of the potent brew from bags still in the pot. It would keep me awake. I took only half a cup to sip at. Unlike aluminum cups these of steel didn't burn your lips. At the time I bought the kit, tinned steel was cheaper by a good deal than aluminum. These cups, brought to the Mahoosucs at Claud's request, although he didn't admit to sentimentality, were pitted where the tinning had worn off or had melted away when set in hot coals. These ancient artifacts of our youth, after I scoured off the rust with steelwool pads at home, added to the ritual of our tea. Right now, however, I set mine aside and accidentally-on-purpose tipped it over on the ground.

We sat again on the bunk's log. We smoked our pipes.

Across the dark valley only Carter Dome caught the last light of the sun, which had set for us. Then the oval of light, away off there, darkened. A plane droned across that southern sky. It glowed silvery from higher sunbeams and vanished. Down on the highway cars were evident by headlights no bigger than single gleams through black pin-pricked paper. We knocked out our pipes, poked off separately to leak for the night, and crawled into our mummy bags.

I was too tired for sleep. I lay on my back and watched flickering reflections on the roof. The firelight faded. The boards blended into darkness. I fell asleep before Claud tuned up—or else he was slumbering quietly for a change.

The whooshing of surf came to me while I was enough aware to understand that it was wind in spruces. Gradually an expanse of sand met the sound of surf by materializing into a beach, and it was South Beach at Martha's Vineyard. A freshwater pond spread in the sand and this anomaly so near the vast ocean with its rollers intrigued me. Ernie appeared in a flowered bathing suit, laughing as I tried to paddle a kayak. She waded into the still water and pushed me in the direction I was aiming but couldn't achieve with the double-ended paddle. Sally had brought the kayak from Menemsha, where we were not staying with her and Joe but in a rented cottage.

I became expert with the paddle after Ernie and Sally lay down on a blanket to sunbathe and talk of many things, girlhood pals. My proficiency improved my day, which had started badly because my morning's work on *Forgotten Democracy*, typing in the one-room cottage while Ernie did housework and read a mystery, had seemed futile, like my earlier casting for striped bass into the flurry of—was it sand eels?—agitating the cove that floated moored boats at Menemsha…gulls and terns overhead…dawn…cool….

I awoke cold. The beach scene vanished. The sound of surf was more of a hissing—strange how different from salt water, no, strange how different from the wind in the pines sighing. This was more of a swish through the branches of short needles. I sat up slowly. I was lame all over.

The wind made me uneasy. It had shifted, and unfavorably I thought. I pulled on my wool shirt. I ached. Across the shelter Claud snored in choking gasps as though a panther had him by the throat. Shivering, I hugged myself. A faintly lighter darkness showed me the front of the shelter. A vagrant gust made the ashes in the fireplace glow for an instant. I lay back and pulled the sleeping bag around my shoulders and over my head. Zip it up by the thong on the steel tab and go to sleep…if you can forget the past and stop worrying about the distance and heights that face you for tomorrow.

Was the trip to Martha's Vineyard only a month ago? A vacation within "retirement" confused the visit, and what would you use for money if the writing didn't pay off? Damn fool gamble at age 51; you had been making $8,000 a year even if the job was probably killing you. Ah, but the addiction to writing; what was it that a Maine poet had to say about the dubious undertaking of expressing your life and the world? Sleep may come before you remember...

"Art's long hazard, where no man may choose/Whether he play to win, or toil to lose."

DAY THREE: SEPTEMBER 2, 1966

THE IRONY OF SUCCESS

DAWNLIGHT, EXCRUCIATING PAINS, HEAVY WOOL SOCKS DRYING overnight somewhere in the bottom of my mummy bag. Clean wool socks lightweight on my feet, not to be put into damp boots, save 'em for the next night. Heavy socks dried some....

Booted, I collected the pots or pails, which no porcupine had raided in the night. Last night's leftover supper occupied two pots, so how do I get water? I remembered the coffeepot by the fireplace, and there must be an empty one...how about filling the plastic water bottles? Yes, but how to carry them...tie them up in my rain parka....

Morning confusion, for this morning person, meant I was tired out. I creaked through the woods to the inlet and back.

Claud had started the fire with fir twigs and birch bark. He was chopping sticks to length on a stump. Tiredness lay on his mind, too:

"There was this fellow used to stop each year at Galehead. Real up-and-at-'em guy. One of those Appies who stood out on the porch and breathed deep of the mountain air and so on. Flexed muscles and jogged back and forth. Gray-haired and wiry. I put him up at least once for five summers. Last time he was afraid he'd slowed down. Said that morning, 'When you have a good night's sleep and wake up tired, you're getting old.'"

We thought about that during breakfast. Tea with dried skim milk and sugar, pink apple pudding quite ghastly by daylight. I dunked left-over biscuit. Noting that Claud did the same, I said, "This'll stick to our ribs for Mount Success."

"No protein." He busied himself mixing scrambled eggs and slicing bacon.

I warmed the leftover hamburg-macaroni.

We ate slowly. The bacon was good. Plenty of tea.

After my third cup I studied the *Guide* pages. This informed me that we were 11.4 miles from the railroad bridge in Gorham. Destination for the night, Carlo Col Shelter, was 16.8 miles. The tenths of miles in such rough country amused me, thinking of someone encumbered with a measuring wheel. And our day's hike was amusing, too. A mere 5.4 miles. But Carlo Col Shelter nestled below Mount Success on the far side, I knew not where. The concept of "nestled" might be wishful thinking; it could be exposed in wind-whipped rain.

To pack my Duluth I first unpacked it so I could slide in the folded sleeping bag to protect my back. In earlier days a blanket had saved my back from canned beans and the ax. I sheathed the Hudson's Bay and began repacking my share of the grub. The pots would go in last, bagged against the soot, after I put out the fire.

A touch of apprehension sent me outside to guess the weather. Un-clear skies could mean nothing, or could threaten us with rain. I looked across the valley to mountains south and west. The barren ridge of Shelburne-Moriah showed its ledges. The peak of Moriah rose above the green of spruces. Farther away Carter Dome appeared dull in outline as did the adjacent summits lined toward me. Nearby clarity allowed me to see down to the asphalt ribbon of Route 2. No white fog from the night lay along the Androscoggin River. The day, I knew, would be more promising had cottony vapors obscured the highway and houses down there. The sun was hazy as though not trying to shine.

Claud began to whistle inside the shelter as he packed. The tune was "March Militaire." It meant he was almost ready to move on.

I told him, "Today we have five-and-a-half miles. Only three miles to the top of Success."

"Only?" He was strapping down the cover of his pack.

"Well, at three thousand five-ninety feet that's not much higher than Smarts and Cube in Orford where we started. No trouble there."

"No trouble except on Smarts, last day of December, nineteen twenty-nine."

He smiled, not at that close call with freezing to death, but because he loved the old log cabin, low and gloomy as it was, once the fire lookout's abode and as primitive as the tower of spruce poles.

We had been young. That's why Smarts and Cube gave us no trouble except New Year's Eve 1929.

I said, "And the cabin door, after we got to it through the snow, frozen in the ice...never mind that. Here at Gentian Pond we're about twenty-five hundred feet. So we have maybe eleven hundred feet of climb. That's only a hundred more than the thousand that you say is the climb up South Twin from Galehead Hut."

"This'll be three times as far."

If he wanted to make the worst of it, I'd help. "And the *Guide* calls the trail 'rough in places.'"

"I'm beginning to think it's all rough in the Mahoosucs."

He prepared for the ordeal by lighting his pipe. I kept rearranging the stuff in my pack in hopes of easier carrying. There was none. He puffed out smoke and tapped the glowing tobacco with his thumb, saying, "Three miles, and then two and a half to Carlo Col Shelter. We ought to have time for locating the wreckage of the DC-3 on Success."

"There's directions here in the *Guide*. Sounds possible, but I'll wait to see about time and my strength."

Water from the pond was easy, and I used plenty out of the pots to douse the fire. The spout of the coffeepot poured a stream among the stones. I knew that Claud was thinking I used too much water—I might crack the rocks, or maybe one would burst. Steam rose from them. I went for more water and quenched the steam. Silly, but steam and smoke look alike. If I leave smoke behind at a camp I worry.

Claud asked, "Is the sun up enough for a picture?"

"Ought to be. Nine o'clock already."

"If you'd stand over there with the ax I'll get a picture of you both, and the shelter."

"I should take you this time."

"Nah, I always look like a bear with a sore paw."

Soon after the picture we hit the trail—gently. Claud walked ahead. I could tell by the way he carefully placed his boots and pushed with his hips that he was straining against aches. I felt sorry for him because he hated growing old. Mixed with sympathy was a touch of guilty gladness that I was not alone in suffering. He carried the bigger load—which he refuse to share—with the oven and more of the grub.

Yes, we took it easy. How? Pauses frequent. Gasp for breath. Climb a steepness. Admire Gentian Pond below us, blue-green in its wooded cup. Climb again. The pond appeared farther below us, and again still farther. Steep. At an open ledge we rested and talked of a picture. I said, "Nope. Clouded over. Not enough light for a color picture, but you can try."

"I hate to waste film. Too bad. That's quite a sight down to the pond and beyond with the mountains. Glad I saw it. Maybe never again."

I disregarded the pessimism. "That's the trouble with color. I wish I'd brought my Bolsey with black and white."

We moved on. The trail led downward. I said, "This is a damn poor way to climb a mountain."

"Laid out by a specialist in difficult routes. You watch, in two minutes we'll be pushing up again."

We were. Then stepped downward again. Climbed again. After several of these I had done my day's hike. Mount Success was an impregnable fortress.

In the brushy bottom of one of those descents we came to a spring. I dropped my pack. This must be the *Guide's* "water in the col beyond the second hump, and then attacks the side of Mount Success." The *Guide* lost track of humps; I guessed four. But how about the next water? I read ahead. No mention of water before our day's destination, Carlo Col Shelter. Here was the last water of the day. We must tank up and fill our water bottles. Tank up? I felt the empty sensation that water would drain through my body and run out my toes. That's how my strength drained out. I was through climbing forever. Done in. And we hadn't started up the real mountain. Time: 11:00. We'd been at it almost two hours. The *Guide* pages gave three hours for the summit from the pond.

My pack contained the snacks. I unstrapped one buckle only and reached under the cover. We sat on a log and ate chocolate from the thick rectangle of notched semi-sweet. We washed down pilot crackers with spring water. We chomped raisins. We drank more water. I could feel the crackers and raisins swelling inside me.

The little pool was deep enough to fill our near-empty water bottles without a cup. How had we ever sipped almost a pint apiece in two hours—evaporation from climbing.

The plastic bottles had come to Claud's mailbox beside his drive-way. They once contained animal medicine. He looked at his carefully before he began an account of his difficulties with the United States Postal Service.

"The smashing machine at the Laconia post office can't seem to squash these. Glass is its real function. Last week I had a call from a guy who believes in rules. But he was smart. He first off just said I had a package to pick up. Why couldn't they deliver? Special form to sign. Finally I got the real poop. There was a broken gallon jug of horse cough syrup, running through the excelsior packing and cardboard onto a bench and the floor. Sticky stuff, stunk horrible. I said how could I pour it down a horse if it was on the bench in the Laconia post office. He began to carry on some. Rule number two thousand and zero-zero. Ad-dressee of damaged goods is required to pick up same and sign form nine nine zero one two three four. I told him what he could do with his rule and his form."

Claud chewed thoughtfully. "You know, sometimes I say things I shouldn't."

We considered this for a while. It was true.

My mind wandered to an actual device that resulted in broken pack-ages. I said, "Maybe some places they're still using the train pickup—that steel arm by the tracks with a mailbag hung on it to be snagged by a hook on the passing baggage car."

"Like the one we used to watch at the Fairlee station?" He shook his head. "No, those are gone, even the one at the Winnisquam station that taught my wife and me not to mail bottles at the Winnisquam post of-fice. What they've done is to build a special smashing machine in Laconia."

He was really wound up about the Postal Service. After lighting his pipe till the match burned close to his fingers, for he always smoked a load to the bottom, he went on about damaged parcels. "Last week they delivered a box hanging by a string on our mailbox. Inside was a cracked bottle of worm medicine for dogs. I hung it back with a note telling 'em it wasn't all smashed and to run it through the smashing machine again. I guess it's war."

He stood up and knocked his pipe against the heel of one hand. Ashes sizzled into the trickle from the pool. He said, "Let's head up to where we start looking for that DC-3."

Stiffened in our joints—we had made the mistake of sitting too long on the log—we shouldered our packs. These added to the considerable weight in our bellies of water-soaked chocolate, crackers, and raisins.

Slowly we approached the "steep and rough" footing predicted in the *Guide* pages. This description hardly prepared us. A 50-degree, upward angle had encouraged a rock slide the previous spring, judging by the fresh scratches on rocks and trees. At first we marked time, so to speak, in treadmill gravel. Then came complaining words for scrambling over stumps and boulders. We untangled ourselves from treetops. Relief met us on a smaller, earlier slide grown to bushes.

I noted a few chunks of broken ledge that I took to be gneiss. Geology I, I realized, had been 33 years back. This pleased me in a sardonic way because it meant that my mind and memory still functioned, after a fashion.

Claud stopped and asked, "Do you figure this is the trail?"

"No."

"Me neither."

We faced about and I led the way back to a cairn we had passed. It consisted of four stones piled on each other and diminishing in size. It had been set on the upper edge of the first slide, seemingly unrelated to the trail. We stood beside it and pondered the problem. I said, "It must mean something."

"Maybe it means to stop and look around. Let's do that."

He eased into the bushes one way, I the other. I pretended there might be a trace of the trail, if not another cairn.

Soon his voice emanated from the tangle. "Here's a washout and a fan of rocks." Silence. Rubber makes no sound on rocks. "Come look."

Together we found the trail leading out of the gully. We laid up another cairn and broke off branches as our good deed for the day.

About a quarter-mile above this fault in the trail we met a man and a girl descending. She was maybe twelve years old. The man, a rugged individual who looked rather frazzled, asked, "Did the mice and squirrels get our food?"

I answered, "Okay when we left."

"That's good. We're going light to get an extra section of the AT. Maybe next year from Carlo Col to Grafton Notch."

"Not me," the girl announced. With thumbs she shifted shoulder straps.

He apologized for her. "My daughter's a little tired."

She gave us—Claud and me—a look combining resignation and discouragement. The expression indicated her opinion of anyone on this trail—crazy as her father, but harmless, if somewhat contemptible.

Claud asked, "How far to the summit?"

"About twenty minutes."

That sounded good to me; he knew that time in the mountains was more reliable than distance. "Could you see off?"

"The weather's closing in the views. If you hurry you'll still see along the range." ·

Claud sought more information. "Did you find the DC-3?"

"No, I didn't take the time to look." He turned away. "So long now."

"Good luck," I said, and to myself, "Hurry indeed, ha-ha."

The man and his daughter stepped rapidly downward among the trees. Their aluminum tube frames and orange nylon packbags vanished last.

I watched Claud disjoint his pipe and blow through the bit. The process was not so much a clearance as it was a gesture commenting on hikers who rushed along trails just to say they'd done part of the AT or had surmounted a summit.

We slogged upward steadily for 20 minutes by my watch. The forest continued to enclose us. The spruces grew thickly together and blended with fir-balsam, mountain ash, and birch. The man must have meant his time descending, the way they had come. He was young, maybe early thirties. She, although tired, moved with a body as active as it would ever be. We climbed on.

The air became damp. Short little plateaus held black muck and sphagnum moss like green sponges. We came to a clear pool in the moss. With mutual inclination we dropped our packs. I said, "More lunch," and produced crackers and cheese.

A few chomps of that dry combination started us eyeing the pool; we shook our heads and sipped from our bottles.

I was staring up the trail without enthusiasm for the next steep pitch when I caught a glimpse of motion on the ground under the evergreen branches. The moving light and shadow materialized into a small dark chicken. The bird wandered into the path. There it caused in me a quick excitement of recognition. I was watching a rare spruce grouse.

Unmistakable were blackish feathers streaked with gray. The bird nipped off a spruce needle and inspected a fern before cocking its head at the ground in search of bugs. So close it was across the pool that I saw the red fleck of comb-like skin over the eye. A male.

Claud slowly took the camera from his pack. The grouse paid no attention. A ruffed grouse would have been off with a roar of wings. Claud raised the camera, whispering, "Haven't seen one since Galehead, coming down my last day in nineteen thirty-eight, on the Garfield Ridge Trail just below the cabin. Saw 'em every summer since I went there in nineteen thirty-four."

I myself had a vivid set of 1934 pictures flashing across my memory screen—Michigan's Upper Peninsula, and Brush Cutter Doan of a survey crew aiming a .22 Colt Woodsman at the head of a spruce grouse in the cedar forest. The boss, who owned the pistol, had started the shooting. The cook baked several. Tasted of cedar.

But before that, 1931, at treeline above Mizpah Spring Shelter on the Crawford Path, as Red West and I headed for all the Presidentials that long day, a spruce grouse hen posed for us on a rock against the sky and clucked to her chicks.

I said to Claud as he fiddled with the camera, "Open it way up, and slow. Damnation, he's walking away."

Claud crouched toward the woods. "I'll see if I can head him back into the light." He pushed aside branches and disappeared.

There came to me, alone, a vain sense of time lost since that spruce grouse on the Crawford Path, since my summer of surveying for the General Land Office, my first job, as was Claud's at AMC's Galehead log-cabin hut.

Staring beyond the pool in hopes that the grouse would again emerge, I realized that not time lost haunted me but lost youth and opportunities for more of my woods and mountains. Maybe I should have gone into forestry after Dartmouth. Maybe I should have tried harder at geology and botany as possible careers. Maybe this and maybe that. I told myself that I was too late, just as I was too late for the Mahoosucs.

Perhaps Claud could turn the grouse back to the patch of light beside the pool. While I waited, the sun went in. Both Claud and the grouse had been gone a long time. So it seemed. I felt a silly panic at being alone. I told myself, "You must be really sick, you old woodsman, relax. Woodsman, hell, you never were a woodsman, not like him. You're alone and your partner lost in this vast wilderness— you're a tired old fart."

The spruce grouse came doddering toward me under the spruces, clucking in a minor key, hesitant with slow stepping claws.

A diet of spruce and fir seems to give spruce grouse a reluctance to react against puzzlement.

Shadowy Claud appeared among the branches. He knelt and sighted through the camera. The bird stepped into the open by the pool but kept moving instead of posing. To stop him I took off my hat and gently waved it. Although the sunlight had gone, a picture might be possible.

With first one eye and then the other our bird admired my show. Claud kneed himself closer. This diverted our bird from my hat; the annoying creature following was very close and maybe dangerous. I wanted to shout at the "creature," "Take it!"

The bird flew off. Even a spruce grouse will stand for only so much harassment.

And yet we were pleased about the incident. The grouse had been an exciting token of the wild. Besides we had lunched, and I had rested.

Claud put away the camera. "We can't be far from the summit now. Those spruces are getting smaller."

"Maybe we'll find the wreckage. I think we can take time."

Proceeding up the steep pitch, we used 20 minutes to reach scrub spruces we could look over. They grew intermittently among the ledges west of the summit, itself a rocky crag still a few minutes away.

Claud had been leading. He stopped. "We've got to decide how to go looking for the wreckage."

"Wait till I read the *Guide* pages." I took the crude booklet from my shirt pocket. "It says, umm, 'about three-tenths mile south and west of the summit'—that's us I guess…umm, yes, scrub growth before the ledge. Here it is for the DC-3, quote, 'one may follow the line of scrub south for about fifty yards to the trail that leads to the wreckage' unquote."

"Sounds easy. Come on."

For some reason I hated to leave the path. "Maybe not so easy. The crash was twelve years ago."

"Sure, but the *Guide* came out in sixty-three."

"You know how editions keep the old text year after year. These directions could be from two years after the crash. Hell, when we started for the mountains in the summer of thirty we used that nineteen-seventeen edition. Bet the so-called trail has grown up and the scrub has spread onto the ledges."

He saw through my prevarications. "Shit, it says fifty yards from here. That ain't much more than a shotgun carries bird shot. There's a plane in that scrub. It'll stand right out. Aluminum is silvery. What you worried about?" He watched me with serious eyes from under his hat brim.

I didn't want to tell him that I had no strength, not to waste anyhow on a pile of junk. "All right," I said. "Goddamn it, let's try."

We left our packs near a cairn where the Mahoosuc Trail headed up to the distant rocks against the clouds. Claud took the camera. Although I knew he could find our way back to the path, I made sure my old brass compass was in my pants pocket. Deserting the packs for a plunge into that scrub made me queasy. I also worried about the clouds spreading over the sky. They might not be threatening, and then again they might shed rain on us. I thought longingly of comfort in the shelter at Carlo Col, somewhere ahead another two-and-a-half miles away over unknown rough terrain. And I followed Claud.

After 50 yards along the east edge of the scrub—I assumed he esti-mated it as 10 yards beyond extreme shotgun range—we began searching for the trail to the wreckage. The ground on our left spread away toward the summit's rocks. Flattened spruces lay across the gravel and stones. I took them for black spruces creeping to escape violent winds. Matted roots grew from patches of scanty black earth to feed hardy heath such as sheep laurel, Labrador tea, and mountain cranberry. A few yards east of this open land rose ledges that layered themselves upward with occa-sional clumps of head-high spruces clinging to crevices.

On our right, no pathway appeared in the tight scrub evergreens. We found faint traces of boots on the turf, although not actual tracks but a worn look that could have been game trails, had there been vee-tracks of deer or moose. Here and there at random we found little piles of stones, two or three in a heap, hardly worthy of the name cairn. We wandered along this easy ground hoping for an opening into the impen-etrable hedge of spruces. Nothing.

We took a compass bearing, mainly for our return. Then Claud bored his way into the scrub and disappeared. In following I encountered a thousand switches binding my legs and arms in the first six pushing steps. Lovely green boughs were also tough and springy as steel. Scratchy wires of dead limbs and twigs clawed from below the branches of green-ery. Direction meant nothing. We soon became separated. I began to worry about escape, so I bent spruce sprays till they hung down, partly broken, to mark my backtrack.

I kept watch for the brown of cut boughs, for slashed stubs, for trimmed trunks. The scrub looked primeval and ageless. Several yards of fighting brought me to a horizontal ledge hidden in a mass of green needles. I felt it with my boots but couldn't see it. So I stepped off the edge. My shirt tore on the sharp butt of a branch that obviously had been cut off some years back. Then I saw another angled stub. Next to catch my eye was an ax blaze, small because the spruce trunk was no more than three inches in diameter. Dried pitch clung to the exposed wood. Be-yond this tree appeared a suggestion of an opening.

I hollered, "Blaze here!"

No answer.

Claud progressed, judging from the sounds, through the almost-impenetrable thicket with the same patient power that he used to follow deer tracks through the close stands of sprouts and striped maple and birch and fir on Crystal Mountain above his camp. For myself, when I found no more blazes, total letdown engulfed me. I began to slump. The spruces supported me. Discouraged and weak, caring nothing for the wreckage, I began to burn with fury so helpless and childish that I struck out at the spruce tangle to make it release me by wilting under my ineffective slaps.

I wanted to rush back into the open, but which way? The branches I had broken did nothing to relieve my fears that I couldn't find the way back to freedom from the spruces. I must find the route, the packs, the trail, hurry to my night's shelter. I felt a bewildered, trapped panic. I looked up as if I could escape that way. The clouds had darkened. A wind began to sweep over the mountaintop.

Somewhere beyond me came indistinct words: "Yes, blazes, must be old way...trail, well, maybe...."

I felt calmer at once and pushed on a few steps. I could feel more rock under my boots. I saw spruce tops below me. I stood on some sort of drop-off. Claud's checked shirt and old felt hat protruded from the green branches. He held up one hand.

"Listen."

I could hear faintly a metallic clinking sound. It came again, and stopped. The whispering of the breeze in the millions of spruce needles had increased to a hiss. Claud's shirt and hat eased ahead until, in an odd way, he became wholly visible. I realized that he had stepped into an opening.

I scrambled, then swam through the branches down the bank to join him. We stood silently in wonder before the expanse of aluminum. A somewhat irrelevant notion came to me: "How strange it is, exposed because trees in twelve years have not overgrown this silvery coffin for how many people?"

Then I recalled the elevation, the exposure, and the slow growth of treeline spruces. There was still evidence of the plane's skidding down to its fate. Trees mowed short by the plane had not put out new tops. Scarred ledges still retained the gouged lines ground in by the undercarriage.

Because still of a metallic glow, the dented aluminum might have slid into the mountainside only recently. I saw that the woods had indeed healed. No trees showed white scars of fresh scraping. No wilted leaves clung to the scattered birches. But wait. Hadn't the plane come down in winter? I should remember the news item in the *Laconia Citizen.* Was it in 1954? Moved to our house on Gilford Avenue 1951 after 10 years in the five-room apartment. At Scott and Williams I was foreman of Department 14, heat-treating...maybe remember more....

I stared at the wreckage of the great bird crumpled here in the wilderness. The feeling of a recent accident came strongly. I had the illusion that the people, the living and the dead, had only just left the scene.

A flap of metal clanked loudly in a gust of wind. It suggested a loose door on a house from which the mother and father and children had fled a disaster.

We made our way around the tangle of wreckage. At first the impact seemed a cause of all the damage. Neither of us knew anything about planes. I probably had been in them more than Claud. Maybe not. We decided that the fuselage had also been sheared by either rescue efforts or salvage work. The crash had torn loose a wing. It lay with the faded number on it—N128 or N138.

Where the wing had wrenched loose, the torn body gaped like a jagged cave. It made incongruous the windows and the doorway.

I noticed that a few birch saplings had taken advantage of the cleared spruces to spring into the light, only to be twisted by icy gales.

How little I remembered of the news that I felt sure I had read. What had I been writing in 1954? Was I still sending short stories to Carl Brandt? No, you damned numbskull, that was the year you worked on *Amos Jackman.* You were so excited about being a novelist that you probably didn't read the daily paper. I asked Claud what he remembered.

"Well, the live ones were rescued after a couple of days. Helicopter. At least two died. I remember a piece in the *Citizen.* Red Dunn and Malcolm Newton climbed up here. They'd been cutting Christmas trees in the valley somewhere. You knew Les Hibbert at Scott and Williams, didn't you? He piloted a small plane, scouting the location."

"I wonder that anyone survived. You can see where the plane struck this southwest shoulder. Another twenty feet and I bet it would have cleared easy. Instead it bounced and mowed off all the growth from that ledge and struck nose-first on this little rise of ground."

We couldn't tell how much breakup had occurred, but seemingly only a miracle could have saved the pilot.

I learned later that he had survived, although I was told he never flew commercially again.

We began exploring and found the salvage track, 15 feet wide and unbelievably steep toward Shelburne. Treaded vehicles, Caterpillars, must have towed sledges for taking away all valuable parts. In the track were sprouts and brush two feet high.

We made our way back to the wreckage.

Claud handed me the camera. "I'll get in on this one."

He posed against the aluminum, self-consciously as always, hands behind his back because he had taken his pipe from his mouth. The picture-to-be, framed in the finder, looked too dark. I lowered the camera and watched the clouds. To keep him from getting restless I called over, "There'll be sun in a couple of minutes." He moved anyway, and began examining the wreckage more closely. I squatted in the scrub. Although wind hissed over my head, the wiry branches hardly moved.

Staring at the wreckage I was impressed by the flying machine's frailty. Transitory human flight. Evidence lay about us everywhere. The tinny sound of flapping, torn aluminum contrasted with the enduring spruces. Insecurity was embodied by cylindrical seats from which fluttered synthetic fibers ripped out of the upholstery. The tail section had wrenched apart, revealing what I took to be the cupboard for supplies administered by the stewardess. A metal box contained the toilet open to the world. Humans who required these necessities had just departed from their temporary passage through the skies.

Sunlight illuminated the fuselage.

Claud stepped to a pose. "How's this?"

"Good." I took the picture.

He vanished into the cabin. When he emerged after a time he came over to me. "What do you think about fools' names and fools' faces?"

"This isn't exactly a public place."

"I figured you wouldn't mind. I wrote 'em on the cabin walls with the date."

"Good. We sure as hell earned the right. Maybe someday we'll hear about other nuts who came here."

Claud led the way back through the scrub. Two gray jays flitted and alighted silently near us in their ghostly flight and perching.

Out on open ground we rested.

Plowing through those branches had left me confused as to where I was. I began to lay up two cairns whose rocks had toppled over. I thought they were supposed to mark the Mahoosuc Trail.

Claud told me quietly, "We aren't yet on our trail, you know."

I stopped and oriented myself. "I thought we had crossed into it. These must have marked the trail to the wreckage. Don't mean a damn thing now it's grown up." I kicked apart the stones.

We walked the remaining distance easily to our packs. The gravelly barren ground crunched under our boots.

I settled into the leather straps and relished the sense of having all my needs accommodated by the Duluth's contents. Well, with what Claud was carrying. I felt the weight bearing down. I tried to concentrate on the future rest at Carlo Col Shelter.

Nagging me, however, came the realization that we had miles to go, which were never walked by Robert Frost. My watch said almost three. The wind felt like snow. No sleigh and little horse to pull me.

The trail led us across open ledges and into short corridors walled with green spruces hardly high as our heads, and they soon dwindled to three-foot mats. The boggy patches were mostly dry. As we ascended the last open rock, luxuriant cranberry vines spread from the seemingly sterile cracks. Red berries clung bright and inviting.

Half to himself, half to me, Claud speculated about the plentiful bits of fruit. "Maybe I ought to pick some to take home to my wife. She wants to make sauce for wild duck, if I manage to hit any this fall."

"If you don't, the sauce would go good on those Pekins she raises." I showed him my watch. "Carlo Col Shelter for me. You'll find enough berries on Old Speck the last day, and they'll be fresh."

"I guess you're right."

He walked on. We stepped down off the ledge and entered a narrow aisle in the scrub, where black earth led into a barren hollow a few yards across. In wet weather it would contain a puddle. Now a dry crust overlay soupy humus surrounded by heath plants that thrived in these strange accumulations of decayed sphagnum moss and leaves, which must be ages old. Roots like brown tendrils interwove to form a sort of turf. We learned to avoid the crust after the first encounter—brown ooze into my socks and almost too deep for Claud's hunting boots. We skirted the edge by walking on sheep laurel and the flattened branches of black spruce known as *krumholtz*. We trod slowly. Claud motioned at the sheep laurel bushes.

"That *kalmia*," he said, "helped me through my poisonous plants out to Michigan. The old bastard who taught the course used pressed specimens in transparent folders. They were old. By God, the leaves slid around inside and shed powder. They didn't look like anything. I identified the species by stains on the folders. I was the only one in the class who answered *kalmia* right. It had a fly speck on it. Never knew a sheep to eat the stuff."

"Lambkill."

"Them neither."

I pointed to the black earth and a dog track. Coyotes, new to New Hampshire, intrigued me, so I asked, "Is it too fresh for that Dalmatian mentioned in the AMC register? Maybe coyote?"

"Injun Joe say spotted dog. Blunt toenails. Coyote toenails sharper."

"I'd like to see a coyote."

"Maybe we'll shoot one up near the camp on Crystal Mountain this fall."

We began the last ascent to rocks and low clouds. The sky was settling on us. When we stopped for breath at the summit-cairn with its sign, we saw around us gathering mist. No indication of the Presidential Range off southwest linked us with familiar territory, only clouds. To the north somewhere must be our final peak. Old Speck's 4,180 feet hid from us in more clouds. We did see unexplored ridges, summits of impenetrable spruce, and shattered cliffs extending away off into mist as total wilderness.

A path of blue was too low for sky, so it suggested the presence there of mankind because it must be Success Pond shown on the map. There ended the Brown Company's truck road from Berlin. The water looked infinitely remote.

I thought that the vastness should have been challenging, exciting with unknown country and adventures. Instead it looked exhausting and threatening.

Claud said, "Lots of country out there. What about a picture?"

"Well, it would show we've been here. Not much else. We could call it 'Misty View from Mount Success.' It might look like one of the paintings of a namesake of yours. But he spelled it with an 'e,' being French."

"Oh, French. I got a French-Canuck son-in-law. To hell with a picture."

I was glad. Picture-taking for Claud involved decisions and lost time. The last thing I wanted was to linger.

We began a long, slow descent through scrub spruces overhanging the trail, which we felt for with our boots. Our heads were in hazy cloud. Then I realized we must be climbing again. My legs at once told me so. I wanted to rest so called ahead, "Wait a minute. There shouldn't be a ridge here. I'll look at the map."

He stopped while I caught up to him and unfolded the map and handed it to him. I scanned the *Guide* pages. I said, "Nothing in print about it, just that we've been descending. What the hell uphill is doing here I don't know."

"Not enough detail on the map." He handed it back to me. "Just the style of the Mahoosucs. We better get at it."

So we climbed over the ridge and down the other side among taller evergreens and scattered small birches. We entered a depression in the slope. Ferns grew tall on the left. Fading from green to rusty yellow, they almost hid a side path. Above it a sign nailed to a fir told us: "Success Trail." I knew from the map and *Guide* pages that the Success Trail was the first of several north routes to the road for logging trucks between Brown Company mills in Berlin and Success Pond. My immediate reaction said to me, "Think of escape. You can get out of this perpetual up-down of the mountain range you would have avoided by staying home."

Escape?

Not now, but there was a trail down from Carlo Col Shelter.

Escape? Not now. Press on. Couraage, mon braave. Excelsior! Once more unto the breach, dear friends! Play up, play up—and all that shit.

The Mahoosuc Trail led down from the little depression, then up.

We were approaching the peak shown on the map and marked 3,330, presumably the elevation. Blessedly the trail swung easterly and became more level until we began a gradual descent.

As I stepped down among the white birches and green firs I noticed above me red clusters of berries. They hung from branches of mountain ash trees. Still not fully ripe, they would soon attract birds. Robins could feast on them for days before flying south.

East of Claud's camp near the Connecticut Lakes, we once had tracked deer on six inches of snow halfway up Crystal Mountain through a growth of mountain ash trees where red-breasted robins plumply gorged on the berries in November....

My ruminations on the eating habits of robins ended because Claud, who had been slumping ahead downhill, stopped at a large sign on two trees. This impressive set of boards I estimated at two feet high by four feet long. Big letters announced for AT hikers and all others that New Hampshire and Maine joined here. With smaller letters and numbers the sign gave us distances from Springer Mountain in Georgia to Mount Katahdin in Maine.

In that wild forest of evergreens high up on the Mahoosuc Range, we stood quietly, just staring at the sign. I thought not about youthful talk of walking the entire 2,000 miles but about Katahdin and our adventure there in 1931. Claud, too, for he gave a snorting half-laugh and asked, "Remember when I drove the Model T through that stream where the gravel road ended? I thought maybe the bridge had washed out."

"Sometimes I lie awake at night and laugh about it."

"That bearded Frenchman on the cabin porch laughed long enough for us to get over and ask where in hell was Mount Katahdin."

"It set him off again. I couldn't believe the horses wandering around the clearing and out in the brush. One of 'em stuck his head in the tent the next morning. Monster logging horse. You never woke up."

I began to laugh. I could still hear the hoofbeats pounding away after I waved my shirt at him. Then I put on the heavy wool shirt. Frost lay on the ground that June morning.

Claud asked, "What was the name of the stream? Next day we followed it beside the tote road all the way to the Hunt Trail."

"Sourdnahunk. Ten miles."

"If we'd had enough gas the Model T would have taken us there."

"Remember we met an old guy and a little girl in a buckboard near Kidney Pond Camp. If a buckboard and horse made that tote road, Lizzie could have. But we walked it." I sat down, saying as I pointed at the sign, "You realize this Mahoosuc Trail could be a link to Katahdin?"

He studied the distances, repeating them to himself, then said, "Not for me it couldn't. Almost three hundred miles...and we've been there." He reached into his pocket for the can of Velvet. "I get a funny sensation thinking back thirty-five years to that trip. Not just the certainty I'm getting old, but facing obstacles."

"You mean overcoming them."

"Well, yes. First getting out of Orford with the old man's Model T Ford. Then two days drive to Greenville on Moosehead Lake where the outfitter told us we had to have a guide or we couldn't build a campfire. Then the game warden warning us and impounding the fishing tackle because we couldn't afford licenses. Then the gatekeeper McGinnis at Ripogenus Dam had to be pestered into letting us through."

Like Claud I needed to review this much-recalled trip. I said, "The bearded Frenchman laughing at us was a relief. But we waited till after dark to touch off our fire, and we hid it with rocks and a kettle of water. I kept feeling we had to hurry and climb the goddamned mountain, wherever it was, and get out before we were arrested. All the same, we should have taken more trips like that."

"No money."

"And not enough time for everything. Choosing is the problem. I think we chose right, as near as possible."

"I suppose. But there's still some time. I'm going up and climb Katahdin again. Camp like we did at the base of the mountain. Katahdin Stream, wasn't it?"

"Yes, and canned beans and rain the next day walking back to the Ford. This time we wouldn't be alone."

"Well, let's go anyway."

Certain that I'd never climb Katahdin again, I nevertheless agreed. "We'll do it."

And then something told me I wasn't through climbing mountains or overcoming obstacles. I felt borne up on hope that I could, because we had acquired a lifelong system for mountains and obstacles. Persistence.

Of course in the process we had also acquired a necessity for wild-wood adventures and wildwood solace from the Real World. I felt a great lift in all this, and from our shared past, plus a new satisfaction in our footwork over the earth.

Claud puffed on his pipe.

I stood up and saw a metal marker on a tree indicating the state line. I had learned from my research into the history of the Indian Stream Republic that the compass bearing of the line was north ten degrees west, and that it ended on the height of land north of the Connecticut Lakes. The great birch blazed by the surveyor could not be found after the Treaty of Paris, causing arguments and threats of war with England.

Claud started off and I followed. The acrid-mellow smell of fire in burley tobacco made me want my pipe. No, I needed all my breath clear to keep up. Even so I began to drop back. We were climbing again.

We slowly achieved another ridge. This tapered off in a ravine of jumbled rocks. Claud disappeared. I concentrated on controlling my legs and boots along a gaping crevice.

We might have been struggling through a bombed quarry. Escape was possible only by pulling ourselves out with spruce branches and roots. A few yards farther brought us to another blasted ravine—literally blown apart by vindictive giants.

Claud's expletives drifted back to me, ending with, "I never intended to get into a stone labyrinth."

With scrabbling boots we levered ourselves out of rocks that did provide the necessary handholds. Trembling knees took me onto bare ledge. We stood on an outlook surrounded by low evergreens and Labrador tea bushes. The extensive view northward was releasing. It included gray Success Pond, gray clouds, and untold numbers of trees. On the ledge near our boots lay a pale gray bobcat turd—solid hair compressed like felt. My wandering mind formed a question.

"Tell me, doctor, why do bobcats do it?"

"Ask Injun Joe."

"All right I will. Injun Joe, why bobcat shit on rock?"

"Ugh, Injun Joe ask bobcat. Him bobcat say, 'This remain to be seen.'"

"Thank you, Injun Joe. Now, doctor, why don't bobcats choke on hair balls like house cats?"

"Get me a bobcat to dissect and I'll show you."

"There must be several out there toward Success Pond."

We stood silently looking across the forest. I realized we perched on a small cliff, but I was in a different world and time. After a while I reminded him of another shared view. "This is sort of like that day we climbed Eastman Ledges and looked out over all those trees stretching from Quinttown into Wentworth and Dorchester. I suppose that was nineteen twenty-nine. God, how I wanted to explore that territory."

"Well, we did."

"I know. And I don't give a tinker's damn about exploring out there."

While I mused on youth and old age, and our shared adventures, my old friend moved to the edge of the cliff and peered over. He said, "I wish I was as limber as then. How's anybody supposed to get away from this fine panorama and down to Carlo Col Shelter?"

I stepped to the edge. "Sprout wings, I guess."

We teetered gingerly, searching for breaks in the rock face. This was the worst drop-off we had encountered. Compared to my physical condition twenty-fours hours previously, confronting the rock gap at Gentian Pond's outlet, I felt nearer collapse. This, as always, put me in a jocose mood that held off hysteria.

Claud's grim expression I interpreted to indicate his unflinching weariness. I also recognized a twisted determination as the prelude to an act of desperation beyond anything at Gentian Pond.

It turned out to be similar.

He took off his pack and knelt on the granular rock, hands supporting him while he stared over. Facing about he eased his boots out of sight. I offered a hand. He shook his head, scowling.

I had to say something. "If you fall you'll land on Carlo Col."

The levity irritated. "Shit on Carlo Col."

"You're no bobcat, but go ahead—if we ever get down there."

"This here problem is what remains to be seen."

Large hands gripped a crack in the ledge. He lowered himself, relaxed his hands and slid sideways.

Then, "I can touch with my feet. I'm on a shelf. Pass me the bloody packs. Come on the same way. If you can't touch I'll grab your boots."

I couldn't and he did.

We sat down on the slanting shelf with the packs hugged to our bellies by left hands. The right hands clung to a series of spruce seedlings no bigger than my thumb. Only one pulled out by the roots and dropped Claud the last five feet to solid earth.

He struggled into the packstraps muttering to himself. I landed several yards away. His words became plainly audible.

"Any son of a bitch who laid out a trail this way...."

I heard a disturbingly bitter and useless string of profane comments from the depths of his unadmitted exhaustion, a futile bulwark against a rising tide of pessimism.

Onward seemed the only way to reply. I walked ahead. A vague path wound among jagged rocks and through dark evergreens. I strode out as rapidly as possible. We must be entering the final depths of Carlo Col, and yet were we? I could see looming above treetops the outline of another mountain. I began thinking, "Christ-almighty, not for us, not today. We'll have to camp right here."

I tried to focus on a white rectangle at eye level. A trail sign. Claud joined me. As though we couldn't read, we glared at the printing about the Carlo Col Trail and the shelter. We both realized that our night's rest lay somewhere on the side trail angling down. The shelter was supposed to be a quarter-mile away.

Claud pointed out our predicament. "Look at that. Just as I expected. Downhill steep. Why not a shelter here? Gotta be water. We'll have to climb back in the morning. Crazy fools."

I felt too relieved to be upset. The shelter was down there someplace. I started down.

The trail took to the dry bed of a seasonal watercourse about one step wide. Trees growing close made impossible the avoidance of rock shards that could twist your ankles. Thighs trembled going down. An aching left knee. The return of my wracking headache. Utter weariness.

Yet I was vividly aware that I had come to this sorry pass of my own free will. I felt a laugh coming at that word "pass." Ha ha. It meant also a col, a notch, or a sorry gap, last gasp. Getting silly. Yes, of my own free will. Nobody to blame but myself. In an internal opening of insight, I was caught by the notion of "voluntary servitude." This thought turned me to feeling a smug virtue at not complaining.

The trail led down and down. We said nothing. The silence became oppressive. In time to my steps I began chanting, "Maa-hoo-suc, Maa-hoo-suc."

The words were in another language, presumably Abenaki. I felt sure they expressed Indian distaste for a journey through these parts. The three-syllable sound carried an obscene consignment to the Indian equivalent of Hell. I tried variations on the emphasis. "Maa-hoo-SUC, Maa-hoo-SUC." Then I dwelt on the middle syllable. "Maa-HOO-suc, Maa-HOO-suc." I liked the middle emphasis better. This amused my floating brains, while I stepped down into a forest of big trees—beech, maple, yellow birch—and knew that I couldn't make it back uphill ever.

"Maa-HOO-suc, Maa-HOO-suc!"

Continued descent started Claud talking again. He found new ways to rail against his fate at the mercy of bloody fools who laid out trails. The prospect of retracing the trail upward gave him the most painful sense of injustice.

I tended to defend the poor locator of the shelter, but only to myself. Doubtless, I thought, he had searched the col and found no water there. But had he searched thoroughly along this slope? Not to Claud's interpretation. Claud occupied himself with denigrations of his character, common sense, and method of looking for water.

But somehow I couldn't bitch. I might have felt better for some bitching. I just didn't feel any good strong urge. Bitching is a sign of determination. It's a sign of fight, will to win. It shows grit and depths of strength despite odds.

I was ready to give up, though I didn't know it. I whispered, "MaHOOsuc, MaHOOsuc."

At last I noticed that my boots squished in water among the rocks. I was walking in a feeble trickle. I stopped at a little pool. Above it a tree-sign with the word "Shelter" pointed to a steep bank. Such a wooded wall could very well have gone by, we were so concentrated on our pains-taking, slow boots.

Claud growled, "That bank is the last goddamned straw!" He charged at it.

The soles of his Bean boots were slipping. Their chain-tread had smoothed from time and miles. In the mud he fell to his knees. I could see the rubber of the soles; chain-pattern was a slight bas-relief. He remained for a moment in a position of prayer. Yes, he was invoking the Deity and found strength to set his hands and toes to scrabbling him over the top.

I dug in the edges of my boots, and slowly, but upright, I understood the same insult that he felt, perhaps for the same silly reason—the concept of a final indignity.

We stood gazing at the shelter.

The old log walls, the open front protected by an overhang, the inner bunk, were replicas of those at Gentian Pond, although I judged them to be less used. I noted an appearance of decay, of abandonment. I looked up at the roof and doubted it would shed all the rain if the threatening clouds opened up. Only disordered stones marked the fireplace. Surrounded by tall and gloomy maples, beeches, and yellow birches, the shelter lacked the airiness and vistas at Gentian Pond.

Claud slung his pack inside onto the bunk. "Bastards burned all the wood. Not a stick left for the next guy. I'll go look for some."

He ambled off.

The front log of the bunk irresistibly drew me. I shed my pack beyond it and sat down. I slid back till the fir needles cushioned my bottom. I thought of leaning back against the pack for a doze.

Maybe I did so. Claud returned from exploring the forest.

"No wood. Lemme have the ax."

I pulled it from my pack, untied the sheath, and handed him the grip end.

Several chunks of logs lay about the clearing. For ordinary hikers the blocks presented too much work, or more likely were beyond their tools. Hikers now didn't carry axes. I wondered who had sawed the lengths for splitting. Probably a trail crew.

Claud's desperate pounding on those chunks sent me into the woods to find kindling. There must be squaw-wood somewhere. I searched for dead branches within reach on trees. Sticks on the ground would be damp. Maybe I'd find saplings killed by shade from taller trees and left standing dry. There had to be wood that I could break up. No, nothing but big trunks loomed before me as I walked. There must be a windfallen dead maple with small branches ready for flames. None.

No undergrowth of mountain maple or moosewood offered their dead twigs in the forest's understory. There was no understory. Nor did I find spruce or fir with kindling twigs left behind by higher ever-green boughs. I kept on down the slope behind the shelter. The air smelled of dank woods and rain. We needed dry wood for the night and morning.

I came to a rough board box, the outhouse evidently. We had not discovered one at Gentian Pond Shelter. As I examined the structure I realized that the term "outhouse" was inadequate and inaccurate. The right word dawned on me. It was "throne."

These wooden boxes provided by the AMC at its Mahoosuc shelters possessed only utilitarian value, or so I at first thought. And yet there was an elegant simplicity that might have appealed to Henry Thoreau. I wondered how he had dealt with the problem. I could recall no mention of a privy in *Walden*.

The AMC solution consisted of a three-foot cube of boards placed over a hole in the ground. The opening in the top appeared under the cover, which conveniently had a cleat for lifting it. Two boards nailed to the sides of the box protruded to offer hand-holds for two men when moving the box to its present location from the shelter, where probably it had been nailed together from leftover roof boards, and also for moving the box when a new hole was required.

The height of the box brought from boyhood memory those old water closets built of wood around a porcelain bowl with an oak seat and lid. I remembered the first requirement to sit up there. Short legs had to spring me upward to place the bare buttocks on the seat, which was also too large.

This box's elevation made me wonder if my legs were even now long enough.

Beyond the throne I passed downhill into thickets of spruce and mountain maple. Dead branches and small twigs gradually became an armful trailing behind me. I stopped at a great white birch so old that its bark hung in curls, as though shedding. I yanked off several loose swatches.

Ready and anxious to return, I was unable to orient myself to back-track. In the gloomy forest all the trees and bushes looked alike. My sense of direction had been ailing for almost 10 years, as I learned at Claud's hunting camp on Crystal Mountain. Now a mild panic seized me. I was imprisoned by inescapable mountains. I thought of hollering. It wouldn't do. I'd wait until I knew the shelter was really lost. I had yet to think of *myself* as lost. I looked around. I recognized, I thought, a massive yellow birch so shaggy that in passing it I'd recalled tales of lumberjacks tricking a tenderfoot into climbing such a tree, then setting fire to the loose bark.

Again I walked past it. After a while I came to an unfamiliar rise of ground and decided to turn left along it. Something told me I was veer-ing too far toward my right.

The guess brought me to the shelter.

Claud had reclaimed the fireplace by removing blackened stubs that had plugged it. He was laying up the scattered rocks. He looked at my armful of dead branches and asked, "Where?"

I wanted to minimize any success I'd had compared to his search. He could himself, seriously enough, belittle his abilities. So I said only, "Quite a ways beyond the shithouse."

"House?"

"No, throne."

"Ummm." He flared a match on his thumbnail and held it under the bundle of spruce twigs I had twisted until the tough little fibers clung together. They were damp and declined to crackle into flames. I tore up birch bark. He lit another match, which brought oily smoke from the white wisps. The campfire began to glow in the sheltering stones of the reconstructed fireplace. Mountain maple sticks, broken and laid on in a wigwam, caught fire. He placed the split chunkwood in alternate layers right and left.

Flames waved upward. As ever when I saw them in a new campfire, the flames and the smoke, and even the resinous prickle in my nostrils from the spruce, and the warmth, made me feel better. The hostility of the forest backed off.

I gathered the pails and a cup for scooping from the little pool near the trail. Over the bank I went. While I cupped the pails full I heard Claud chopping more wood. I thought that an ax for him was a weapon against the wild. An ax made possible a good fire.

And our fire was burning down to cooking moderation. I set the coffeepot in the coals, and laid out tea, dried milk, and sugar. Plastic bags had simplified handling grub for camping out. What a collection of sad sacks we once used!—cloth bags in which sugar and salt were sold, some so long they could be knotted on themselves instead of closed with string. They blackened from associating with our cooking kettles, or stiffened with wet sugar and flour and spruce pitch. When did plastic bags arrive? You washed cloth bags; you threw plastic.

Claud stood near the inadequate fireplace. He held the reflector oven. I wondered how he planned to arrange it for baking bread.

He said, "I could rig a platform of logs and stones for the oven. Those stupid bastids who frigged up the fireplace need a talking-to, or well-placed boots."

"The world is full of yahoos. Forget the bread." I slumped on the log at the foot of the bunk. "Must be a package of that Chuckwagon dried stuff we can cook up fast."

"All right. I don't feel like baking." He pawed in his pack, peering inside, and held out for my inspection a plastic envelope of dehydrated chili con carne. "How about this shit?"

"Sure. Lemme have it. I can fix it when I get my glasses and read the directions."

Claud picked up the ax to split more wood. But he was due to light his pipe. He drove the ax, one-handed, into a log, and held a flaming match to the heel of tobacco in his pipe.

I called over, "Says here reconstitute in cold water for three hours. How about just dumping into water and boil till fit to eat?"

"Let's try it." He picked up the ax.

I slit the envelope with my jackknife and shook half the brown bits and globules—meat and beans—into the larger kettle of water. I figured on four servings, the envelope being for eight men. But the powdered sauce lay in the bottom. I ended up dumping it all in.

Then there was the question of suspending the pail over the fire. The luxury of a cross stick on two forked stakes did not exist. Too much trouble to cut and drive in the stakes. I found a pointed pole in the shelter. Shoved into the ground at an angle across the stones of the fireplace, it became the classic "wangan stick" of a woodsman. I had recollected enough of the past to notch the upper end, which held the bail, which held the pail, which held the chili over the flames.

I could tell I was again getting silly, so I spooned tea into boiling water. To insure enough tea I had brought loose-leaf. This seemed the time to brew unbagged Salada, which we used to take camping; his folks chose that brand among American teas, and *not* in bags. The boiling water was in the coffeepot. I set it aside to steep.

Claud joined me on the bunk log. We sat there and drank tea (commenting on loose tea versus bags) with powdered milk and plenty of sugar—well, I allowed myself a teaspoon just in case my pancreas could manufacture some energy out of it.

Cups set aside, we arranged sleeping bags at either side of the bunk as far apart as possible. We drank more tea from the pot, strong enough to clean your teeth. I tended the fire and the chili.

Over the years we had evolved a system for cooking over a campfire. Whichever one of us started the cooking also fed the flames with wood as necessary. If only coals, which might die out before cooking was finished, then finely split sticks or twigs soon flared. Now this caused the chili to boil instead of simmer. I slid back the cover to prevent boiling over. But as the mess stopped seething and I added sticks to the fire, ashes drifted into the kettle.

Claud placed a rock over the butt of the wangan stick. "Might have pried itself out of the ground. Pretty heavy kettle. I wouldn't want that shit to end up in the fire."

"Thanks, I guess I'm numb." I spooned out several beans and blew on them till cool enough to eat. "Well, if we chew 'em enough we can swallow 'em."

Among dehydrated foods in my experience, chili can be one of the best. Not this. The granular beans, the resurrected meat, the acid tomato sauce, and the burning chili powder dropped to our stomachs like personal insults. Then they began agitating our guts. I didn't dare mention Claud's recurring ulcer.

We stopped eating the mess long before we had consumed half of it. I felt no real pain, and Claud, when I asked his reaction, said, "Okay, but pass the water."

Before long we discovered that the beans were windy beyond any of those in various cans we had eaten camping out. Speedier too, we agreed.

He said, "Green Mountain Beans were almost as bad."

"Holbrook Grocery Company," I said, with memories of Pat Holbrook and his wife, Rita, who lived in a new house across a vale in Hanover, west of Sargent Street, where I lived with Mother and Ib the three years I went to Clark School before Dartmouth. Rita a friend of Ib's. I said, "Campbell's Baked Beans were easier to swallow. Slipped down in that tomato sauce."

"My old man wouldn't eat any other kind. Ten cents a can at the First National in Fairlee. He wouldn't trade at Carr's Store. In Orford. He had a lot of trouble with Orford people."

I wanted to change the subject before Claud got started on his old man's other convictions, such as dislike of the moccasins that Claud and I insisted on wearing—"uncivilized footwear for savages."

I hit upon a more attractive subject. "Remember the box of four-oh-five cartridges on the shelf in Carr's Store?"

"I never could figure why Henry Carr stocked them. Teddy Roosevelt took a four-oh-five to Africa."

By the time we eased ourselves into our sleeping bags we had talked about most of the merchandise in the store, including penny candy and ax handles. We discussed once more the accident with a shotgun that had deprived Henry Carr of an arm below the elbow. Hunting and crawling through a fence, the story went. Not the best talk before going to sleep. I didn't mention again that Ernie's father (Dartmouth oh-one) had been in the Mary Hitchcock Hospital with the flu when Henry was brought in screaming.

Silently we lay in our separate corners and considered, I know I did, the chances we'd taken with firearms. I was sure of his thoughts when he said, "For kids, we were careful, and lucky, without any man to teach us."

I had some reservations about the word "careful," at least as regards targets, but instructors we had indeed lacked.

About the "lucky" I said, "God looks after idiots, drunks, and kids...sometimes."

"Sometimes is right." He was silent for a moment. "Sometimes not. Maybe set the whole crazy shebang going and went off and forgot it."

"That has been postulated. I'm with Francis Parkman, a reverent agnostic."

"Maybe someday I'll get reverent, though I doubt it. Good-night."

"Good-night."

Then from him, "You ever read anything besides *The Oregon Trail?*"

"*England and France in North America.* I also got his account of leaving Indian Stream Territory and crossing to the Magalloway River."

"Loan 'em to me sometime." He began snoring.

For me, restless sleep.

A mummy sleeping bag unzips only halfway down. In one as snug as my reconditioned Air Force surplus, flatulence can be as deadly as is implied by the GI name "fart sack."

Added to the gas was my pounding headache. For a long time I couldn't sleep. At last between stench attacks I raised my head high on my pillow of pants, shirt, and boots. In the breezy air I managed some deep-breathing exercises and passed into a floating sleep, drunk on oxygen, interrupted occasionally by Claud's thrashing at the far wall, punctuated by double-ended noises.

I was also haunted by a sense of utter inadequacy to fight the mountains that surrounded me.

DESPERATION

INADEQUACY WAS STILL MY DOMINANT SENSATION WHEN I AWOKE. At once this was supplanted by the conviction that if I moved I would die. Next came certainty that I would die anyway.

I felt a vacancy in the head. This was peculiar because it contained a steady hammering. Slowly I realized that a bursting, up there, would bring relief and be a blessing, either my head or a blood vessel somewhere. The pain centered in my forehead. At rare intervals a popping inside my head, above my nose, would temporarily relieve the throbbing.

Recently in the mountains I had experienced this series of tiny explosions, like elves wielding pins at balloons. The relief felt as if draped with the droopy skins of balloons. These smothered me in lassitude that refused to allow me to move my aching body. I had no more gumption than a molting chicken huddled in a thunderstorm.

And outside rain was pouring down.

Claud snored on.

I had felt chilled in the night and had wriggled my arms into the sleeves of my red and black wool shirt. Now a cold wind blew in the open front of the shelter. Water dripped from the eaves into the edge of the fireplace, whose stones were barely visible in a murky and dismal light. The forest beyond loomed dark and wet.

I thought of lying there forever. I could never get up. I was limp. If I did get up and went out I would become soaking wet as a prelude to freezing solid. I was beaten. I was an old man. Stupid me, to think that I could enjoy camping out with Claud as we had done when we were young.

Then I remembered the trail past the shelter. It led down to the Success Pond Road about which I knew nothing except that it would be an easy surface for my battered feet and legs. Maybe even a ride with a driver of a logging truck heading loaded with pulp to Berlin. Ah, yes, Berlin and forget the stink...a motel, a hot shower (if not a soaking bath), and a double shot of vodka, a steak dinner....

Abruptly I felt like a quitter.

Both my father and my mother had adjured me to complete whatever I undertook. Now, long years later, I knew the rule could be silly. What was Robert Frost's cure for impossible situations—I must have heard it at Bread Loaf, maybe from John Ciardi or Bill Sloane? Cut and run, I think.

Still, I felt like a quitter.

Yes, but I reveled—reveled mentally only because the failed body was past any revelry—in the dream of civilized comforts and luxuries in Berlin, a city that I had always avoided except to pass through. It would have phones; a call home would bring Ernie's welcome voice as it would bring Don and Ruthie to rescue me.

Yet how could I face them?

Dichotomy set in.

The challenge of the strange and fearsome peaks, the cliffs, the alpine barrens that must lie ahead, became so repugnant they disgusted me. Quitter.

No, look, this excursion you undertook voluntarily, so give it up the same way. Turn your back on the challenge. The road to Berlin awaits at the end of the trail past the shelter. Be sensible about your inability to conquer the Mahoosucs. Forget failure's stigma; it's an illusion forced on you by the doers of this world, and they have caused all the trouble. You've tried your best. It was not enough. Retreat. In good order.

And forever after regret it. I understood myself well enough to foresee years of remembering I had made a cowardly and sneaky escape. I didn't care.

Then arrived a thought that did require care: Suppose I went on in desperation and collapsed. Rescue would be impossible before I died, no matter how fast Claud went for help. Then there would be the terrible news for Ernie while the rescuers were lugging out my body.

To hell with the Mahoosucs.

I began to devise ways of convincing Claud that we should pack and walk down to the Success Pond Road. At times he was immovably unconvincible. His quietness over determination to explore new territory could be like the velvet glove over the steel fist. He would gently explain the logic of continuing. The steel would be his heading on alone.

Awake and informed of my agony and of my decision to get the hell out via Carlo Col Trail and Success Pond Road, he growled and grumbled as he rose out of his sleeping bag and put on his hat.

Then he began listing the delights ahead on the Mahoosuc Trail. "Just a short distance to the next shelter. You've got to see Goose High Mountain—it's the most spectacular in the whole range, and easy from here because we are so high up. And Full Goose Shelter soon after. All great country you're too near now to miss. Cozy shelter after an easy day. And we'll have time to cook up a good supper."

I said, "It's four miles over God knows how many of these fucking peaks that keep coming at me again and again."

"All right, we'll take 'em easy and rest a lot so's we can enjoy the scenery. Goose Eye is really special. I've talked to AT hikers. You can see all the North Country clear to Rangeley Lakes. And how many guys ever climb Goose Eye? You don't want to miss that. Maybe we'll see some geese. They gave it the old name, Goose High, because they just barely clear the summit. This time of year maybe there'll be an early flight and we can knock one down with a club and roast it at the shelter."

"Against the law."

"Who's to know?"

"If it's high for geese it's too high for me."

"Can't be any higher than our Smarts Mountain, only more pick-ed."

"Five hundred higher. It's almost thirty-eight hundred."

He was pulling on his boots. "We need a fire."

"Just in case you hadn't noticed, that's rain out there and the mist settling down is cloud. Above treeline we couldn't see ten feet."

I might have added that I had no intention of leaving my chilled corpse on the windswept, rainy, sleety, icy slopes of Goose Eye, or Goose High, whichever applied.

He squatted before the fireplace breaking twigs from the bunk and laying them on a piece of birch bark he'd found under the bunk. A flap of cardboard similarly found kept off the rain. He tucked under a few larger sticks gleaned somewhere inside. When the flames started he quickly stepped out with the ax into the rain. Three blows split a chunk. The dry inside wood fell apart. The fire flared around the splinters.

I crawled from my sleeping bag and worked my boots over the heavy socks I had slept in. I could see that we needed more wood. I thought I remembered a fallen spruce up the trail—or had I dreamed it? More than likely, or I'd have gone after it when I was looking for wood yesterday. Fallen spruce, dead and pitchy? Naa, a dream. Yet from long past, I felt driven by the urge to contribute fuel. Go looking anyhow, over the bank and up the trail. After a few steps along the rivulet into which rain poured after dousing me, I went back for my red rain shirt.

There came to me the certainty that I wasn't going uphill anymore. I stood under the shelter. Firewood was no responsibility of mine. I saw ahead only downhill along the Carlo Col Trail to Success Pond Road and a warm room in a Berlin hotel or motel.

Claud puttered around the fire to make the pot boil, same as he would on any day's start of a hike from a camp. We said nothing more about my quitting the trip. He split wood. For him the rain might not have been coming down, although his felt hat dripped water and droplets clung to his heavy wool shirt. His pants hung in wet brown folds. He placed the pot of chili on the fire. He poured tea. He handed me a steaming cup and pointed to the sugar and powdered milk that he had laid on the bunk log. The fire blazing up made his shirt give off vapor.

Breakfast was the last of the chili and two more cups of tea. I felt better. I felt good enough to argue with myself: "You know your dream of a warm room and so on in Berlin is only a dream. That's a strange place, and you're no good alone in strange places. And you will be alone. He's going on to Grafton Notch. He likes to be alone. You try to follow and you'll end up a basket case. This shelter is the point of no return."

Then came a surprise.

He held up a can. "Time to eat these."

I read the label to myself and it told me, "Plums in Heavy Syrup."

Aloud, "By God, I'd forgot them."

The can had appeared in the trail sometime after we passed the man and his daughter. The can was a real find, a bonanza, because we had agreed at home not to bring any canned fruit. Or rather, Claud had reluctantly admitted he would be carrying enough weight without his usual can of peaches or pears in heavy syrup—and a large can at that.

That can of plums had caused us to speculate how it happened to be in the trail. Accidentally from the man and daughter seemed unlikely, considering the swanky packs with zippered pockets and all. We had decided that maybe the girl had jettisoned some of her load. Maybe she detested plums as much as their weight.

Claud had slipped the can into his pack, saying, "Sort of manna from heaven, not from the girl. Don't make sense they'd carry it and leave the other stuff at Gentian Pond."

I said sententiously, because too tired for any interest, "It will remain one of our many mysteries of the woods."

"Well, we're going to eat 'em."

He declined the can opener on my Scout knife and slit around the top of the can with the blade of his jackknife.

"A few days ago," he said, "I castrated a bull calf with this."

I knew this wasn't true but if it had been I wouldn't have cared. I could smell the sweetness enhanced by the fruit scent of ripe plums. I set out our tin cups while the luscious purple syrup made my mouth water.

Claud began spooning plums from the can. "One for you, one for me, one for you, one for me. I hope they come out even. Otherwise I'll have to cut the extra in half with this knife. Ahh, sho' nuff, four apiece. Only. Damn small can."

Spoon poised, he peered inside.

"Now," he said, "syrup for you, one spoonful, syrup for me, syrup for you, syrup for me, drop for you"—tipping the can—"drop for me."

"You could rinse out the can and drink it."

"Good idea. You swig your half first. And I'll be watching your Adam's apple."

"You can have it all. I want some of this."

I sipped from the cup. The rich sweetness spread throughout my mouth, giving off the bland aroma of plums, which I had never cared for as too cloying and fulsome. Not now. If I ever again (I thought) have a taste of Benedictine with its swift warmth it'll remind me of this infinitely more sybaritic delight.

I ate those four plums slowly. Gradually my body let up complaining each time I took a stumbling step in the shelter. I stopped bumping my protesting head against the rafters—great place, an open-front shelter, to knock yourself silly. I gladly accepted the sensation that my stomach and intestines were extracting nourishment, even energy, from my nongourmet breakfast.

My short memory of unpleasantness is faster than normally human. This is my good luck. Unlike Claud I seldom dwelt on the injustices of the world, such as the rain outside. And yet he wasn't bitching about it. For God's sake, was he happy to be here? He whistled a tune that I thought was from *Pinafore*. Perverse cuss.

The rain let up enough to allow me a foray to the throne. The lack of wetness was overhead only. Soaking bushes drenched me more than I expected. An old woodsman should have known better. Then the chilled seat reactivated my concern that I couldn't survive in this mountain fastness. Yes, indeed, Carlo Col Shelter was the point of no return. Go on and you probably have three more days of this.

Back at the shelter I found that Claud was all packed and smoking his pipe. I said, "You know we're crazy to go on with this. Look out there—more rain."

"We've got wet before, and we're wet already."

"Let's stay here and rest up for a day. Don and Ruthie will wait overnight at Grafton Notch."

I knew I was unconvincing. He puffed out smoke twice. The adjective "adamant" came to me.

But he reasoned with me, removing the pipe. "Look at it this way. You can go one more day, and then if it's too much, you can take the Mahoosuc Notch Trail to the Success Pond Road." Again he puffed twice. "But then you'll want to see the notch. It's the wildest, most remote notch in the mountains."

I thought that by comparison to all this my escape dream had been very shoddy and without honor. I began rolling my sleeping bag, recollecting that I had to fold it carefully to pad my back from the ax and kettles and grub.

I would try the slope of the trail above the shelter to its junction with the Mahoosuc Trail. There I'd make up my mind whether to keep on like an honorable fool or quit.

We climbed slowly. The rocks were wet and slippery. Every bush shed water on us. Fine rain condensed out of the saturated mist in which we moved. Claud led the way. After a time he began commenting on this quarter mile that seemed a mile. The figure was dreamed up by the perpetrator of the location for the shelter. "If he had a measuring wheel he must have left it up at the junction."

I could tell by his short steps and the way each hip hoisted him onto each forward boot that he was enduring the same excruciating process of limbering a fifty-two-year structure of bone and muscle as I was. Our speed matched that of ancient turtles.

At the junction with the Mahoosuc Trail I realized that the rain had stopped. Claud didn't stop. He turned left, up Mount Carlo.

After missing two steps I followed. There had been reassurance in my climbing that mile-long quarter, but relief was the dominant feeling. I said loudly, "The die is cast."

Claud called back the Latin of it.

We were in evergreens whose branches held twice the water of the leafy bushes below. The trail badly needed trimming. We moved up into gray wisps of thicker clouds. They swirled past on cold gusts. Claud must have suspected that my courage was failing. He began talking about the meal we'd eat that evening at Full Goose Shelter.

"We'll have real pea soup."

"You got peas?"

"No, but I brought the onion. I figured on your lugging along your extra grub for emergencies, peas, beans, lentils, that starvation holdout you always bring."

"This time they're yellow split peas."

"And I have that slab of my bacon."

He and Louise each summer raised two pigs, which they hired a professional named Southwick to slaughter and cut up for their deepfreeze, for sausage-making, and for pickling and smoking the hams, shoulders, and bacon. Claud had remodeled an old ice-fishing bobhouse into a smokehouse.

He said, "We'll get to the shelter in plenty of time to start 'em all simmering. I'll set up the oven right, this time. There's a package of corn-bread mix in this Chuckwagon stuff. I know you're partial to corn bread and I can stand it. Not that it'll be as powerful as that frying-pan corn bread you used to make."

"That was corn pone—all corn meal. This'll be more civilized."

"Well, there'll be plenty. It's a big bag of mix. And time for a good fire. The shelter's probably in spruces, but we can look around for some hardwood that'll burn down to coals, birch anyhow, maybe some mountain ash. I'll rig the oven so's I can move it back and forth to get the heat right."

"Sounds great," I said. And refrained from adding, "A hellova ways off." All I said, "Goddamn cloud's bearing down."

We were climbing into thick fog, that's what it was, yet he informed me, "This is going to lift. Feel that breeze? Soon we'll be enjoying our free mountain life. Beats hell out of the Lakes Region around Laconia."

If he could come up with this crap I'd better stop my mental bitching. Nor would I let on that I saw through his talk, which was meant to encourage me. What should I say to him? I saw no spring in his walk either. I might say something about Mount Carlo, but could think only of peculiar attributes.

One oddity lay in the incongruous elevations. Mount Carlo's summit being 3,500 feet, and the shelter about 3,000, we were engaged in no serious climb in the half mile to the "excellent view" we wouldn't see. We dragged along, however, up and up in the spruces. It made no sense. Half a mile wasn't this long.

Claud, pushing ahead, saturated himself in the dripping green branches. I brought my creaking carcass behind him. Another oddity was, for an unknown reason, my increasing strength. I was puzzling over this welcome sensation when he stopped and moved aside.

"You better go first. That breakfast of chili is building up to a gas attack."

"Well, you better wait after me," I told him, "till the breeze clears the trail. I ate the same breakfast."

He nodded and I went on alone.

I soon noticed the illusion of strength fading. There was the trail, steep and rough, ahead of me. I drove myself to a protruding rock I could see above me. Then 10 more steps and I had to rest. I thought seriously of sitting down. Claud caught up, shifted his shoulders to ease the packstraps, and told me in his parody of French Canuck accent, "En avant."

I agreed, "Marchons!" We proceeded noisily. I proclaimed pontifically, "Let us be up and doing, with a fart for any fate."

This parody made me feel better. I stepped upward into the narrow trail, where a dose of unshaken wet branches incongruously reminded me of dry ice—another peculiar attribute of this climb. I continued to a ledgy shoulder.

Instead of stopping to enjoy the lift of a sweeping panorama featuring North Country scenery, we plodded into a misty opening and across bare rock surrounded by cloud of an interesting gray shade. We kept on through dripping spruce woods. The trail led to a bog of black mud.

Along the edge were the tough, exposed roots of sheep laurel and blueberry bushes. They supported us part of the time as we picked our way past the possibly bottomless decayed morass. Beyond us a great flat rock offered a chance to stamp our boots clean. A wasted fastidiousness. We descended into another pocket of the gooey Mahoosuc oddity. Evergreens closed in.

Clinging to branches and looking for roots on which to place my boots, I ran out of both and stood in an open moor or heath. This mountain meadow, I realized, except for its steepness, spread out like pictures of tundra in the far north.

The trail had been worn into the thick turf by boots and erosion, I assumed, although moose and deer probably helped. The depth of a foot or so indicated more wear than seemed likely through the roots and matted vegetation, which when walked upon above the trenched trail cushioned boots like an innerspring mattress. Underneath it all, keeping to the trail, I could see and feel pulverized bits of rotten rock.

In this heath were numerous little bogs that suited cotton grass with its white puffs. Extensive patches of Labrador tea on more solid ground blended with leatherleaf and plants I didn't know.

The moor seemed to cling on the mountainside as we descended or traversed it in the cloud. A sudden drop-off halted us. We looked down upon spruce spires vanishing into misty vacancy. The trail consisted of slippery mud. I started down. At once I had to grab a spruce to arrest my slide. We stopped again, hanging onto trees and staring into the apparent abyss. There was nothing to dispel the sensation of being suspended among evergreens growing over nothingness.

I said, "It's got to be above the col before Goose Eye."

"Can't hang here all day. I'm going to find out." He slid past me. "Ta-ta."

His ancient gray felt dropped from sight through the waving branches he had clung to. I let go and slid after him, hoping the small firs I gripped wouldn't uproot at the edge of a precipice.

No collapse into the void. My boots grabbing for footholds began to pull into aches those front thigh muscles. I didn't sit down in the mud but might have done so had not the trail leveled. Claud was waiting by a pool to the left of the trail—lunchtime.

The dry crackers and cheese, rinsed down with spring water from the envelope, were not enough to suit Claud. He dug into his pack for the powdered strawberry milkshake. I passed him one of the tin pails. Pretending accurate measurements with a tin cup, he mixed a quantity between a pint and a quart. After all, the supply of powder, for practical purposes, was inexhaustible or so I realized by figuring eight men on a week of milkshakes would equal, well, four times two is eight, say a month for two men...oh, forget it.

We added the ineffable scent of artificial strawberries—no real taste except for the sweetness—as dessert on top of the crackers and cheese. Any chocolate would have been superfluous.

Sipping the strawberry milkshake in small swallows that wouldn't gag me, though the first cupful had slipped down easily, I took my glasses case from the pack so I could examine the map.

I said, "Pretty soon we'll meet the challenge of the cliffs on Goose Eye, judging by contour lines here." I took up the *Guide* pages. "Nothing about cliffs in the text. I don't know."

"Whatever's ahead let us attack it with fortitude."

"Sure, if you'll lend me some."

Our way began to slant innocently up into more fog as we sloshed out of the spruces and through deep sphagnum moss, which never quite looked—those green tendrils beside my boots—as though they could have padded wounds during the First World War. Moist cradling for mud worms, yes, or antimold seedbed for tomatoes, yes, or diapers for Indian babies, yes, but wounds?

We entered upon a rising moor. The trail led across several ax-flattened logs laid end to end on bogholes. We balanced our way along, slipped into the black humus, took to the springy turf of peat and matted roots, stepped down onto granulated rock again for a few yards.

Between the bogholes, I wondered how the few hikers in this remote range, mostly aiming their boots toward Katahdin on the AT, I assumed, could wear away a foot of turf to crumbling rock. Then I thought of the obvious tenderness of the turf, mostly dried sphagnum moss and brittle roots of sheep laurel, Labrador tea, and blueberries (or bilberries), and other shrubs whose names I wished I knew.

Back on the turf I realized that my boots sank in with a slight crackling sound. I stopped to look back. I was leaving imprints. When Claud bypassed a boghole on the other side of the trail he left similar tracks. Our crushing of vegetation was especially evident in the crinkly, pale moss or lichens that I called reindeer moss and remembered from Deer Isle. Here no weathered sea urchins dropped into evergreens by gulls, no liquid sound of surf on rocks.

I also noticed that behind us sedges and rushes remained bent. I tried to avoid stepping on the creeping tangles of crowberry. I felt that I was destroying or "hurting" an age-old product of the natural world, an adaptation of remarkable plants to this inhospitable, wind-swept, primeval pile of rocks, where vegetation, somehow starting with lichens, had turned into soil, probably very acid, hence the crumbling surface of the bedrock. I couldn't recall—if I ever knew—what chemical or gas and water made rocks fall apart. How did plants live and endure nine months of freezing temperatures, snow, and ice? Ten thousand years since the glacier ages? And on a rock pile?

Yet they were not tough and hardy. They were tender. What was their secret? I walked on lichens, mosses, and plants that survived by their very delicacy. No wonder a few boots killed the turf down to granular, rotted rock. Tough boots destroyed delicate plants....

I had no time to pause and seek the moral significance hidden in these observations. We had arrived at the foundation of the predicted spire that was Mount Goose Eye. Cliffs emerged from the cloud as a triangular face whose apex disappeared in mist and gray-white fog.

We stopped and began looking for footholds. Claud reached out to test a twisted spruce. I hesitated and as so often happens, this produced an association of ideas that came as a thought. I could see it in quotes: "If you are delicate but tenacious, you survive."

From this general premise something was missing. I kept looking for toeholds in which to wedge my boots...there, the something missing were boots. Delicate tenaciousness will not save you from boots treading on you. Try to escape from boots bearing down upon you....

This cliff, however, could stand it, mine anyhow, if I could. And there were edges for boots, also here or there a little spruce for my fists to grab. The trees were about a foot high with roots of questionable security in cracks filled with eroded bits of stone.

The weight of the pack pulled on my shoulders till I remembered to concentrate on balancing me and my pack above my boots. I began feeling better. The first really vertical ledge offered a chance to test my adrenaline stimulus by scrambling up it.

Claud's rubber boots above me displayed their faint chain tread. At the second face of battered rock, his words came down to me in a simple statement formed into a snarl. "This route was laid out by the same sonofabitch who took us through those bombed rocks above Carlo Col. Goddamn sadist. I'm climbing over there, around that jut of rock."

He circled through scrub and disappeared. Then he called back, "Holy Christ, here's a chimney and no way to bypass it."

I heard rattling rocks dislodged, more cursing. The gray felt appeared, the arms in the cotton shirt—he had given up the wool shirt climbing Mount Carlo. Next I saw shoulders and pack straps of green canvas stitched by Louise, and the bulging green bag. A Bean boot appeared and jammed itself into a crevice.

He rose up in it—yes, it was a chimney. Wedging himself upward with boots and elbows, he finally seemed to be hauling himself up by handholds.

And must have, because I saw the chain treads pushing air as they groped for and at last found adherence with which to push him into scrub branches.

When I clung there in the chimney I did manage to insert the edge of my boot soles onto, and into, one-inch shelves and cracks. They allowed me, with a hand-hold grip on an upper shelf, to stretch out at an angle where I could flop without sliding back into the depths. Momentum zero. I struggled out of my pack before I could crawl, dragging it, to a panting stand-up.

Claud had disappeared into low spruces and lower clouds.

The trail ahead of me could be described in mountaineering terms as "less demanding."

It was a relief, yet demanding enough until I topped out on a ridge and saw the cloudy outline of a man with a bulky pack slung low. He stood beside a post. Another two steps brought me close enough to read the lettering on the white sign. It told me "Goose Eye Trail."

This was startling and confusing. I had been ready to feel exultation at conquering Mount Goose Eye by the demanding Mahoosuc Trail. Momentarily I stood in a dream world beside a stranger carrying a Duluth pack.

So he must be Claud. Gradually I realized I had achieved only a bare ridge somewhere below the summit of Goose Eye. I had to go somewhere else. Yes, to Full Goose Shelter and rest. But which way? I tried to visualize the map. I couldn't recall any "Goose Eye Trail."

Claud was gazing to the left into cloud. He said, "We ought to go to the summit."

This oriented me. Our trail to the shelter and rest, the Mahoosuc Trail, led off to the right into the fog, but must be the way for us.

He repeated, "Get to the top, now we're so close."

"In this frigging cloud? Bullshit. You're crazy."

"Don't you want to say you were on the summit of Mount Goose Eye?"

"Not in the least."

"We ought to, you know."

I sensed that his heart wasn't in the "ought to." I turned to the right, easterly, and walked into the cloud and past the sign that dimly appeared for the Mahoosuc Trail. I felt relieved to know I was on the way at last to Full Goose Shelter.

Behind me he merely said, a little sadly, "I really wanted to hit all the summits in the Mahoosucs, but I don't care so much now. Can't see anything." Silence for a few steps, then, "We can come back sometime and climb it on a clear day from the Success Pond Road."

I didn't reply with forced agreement. The prospect angered me in a twisted way. I hated this mountain that had almost beaten me. I was furious at my inadequate body, at aging, at the approaching mountains ahead.

And yet there was a gnawing desire to stand on top of Mount Goose Eye. By a quirk of memory I could recall the *Guide* pages for the trail approaching Goose Eye, in which the text had read: "It comes out on the open ridge about 200 yds. E of the main (W) peak, which is reached by the Goose Eye Trail...." Two hundred yards was only twice the length of Claud's rifle range in his pine woods. Not far to the summit really, but exhaustion told me that even without a pack, 200 yards uphill, and back—call it a quarter mile—was not a choice I could accept. Shit, the summit represented no accomplishment, just final collapse of my aching legs.

And eastward proved to be nearly level in low scrub, yes, and downhill somewhat. The wind was only a sharp breeze. No rain, which would have been an unnecessary addition—we were soaked by cloud and sweat. Now, dripping branches soaked us again.

On that ridge, luckily after we emerged from the scrub onto barren ground, cairns guided us through the cloud. For short distances I followed the trail worn in the turf and mud. Once or twice I noticed again dog tracks and the cleated impression of a Vibram sole.

Occasionally I thought I detected smaller footprints. A child? Mystery. I bent to look, and Claud hauled up short behind me, saying, "I'm sleepwalking. Almost ran you down. What you got?"

"Track of a very small boot, faint, but look there. Only a kid would wear a boot that size. What say Injun Joe?"

"Him say one print ain't a trail. Rained in some but even so, not much weight in boot. Him say track of Irish leprechaun."

"They don't make tracks."

"Small boy then. There's another."

"How old?"

"Much rain last night. Not made today. Dog track older, like big boot."

"That dog and the owner look to me traveling fast. We'll never see them. But look here—another big boot track, and fresh as small one."

"Not so big as dog-man's. Whole goddamn Mahoosucs getting crowded."

"Looks it. Let's go."

I moved on, speculating about a kid up here. Seemed impossible, in this cloud, in this vacancy of mountains. I stepped across more tracks and knew that Claud would notice them.

These muddy places proved to be in a col. After them we began climbing steeply. I had read of East Peak. This must be it, a narrow cut in spruces ending in a rock scramble. East Peak of Goose Eye must be a bare pinnacle surrounded by stunted evergreens.

I pulled myself onto rocks and saw a cairn. It caught wisps of cloud blown by a wet wind that gave me an instantaneous shudder. Claud joined me. We stood there panting and looked at cloud-obscured rocks. He expressed my growing concern. "I don't see another damned cairn, or sign, or painted arrow, so where the hell are we?"

"I figure it's East Peak of Goose Eye. I think the trail turns north off East Peak."

He took his brass compass from his pants pocket, lifted back the lid, and watched the floating dial settle. He pointed left. "I've had enough of this bloody wind. Let's get out of here."

Compass in hand, he strode off.

I was taken with a sudden uncertainty about the "north" I had quoted. I hurried after him and caught up before he disappeared in the cloud.

"Wait a bit. I better check the map and the *Guide*."

We looked at each other, wet and cold. We'd both have the shakes soon, but I had to know for sure our direction. Claud took shelter out of the wind by the lee of an upslanted ledge and crouched on his heels. He looked at me with stolid resignation for my perpetual wanting to be sure.

I dared not squat for fear of leg cramps, so slid out of my pack and sat on it. I pulled from my shirt pocket the damp *Guide* pages and the little map. Accuracy required my glasses. Putting them on revealed that my fingers were too cold for simple motions.

Numbness wasn't right for summertime. The third day of September ought to be summertime. And only 3,500 feet up.

I jammed my hands into pants pockets and watched Claud's slow fingers loading his pipe. I said, "Look out when you stand up in the wind."

"I got more experience than when I was sixteen."

We were sharing the memory of his lighting his pipe above treeline on Mount Washington by huddling under the flap of his pack, the first Duluth from Sears Roebuck. Standing up he puffed only once before the gale snatched the tobacco from the bowl, a smouldering clot glowing red for a vanishing instant. We had leaned into the wind convulsed with laughter.

My hands warmer, I turned pages and carefully unfolded the map. Northward proved to be our route. I looked up. Claud was pointing with his pipe. I saw through breaks in the cloud a vast heath slanting down. And no trail, no cairns. Suppose we descended at random and couldn't find the trail at the far fringe of scrub spruce?

Yet move we must or chill to death. We stood up together. Claud's wet cotton shirt plastered his chest and his shoulders outside the packstraps. My coarse work shirt felt less wet than he looked. We started walking down. Claud held his pipe in one hand, palm curved over the bowl. When I paused to look for traces of hikers, he would take a puff and stare ahead, too.

After the second or third examination of the terrain, we began to see low, four-stone cairns emerge from the cloud on this sloping alpine meadow. They appeared in no regular line. A few boot tracks here and there suggested that hikers had different ideas as to the whereabouts of the trail and had marked various ways down. The trend seemed toward the east end of the meadow or heath.

Finally down at the scrub, we came to a blank wall of impenetrable branches. The green tangle stopped me and I reacted with total dejection. In the depths I remained speechless and stationary. Once again at a critical moment, Claud walked past me along the edge of scrub. I followed. I think he saw nothing more than I did and was urged on by the necessity of keeping in motion just to stay warm.

We came to an opening and a white blaze of paint. Another spruce showed scars where branches had been trimmed. I almost sat down in relief.

Claud made a little bow, "After you, my dear Alphonse," and waved me into the opening. Maybe he knew I had been for a moment ready to quit.

I managed my bow, and replied, "On the contrary, my dear Gaston. Allow me to follow you."

Which he did.

We relaxed on the trail.

The spruces in their scrubby density soon became taller. We walked through a sizable array of trees, maybe 15 feet high and six to ten inches through at the bases of the trunks. A thick carpet of sphagnum moss cushioned the ground. In a small, wooded ravine our boots squished into the moss as we came to pools of water. All of a sudden I felt a hungry weakness. "I gotta eat again."

"Past time for me, too."

He probably could have gone on for hours.

A cold wind blew through the spruces. I pulled on my worn, hooded rain shirt, hip-length. The coated nylon fabric gave no warmth but would cut the wind. Its red color suggested heat.

Claud began mixing pink lemonade from one of the packets of sugar and chemicals. He cupped water out of a pool and stirred the mess in the coffeepot. There was no *kalmia* growing around the pool.

Nearby, beside the charcoal of a dead fire built on rock, someone had chopped and sawed up four-foot lengths of spruce and stacked them almost two feet high and braced against a stump two feet away. Some job for a hiker. Who? Why waiting to be burned? The stack was neatly done, the ax marks expert, and the saw couldn't have been a backpacker's saw for dead branches.

I said, "Not chawed by a beaver."

"Nor a Boy Scout's hatchet. How about the saw?"

I examined a butt. "Done with a pulp saw, betcha."

"Mystery." He poured cups of pink lemonade. "Can't figure a trail crew wasting time and energy like that. Mystery."

We drank the sweet, lemon-flavored water. Ice-cold from the pool, it made Claud say, "I could use one hell of a big fire." He was eyeing the stack of wood and the handle of my ax sticking from the corner of my pack at the joint of the wide flap. I felt a panic, knowing his dedicated enthusiasm for a rousing fire in the cold and rain—hell, any time. And now he could start a blaze with the ax and his large supply of matches by splitting the spruce sticks to their inner dryness for tinder and kindling. I must have somehow registered my fear that we'd be caught by darkness far from the shelter.

He said, "We better not take the time."

He was making a big concession to me, and in a sense turning from the challenge of the wet cold, which I knew he wanted to drive back with his flames. The distance to the shelter probably had little effect on his decision, for he reveled in the heat (although without comment or demonstrations) of a blazing fire and the inner comfort of scalding tea. And he must be very cold and tired.

We once more ate cheese and crackers, this time washed down with the chilly, so-called lemonade. I hoped for some energy from the sugary yet tart sweetness. I realized I was drinking a circus or country-fair treat—pink lemonade.

Ernie and I had sipped it at the World's Fair, Tunbridge, Vermont? Yes, when Ernie and I went with her brother, Lou, and my sister Ib...yes, summer of 1936 when we were a commune in Orford...and I won Ernie a doll by ringing the bell on a lucky swing of a maul.

Maybe the sugar worked, or my lucky past. I began to feel better.

Boreal chickadees flew close to inspect us. Claud held out cracker crumbs. They had not been trained to handouts from hikers, although one lit on a twig to examine the toasty brown bits before rejoining his companions in their diligent search for larvae among the spruces.

Off in the woods I saw on the ground a silent thrush. His quick bill tossed aside birch leaves, not by plucking at them but with quick flips and pecks at revealed worm or bug. I saw above the thrush the bare branches of the birches growing among the spruce and fir. The season was early up here. Pale tan-colored leaves made me feel the urgency of autumn. I was also seized by the cold. After food your blood concentrated at your stomach, or so I'd been told. And I felt cold trickles on my back. Did my red parka...why did I think of it as a rain shirt...archaic term from fishing days...did it leak?

When I took it off to shoulder my pack—Claud was about to move on—I held up the red cloth. Cracks in the waterproofing showed plainly. I had loaned it to Penny for her summer in Germany assisting at children's camps with the Unitarian group. I myself had folded it or rolled it many times to shove in my pack.

I set out for warmth as well as for distance.

We began to climb again. This must be North Peak. The spruces dwindled to head height then retreated into the ground. We stepped into another barren heath, presumably too exposed even for spruces. The dwarf plants reminded me of those in sections of the Alpine Garden below Mount Washington's cone, but here tipped at an angle with few imbedded rocks, and none of the rock slabs towering above. The heath extended upward through the wisps of cloud. I supposed, and hoped, that the limit of my vision was the highest ground of North Peak.

We went at it steadily first-off. Soon the pitch of the slope shifted us into our one-foot-before-the-other pace. I had warmed all right with the exertion, and although puffing, began enjoying myself in the wild setting.

Obviously, given a sunny day, this hike over the three summits of Goose Eye would be an exciting adventure in a semialpine environment. There would be views open to northern forests and lakes. Even today, nearby, I could see a bird who might have been more appropriate in Labrador, a slate-colored junco. If I had the time I could look for his—more likely her—nest. She had flown from an undercut in the turf. The white edges of her tail showed clearly. Once on Mount Chocorua I had found a nest in a similar spot, but now I hurried on. Besides, juncos don't build nests in September.

I had no air in my lungs, gasped, stopped. Ahead, Claud rested.

He asked over his shoulder and from under wet felt hat drooping over one eye, "How high is this sonofabitch?"

"Three thousand six hundred and fifty."

"Feels like we been climbing from sea level." He shifted his weight from left hip to right. "I'm getting old. I used to run from Galehead Hut a thousand feet up over South Twin and along that ridge to Zealand Hut and back, seven miles one way. And in those days the trail dipped down to Zealand Pond. Just for some foolishness like stealing a stove lid or egg-beater off the crew there because they'd swiped something of mine. I guess that started in thirty-four when I was learning Galehead from Dick Dodge. Well, it went on between all the huts."

I didn't mention that Dick had been a classmate of mine. Claud knew it. We seldom talked about our different colleges, a mutual acknowledgment that mine had been elite and UNH wasn't, so it lay in the area of our differences and unshared past.

We stood there in the drizzle like donkeys resting under loads. I thought of asking him about the AMC donkeys packing supplies to Galehead but he began moving upward step by step. He was too tired, I could tell, for a real rest and the comfort of his pipe.

We stopped often, again and again. Wet and cold, we wanted only the shelter. This bare peak intervened. We had to climb over it. The trail here was a gravel path naturally formed by the decomposition of rock, which was crumbling from millions, more or less, of years. The harsh crumbs crunched under my boots. Claud walked softer.

Assurance that we had reached the summit came at a large cairn built waist high on North Peak. We had also achieved a biting east wind, into which Claud turned without hesitation. A scattering of little cairns led off that way across another barren ridge. Again low spruces gradually lined the trail beyond what had to be called treeline, not from elevation but from exposure. Wide patches like trimmed branches lay flat on the ground. Black spruce, I figured, brushed against the earth by the prevailing winds blasting, unlike ours, from the northwest. Taller spruces leaned away southeast, and put out longer branches on that leeward side. The trees looked ages old yet sturdy. Endurance was a way of life.

Now we were going down at last. Steeply we entered a cut in the scrub. Mud and rocks offered minor obstacles as we made our way into an area of tipped ledges. They forced us to pull ourselves over and past. The spruce and fir grew larger here, taller, and with spreading branches.

Moss, in wisps like Chinamen's beards, hung gray and fine from twigs, a lichen, more likely. *Usnea.*

Our path in the woods ended at a wall of evergreens. A vertical rock face rose to our right. I judged it to be eight feet high. Evidences of climbing were scuffed roots at the top. As we looked close we noticed the marks of scrabbling boots on the turf that clung to the edges of the rock.

These taunted Claud enough to arouse him into a sudden charge at the face, hands and boots clawing, fists gripping branches.

I followed as best I could.

At the top we found ourselves on a little flat in the woods. We faced a perfect haven. The phrase came to me as incongruous yet heartfelt for the dilapidated log structure—Full Goose Shelter. We dumped our packs inside. Then we dumped ourselves beside them on the bunk. The scent of dried fir boughs wafted upward.

Prodded by the cold, we stirred. Claud asked, "How about fire and water?"

I looked at my watch. "No hurry. Only three-thirty. Not as far along as I had thought."

"All the same, I want a fire."

I took the ax from my pack and handed it to him. He walked off to an ancient spruce stump. In my heavier shirt I wasn't as cold as he must be, but I was probably more tired, so I sat on the front bunk log and pulled on the red parka. I wanted to add up our mileage. I assembled myself with glasses, *Guide* pages, and map.

This day's hike, four summits, distance 4.3 miles. From the railroad bridge in Gorham, distance 21.12 miles. The pages of the *Guide* gave the time for the total distance as 17 hours, say about two days of hiking. We had been walking three-and-a-half days, figuring start at about noon, August 31st. That drive from Laconia the first half of the 31st seemed like an aeon away.

Since we saw the watchman at the powerhouse, and the man and woman on the trail to Mascot Pond soon after, we had encountered only two human beings, the collector of AT mileage and his daughter who may have lost the can of plums. Now we were totally alone. And content to be so, at Full Goose Shelter. I looked about, moving gently.

The shelter faced across a ravine to the shoulder of Fulling Mill

Mountain, per the map. I wondered whoever, there, built and operated a mill for raising a nap on cloth…but never mind.

The view, on a clear day, probably gave away downward, and likely out of sight, to the beginning of the highway through Grafton Notch. This seemed unlikely because the scene—under the lowering clouds, forested, precipitous—appeared wildly remote and rugged. The dark ridges of spruces toward Goose Eye Brook and Bull Branch vanished in rainy fog.

I estimated on our map our elevation to be somewhat above 3,000 feet. The air sluiced into the shelter as a cold draft from the east. The ravine channeled it in a peculiar, windless way.

I was clammy wet but decided to get the water before changing to dry clothes from my pack—if they were dry. Duluth canvas packs soaked up water. I gathered our kettles, plus a tin can with a wire bail from the shelter. Where was the path to the spring?

I found a little sign on a tree. Labeled "Spring," it pointed to a break in the spruces. The path at once headed down. It descended and descended to a clear pool. I squatted and cupped water, slowly. With equal moderation, favoring the headache that began to pound, I climbed back with kettles and can stretching both arms.

Claud, chopping, bent over a stump. I announced, "*De profundis.*"

He replied with Latin that I couldn't follow, except maybe the English word "wild," which must be "wilde." I didn't care. Hell, I barely made the shelter and almost spilled water as I disentangled the bails and set kettles near the fireplace. I sat on the bunk's front log.

Claud straightened up with a slab off the stump, walked a few steps, laid it on the blazing flames, then stood close to dry his wet clothes. How those stump slabs flared! Resin formed torches leaping into the drizzle and cloud.

The shelter, small and adequate for only six hikers, nestled in a veritable bonanza of firewood. Spruce stumps, rotted at the roots, contained pitchy wood ready to be chopped off by a splitting action of the ax. Their length, about a foot and a half, was just right without more fitting. Apparently the stumps had been left by the builders of the shelter; their diameters of a foot or less matched the logs. I guessed that logging had never penetrated this far back and up in the mountains. Difficult distance, even in horse-logging days, must have made such an enterprise unprofitable.

Besides the stumps, which for some mysterious reason other hikers had not burned, there was for us spruce-branch kindling, dried on the trunks of living trees. We were settling into a woodsman's hideout such as we used to dream about as boys. Full Goose Shelter could very well take away the place of perfection from Isolation Shelter south of Mount Washington, site of fabulous trout feasts.

After a time, Claud set two pots of water on the edge of the fire. The fireplace of stones neatly arranged in an open circle, reflected heat back into the shelter while at the same time containing the fire. Two forked sticks driven into the ground supported a green sapling crossbar from which to hang pots. I saw no pothooks.

I could supply that need by whittling them out of birch branches trimmed so as to leave a sturdy twig for the crossbar. A notch carved in the other end would catch the bail of the pot. I had not forgotten how to do this. Claud was more inclined to leave the pots in the coals. Anyhow I was too lazy at the moment and anxious to examine my pack for dry clothes.

Too much fire now for cooking, though Claud was putting together the reflector oven. Flames lit the shelter's interior. It contained the usual bough bed, no fresh greenery there on the bunk, a few nails in the logs, and not much else. No toilet paper, not even for the mice to tear into nests. The log roof had rotted in one corner, from water leaking through a rip in the tar paper. A helpful hiker had propped the roof with a post and had tucked a strip of birch bark under the tar paper.

As for clothing, I was luckier than Claud. While he stood in front of the fire and steamed, he smoked his pipe. I dug from my pack my long underwear, an old-fashioned, one-piece union suit. Also came out a pair of hiking shorts, a change of wool socks, and my heavy wool shirt in black and red squares, known by an unlikely name, buffalo plaid. Well, Claud could have put on his similar shirt. We had been wearing such shirts for a long time—woodsman's standard.

I put on the union suit over my goose flesh, yanked on shorts, shirt, and red parka—a serviceable, warm, unusual outfit. I felt, however, over-dressed, because Claud stood by the fire turning one side, then the other, the probable shivering concealed by his attempts to shrink and expose as little as possible of himself to the cold breeze.

Yet he remained a hulking figure there, outlined against the red flare and the gray smoke. Hands in pants pockets, hat snugged down, legs braced under him, he showed stubborn resistance to the elements. The steam from his pants drifted into the flames and went up with the smoke. The pants hung outside his boot tops. Never did he pull his wool socks over his pants. He always folded the hem in back and tucked as much as possible into the leather tops before lacing them tightly. He formed the habit in winter snows, which collected on outside sock tops. This method often allowed one pant-leg to pull free and flop alongside the tucked one. Or both pulled free.

I noticed a pot of water bubbling and steaming. A short stick under the bail gave me a lever to lift it off the coals. I dumped in from a cloth bag the pound of split peas. Looking at my initials embroidered on the bag I was back in "The Lilting House," the title of Ruthie's first novel about that lower half of a duplex we lived in during the war years and after. Ruthie had made this bag for me back when she was a little-girl seamstress before paper and pencils absorbed her attention. Penny's contribution to my camping equipment, bought from her allowance, had been two black, screw-top jars—Bakelite to me—for peanut butter and jelly, she said, luxuries not for this trip. Penny turned out to be the mature seamstress...well, should we have brought peanut butter...?

I smelled raw onion.

Claud was kneeling on the bunk among the balsam fir needles and old branches, slicing the onion on the front log. Then from a plastic bag he slid out a greasy paper package. The rectangle of bacon, which he laid crossways on the log, added its smoky aroma to the prickle in my eyes from the onion. He pressed his knife easily through the white fat and red lean, but hard through the rind, for two strips, which he trimmed and cut into squares.

I held the frying pan to him so he could drop in the bacon and onion.

Frizzling over the fire, they made me hungry for a plateful of fried eggs and crisp bacon with white bread toasted, slathered with plenty of butter, and, to drink, a mug of strong coffee...real milk, sugar....

When the bacon had started to brown, I dumped it, onion, fat, and all into the pot of peas, which I moved back so it wouldn't boil over. I knew that the peas should have soaked. Simmering (in time) would soften them, and we had time, enough to rest and watch the soup cook.

Claud had been carefully looking over the shelter. Now he handed me a heavy wire pothook, S-shaped and strong. No need for whittling a pothook. I caught the bail and lifted the pot to a position under the crosspiece. By watching the boil I could slide the pot along till the soup barely simmered.

We sat on the bunk's front log and talked about our days in Orford. This was so necessary to us that it had become automatic and unthinking. The shared past began on the summer day when he came wandering into the yard of our house, a plain little boy of six, I think, as was I, who cautiously stared at this strange intruder in my demesne. I was sitting on the board seat of a rope swing suspended from a butternut tree. The board had a vee sawed into each end to catch the loop of the rope. I was shocked to note that the strange boy's short pants were held up by suspenders. Only men wore suspenders.

He spoke first. "You live here?"

"Summers. In the winters I live in New Jersey."

"I'm here year-round, but we came from Gardner, Massachusetts."

Or some such conversation. I don't remember how we verbally became acquainted. I'm sure I must have shown him the garage made from the barn attached to the house's ell, which included a backhouse, a sawdust-filled room of ice, woodshed, and overhead two attics, and above the garage-stable a hayloft. We probably got into mischief. That was typical of our friendship.

Now those days grew vivid because a toad, warmed by the fire, appeared in all his warty confidence from a crevice among the rocks of the fireplace. Overheated more likely, and suffering. Claud picked him up, stroked his back, and tucked him out of harm's way under a log. I had once been cruel to toads with him. Then was I too painfully shy, spoiled, and overprotected to do anything alone so vicious? Perhaps, as in his way alone he might have been. We seemed to lead each other into bad incidents.

Returning to our log, Claud said, "Remember the old wheelbarrow at your place, with wooden sides and iron wheel?"

"Sure," I replied, knowing where his thoughts had gone, as had mine. But I spoke of the wheelbarrow. "I started pushing it when I was so small I had to lift on its handles near the body to get the legs off the ground."

We were silent till I added, "I know what the toad reminded you of."

"Running over those with it."

"Down the terrace in front of our house. Barbarous exploit we egged each other into."

"There were four toads. I was interested in their guts. Scientific experiment."

I refrained from saying, "You were interested in squashing them." His feelings hurt easily, or his half-Welsh pride, and I could never be sure of his reaction to an intended wisecrack.

He, too, dealt with my sensitivities by avoiding them.

We dropped the subject while I wondered how boyish barbarity and sadism had transformed into a career of helping sick animals...and where had mine gone?

As for Orford days, our sharing of memories temporarily restored us to a simpler time before we went our adult ways. Various interests the passing of years had changed.

For instance, I had not continued my youthful interest in firearms, whereas he was becoming a collector of antique rifles and shotguns. Not merely for display—indeed I was never quite sure why, ever since the day he spent two hours at the tar-paper home of Shiff the Gunman near Woodstock, while I, restive to catch trout up in Russell Pond, waited...summer 1941...a single-barrel eight-gauge shotgun for $12.

He sometimes shot it, and Ballards and Bullards and such, on his range. He studied all the old models of Winchester, Remington, and Marlin, one or two of which he used for deer hunting. I had no such knowledge beyond a scattering acquired from him, nor his marksmanship, and didn't care, except I wished I was a better shot.

In reverse, he tried fly fishing and skiing but never went along with my interest in those.

Our shared interest continued in hunting deer, rabbits, and partridge, also in worm fishing for brook trout and ice fishing with shiners and smelt for bait. So our recollections of Orford time together were complicated by relating to the present.

Yes, we still went deer hunting together, south of Lake Francis near the top of New Hampshire. In the fall we drove in his Jeep truck to his camp on land leased from the St. Regis Paper Company. The old topo map by the USGS showed it as "Hurlburt Camp." I carried the map so I wouldn't get lost; the wrong side of Crystal Mountain could put you into Dead Diamond River country. I got lost anyhow at least once. We failed to damage the deer much. These hunts began in 1957 when my devoted service to Scott and Williams for 17 years brought a third week's vacation as a reward. Ernie was very understanding and kept right on at the law office.

All this is a different story, but in Full Goose Shelter I remembered his firing at two deer as we returned to the camp along a logging road. The deer vanished into the brush country of slash and sprouts. We trailed them on bloodless snow till almost dark. Back at the place where he had shot, he paused to look and said, "Plenty room for bullets."

I didn't remind him. We watched the pea soup and the fire. He could dwell too seriously on missed shots.

Instead I asked about the rifle of that day. "You taking your 'scoped three hundred Magnum again this year?"

"No, I've bought a Winchester four-oh-one automatic that handles good. Open sights. Faster than that 'scope. Remember Clint Ansley in Orford? He used one. Got a lot of deer with it."

"He claimed."

"Well, yes." Then after a moment to stir the soup, "I ought to have shot at least one deer when we were kids in Orford. Never did,"

"Me neither."

"Came of trying to learn by ourselves, or alone. Now if my old man had been a hunter, or your father...." He quickly shifted the subject to a pleasant memory, realizing that my father had died before we were old enough to hunt. "Remember your father taking us up Fairlee Cliff? We blazed a trail among the rocks leading to that gully."

"Red paint." I switched us back to deer hunting in Orford. "Remember when we tried to tire those deer by keeping after them till they'd slow down and we could get a standing shot?"

"Kept after them three days."

I was dry and warm and talkative. "You and Malcolm were hardly able to climb up the side of Cube Mountain to his camp that second afternoon when I arrived to keep after them the third day. Was that the weekend Malcolm sat down on the bunk and fired both barrels through the roof? I wasn't there. Maybe chasing those three deer."

"No, earlier that year. Malcolm and I had been hunting partridge in the old orchard in the swamp below his camp. He'd pushed off the safety catch and forgot it. After that I never hunted in front of him. But at the time we thought it was a hell of a joke."

"He tried to be too quick on the trigger. Filled a stump full of buckshot once with me. The stump looked just like a deer getting up from its bed. Scared the shit out of me. I was ahead of him. The wonder is someone didn't get shot."

We dropped the subject, perhaps because we were both thinking of other near accidents, yet we were alive and talking, many years later, in Full Goose Shelter, Mahoosuc Mountains, State of Maine, USA, World....

I said, "Boyhood hunting seems a long time past."

"It is," Claud stood up. "Or last fall. I'm going to start the corn bread."

Before mixing the batter he washed his hands without a basin. This involved extracting a thin piece of soap from a grimy ditty bag, wetting his hands from the can of water, soaping, rinsing onto the ground, drying with his shirt tail, while telling me, "First my mother worked on me about cleanliness, then Joe Dodge reminded me when some finicky old Appie complained about me, then at Michigan to be sure you washed off the blood and formaldehyde. The yellow didn't come off. Then my wife." He measured out the mix. "She's not so emphatic as Joe was. Hasn't got his Navy style."

After he arranged the reflector oven with the pan of batter in front of the fire, he stirred the soup and added water.

Together again on the log we shared a can of kipper-snacks. The long, narrow cans with a key under the wrapping had often contained excursion food for us. We dug into the fillets with the short-handled spoons.

He said, "This cost eighty-two cents. When we started with them remember what they were?"

"A nickel." I savored the smoky, salty fish.

He nodded. "And a bigger can."

I foresaw a lecture on the hellish consequences of inflation caused by Franklin Roosevelt's taking us off the gold standard. Quickly I interrupted.

"Remember when we used an empty can to hold bacon fat and a bit of rag to make a lamp?"

This started us talking about the hunting camp we created from a boxlike henhouse near an abandoned sawdust pile in Quinttown.

The soup and corn bread smelled too good for talking. We served ourselves and ate in silence for a while, till I had to say, "It was still there after the war."

"We'd been away seventeen years, I figure."

"A poplar tree six inches through had grown up and blocked the window," I reminded him.

"If we'd finished the log shelter on Lamprey Pond, it would have been standing, too, that year of forty-seven."

"I'm not sure. Those fir logs had rotted. Chimney in good shape still."

"Ten years after," Claud said, "maybe longer, when I went there with my son Joe, the beavers had flooded the woods. Nothing but the chimney above water."

"No beavers out there, none in Orford, when we built it. No moose, no fishers, no ravens. Got 'em all now. Big improvement."

In all this talk we were telling each other nothing new. We had said the same things many times before. Renewal of our shared past was necessary. I wondered why we kept thus vicariously living it again together. Some deep, gloomy, psychological reason doubtless, which I didn't want to know.

We finished eating our soup and corn bread, all we could hold, and plenty left over. By that time, darkness was making the fire glow more and more.

Suddenly, moving slowly up above the steep bank beyond the fireplace, appeared a head of dark hair and a woman's face.

Gradually the apparition took the form of a whole young woman standing in the firelight. By contrast to our woodsmen's primitiveness she was modern in red shorts and white T-shirt. She carried a gleaming aluminum packframe and orange nylon bag. Yet she was an Indian, or so my bemused mind told me—bronzed skin, high cheekbones, black hair, but tied back in a ponytail instead of in braids.

Equally out of keeping were her Italian climbing boots, and her ragg-wool socks, which had not protected her bare legs from mud.

She wasn't breathing hard. Although her tanned face looked tired she gave the impression of reserve strength.

Her first words were, "Hi there." She unslung the pack and dropped it inside. "May I have a drink? I'm very thirsty."

Simultaneously we stood up.

Claud dipped a cup of water from a kettle and handed it to her.

"Thanks. What's for supper?" She investigated the soup pot hanging away from the heat, and the corn bread pan covered with an aluminum plate.

I said, "Help yourself."

Instead she sat down on the bunk log and loosened her boot laces. Then she pulled from her pack a quilted yellow parka. She shook it until it became fluffy. I thought, "Hmm, goose down. Expensive."

As was the Shetland sweater she put on first.

Claud filled a plate with thick soup and the corn bread.

She accepted it but asked "Got plenty? You've eaten?"

Together we answered, "Sure."

Claud added tea bags to the boiling water in the coffeepot and set it aside to brew.

So I dug out the dried skim milk and the sugar in their plastic bags.

After a time Claud asked, "Tea?"

I knew he wasn't addressing me.

"Thanks, yes." And she scraped her plate with the spoon. "I was very, very hungry. Where are you from?"

My reply condensed our locations. "Laconia. Where you from?"

"Grafton Notch. Really Massachusetts. My aunt and uncle live in Laconia."

Claud took her plate and gave her a cup of tea. Without asking he dished out more soup and corn bread. I passed the milk and sugar.

She looked at us. "Why don't you two sit down?"

We did so, and holding our cups we looked into the fire. She sipped her tea and ate more slowly.

I was about to ask the name of her uncle when another damp head of hair slowly appeared at the top of the bank from the little ravine. Blond hair, then the face of a young man.

Did I detect a slowly dawning expression of disappointment?

His girl was sitting between two old codgers and eating from a plate of food. In this remote difficult mountainside the shelter should have been vacant.

His shoulders and pack appeared. He pulled himself over the edge and stood up. Weary, disheveled, and wet in his shorts and T-shirt, he looked totally alien to this environment. Civilization and cities were much more his habitat than hers, or so he appeared to me. He looked vulnerable, lean, and burdened with his pack. His footgear added to my sympathy. Muddy white tennis shoes and thin socks must have left his feet beaten. Awkwardly he disengaged himself from his packframe. He began to shrink in the cold east wind.

The young woman said, "Robert, put on your sweater. You're start-ing to shiver. Put on your parka and pants."

Shivering he truly was. His hands trembled as he undid the straps of his pack.

Claud placed more wood on the fire. Leaping flames carried the smoke up past the eaves. The dying fire had allowed the breeze to waft smoke toward us. Spruce smoke is eye-watering. Claud offered Robert a plate of soup and corn bread. Robert declined, saying, "Thanks, we brought plenty of supplies."

Claud motioned with the plate. "Into the fire then."

The young woman spoke quickly. "Take it, Robert. Can't you see the man wants you to have it?"

Robert accepted and ate ravenously.

He was older than I had at first estimated—and tougher, despite his weakened condition. Wiry lankiness was his style, or must be for him to climb from Grafton Notch, almost eight miles, and the trail up Old Speck said to be the steepest in the mountains. He and the young woman had also negotiated the rock tangle that was notoriously the worst along the AT, Mahoosuc Notch. He had done all that in tennis shoes. No wonder he sat down to eat.

We were all in a row on the log. Claud and I sat on either side near our sleeping bags by the side walls. They sat in the middle.

The young folks began to unpack their equipment.

New to me were the foam mattresses, unrolled half-length. Eventually I learned they were made of a material called Ensolite. The packs also disgorged nesting aluminum utensils, a little gasoline stove, other new-to-us amenities or gadgets, and packets of food. The kids didn't talk.

I couldn't surmise what Claud thought of everything; certainly it didn't represent our "camping out." Nor could I be sure about his opinions on this liberated female. We never talked of girls, not even back when we were young. Certainly we never talked about our wives, except in a general way, such as their hobbies. I think we agreed that marriage both simplified and complicated problems, but we wouldn't have it otherwise. About the new feminism, I was probably more tolerant than he.

When the kids went for a walk in the darkening woods, the young woman with a flashlight, Robert with their shiny kettles, we did talk about their difficult hike. It traversed such rugged terrain that I marveled aloud, "I don't see how they did it in one day."

"We could have, easy, at their age."

I asked, "How old?"

Claud said, "I heard something about graduate work."

"Twenty-three to twenty-five or so? They can't be. They aren't that old."

"Every year they look younger."

Our examples came back with their dripping kettles and full water bottles.

Claud's fire had died down. The young woman reached into the bunk and picked up the little stove. Her inspection seemed professional to me, yet she said, "I never ran one of these things before. Just bought it at EMS in North Conway." She held it up, a gleaming little tank and frame around a tiny burner. "Is there an expert with backpack stoves in the audience?"

Three males shook their heads. She began to read a sheet of directions.

I suggested, "Maybe gas is first."

"No, I had a guy fill it for me. And I bought that metal bottle full."

Claud took his pipe from his mouth. "If it's like a gasoline lantern I
might help some."

"Here." She gave him the stove.

Robert said, "Presumably, Mary, you must first vaporize the gasoline."

Claud noted a deficiency. "No pump that I can see."

"Of course not," Mary told him. "You open a valve and let a few
drops of gasoline out and light it to start the vaporizing."

Claud said, "I see. Must be this valve, but I think we'll need about a
teaspoon of gas in the little pan. Strange there's no pump."

Robert murmured, "The principle is sound. Vaporizing results…let
me see, yes, in drawing up the gasoline to the tube beyond which you
should be able to light a flame at the burner."

Somehow Mary and Claud, in the aroma of gasoline, lit the stove
without an explosion. The little purring burner heated water in a spotless
kettle faster than I could believe.

Mary and Robert made their second meal of various lightweight
foods, seemingly from a supermarket. Dried soups. Nuts and raisins. A
pastry thing heated in the frying pan. I asked Mary what they were.

"Toasteryums. Really flattened apple turnovers." She laughed, I
thought at my ignorance, but went on, "They're so filled with preserva-
tives they need no refrigeration. Shelf life forever. I hate to think what
they do to you. But very very good."

I declined her offer of one, not so much from fear of the preserva-
tives as concern that I'd deprive them of some of their scanty, sketchy
provisions.

She gave it to Robert, and ate another herself while setting more
water to boil on the little stove. I noted again how shiny the outfit was
compared to our blackened pots and tin cans. But the kettle began to
jiggle a little as the water came to a roiling boil. She tended the balance
on the precarious supports and adjusted the flame. Instant coffee in a cup
was the finish of her meal. Perhaps Robert avoided caffeine, because he

shook Jell-O, a red powder, from an envelope and stirred, then set the cup aside, saying, "To harden."

"Robert, it won't. The water has to be boiling."

"Oh," He tasted a spoonful. "I'll drink it."

I switched my eyes to Claud. He was lighting his pipe.

I wanted to fill the silence, so I asked the space between Robert and Mary, "Where you two headed? Gorham?"

Robert shrugged and motioned with the cup at Mary. "I think not, are we?"

"No," she said. "We haven't the time. Massachusetts day after tomorrow. That means Gentian Pond tomorrow, next day down to Shelburne and hitch rides back to our car at Grafton Notch."

Robert put in as though explaining to a class, "Labor Day causes much traffic for rides."

"Not only that. I have to be back in Cambridge for work Tuesday." She sipped her coffee.

Claud asked, "What do you do?"

"Lab technician for an electronics firm. I fool around with sunshine, you might say. Energy from, that is."

This revelation, and Robert's evident acceptance of it as normal, for he just concentrated on drinking his Jell-O, emphasized the generation gap more than their obvious youth or their modern camping equipment. I turned the talk to Laconia.

"What's the name of your uncle and aunt?"

"Winship."

"Paul and Polly?"

"Yes. Aunt Polly is my mother's sister. Do you know them?"

"Sure, for a long time, but not well."

The rush of memories involving Paul and Polly left me free only to add, when she asked, "They're fine. I talked to Paul the other day in the bank. My wife and I have an account there. See Polly to say hello in town sometimes. Beautiful as ever."

"Oh, good, I always thought her lovely."

"They're a handsome couple."

"I must take time to see them this fall. Robert, let's take a foliage drive next month and stop to see my aunt and uncle."

"I'd love to, you know, Mary."

"It's a deal."

I didn't have any real news of them for her because I didn't play golf nor frequent the country club. I could have told her that Paul and the bank had held the mortgage on the Gilford Avenue house, from which Ernie and I had moved two years ago to the Sanbornton cottage.

Nor did I hark back and say that a failed chicken farmer, looking for a job to support himself, his wife, and year-old daughter, had lacked a decent suit, long ago, and our friends from Lexington days, Dick and Helen, who moved to Laconia before us and located our Belmont farm in 1937, arranged a hand-me-down suit from Paul Winship, this girl's uncle. We were about of a size. Maybe that suit landed me a job as drill press operator, December 1940, at Scott and Williams. I wore to work there, not the suit, but my overalls....

Claud, too, was thinking of old times while Mary and Robert talked quietly. But I knew that Claud was way back when he said, "The wind has come up in the spruces. Remember hearing the sound outside the old cabin on Smarts Mountain? First heard it there and always reminds me. And that's almost forty years ago."

I said, "Thirty-seven, at least."

I noticed that a silence had fallen between our young friends. Mary asked, "You fellows been doing this all that time?"

"A lot of it," I told her.

And we were off when Claud added, "We were fifteen when we found that cabin."

"First time, looking, we got caught in the rain and turned back."

"Learned to start a fire in the rain to cook hot dogs. I can taste them still, that oily birch-bark smell."

"Next try we found it in the spruces."

"An old tramp came in after dark with a big stick in his hand."

"He pretended it was a walking stick."

"I kept the ax handy," Claud added.

"We got quite friendly. He showed us his winter savings, for winter that is, four hundred dollars."

Claud said, "We should have hit him over the head and run with it."

"Risky. He claimed to be checking the cabins for the Dartmouth

Outing Club. Said he knew Dan Hatch, the manager." I felt we had done enough with the old hovel of a cabin on Smarts. "After we got our driver's licenses we began on Washington. Then Katahdin in thirty-one."

Robert yawned. I didn't go on. All Claud said was, "Real wild. We had to walk in ten miles before we started up the mountain."

Mary yawned. "Sorry. Long day. Go on."

But we couldn't. Just as well.

I listened to the wind in the spruces. It did not sigh, like wind in big pines, nor whisper like wind in green leaves. Short spruce needles and rushing air, again on a mountain high up, produced the whishing hiss I'd heard near the plane crash, but now the pervasive sound encased the log walls and board–tar-paper roof. Claud and I had listened to it many other places—especially he had at Galehead. I tried to bring us into the present by asking Robert if he had a lot of time for hiking.

He answered, "Not much. I am new to it, not like you fellows."

I never got any more from him. Guessing, after overhearing a few words to Mary, I put him down as Claud had said, likely a graduate student or an assistant professor. He gave the impression of shyness and possibly a brilliant mind—or not. His silence may have run deep. But he could act with great individuality as we learned in the night.

Darkness took over as the fire died down. Claud laid wood on the coals, more nearly hot ashes. Spruce and fir leave little piles of gray dust hiding the few coals. I felt cold.

With clothes on and boots off, I wriggled down into my sleeping bag. Claud, pipe in mouth, slid his stocking feet into his bag and pulled up the zipper part way until he stretched out on his back and put aside the pipe. We were each lying along a side wall. The fire flickered fitfully for Mary and Robert who sat on the log of the bunk and talked. Firelight passed across the roof over me.

I dozed warm in my sleeping bag, legs and feet beyond the shorty air mattress cushioned on the balsam branches and deep layer of old needles whose fragrance permeated the shelter. Glad that I had brought the outer shell of the sleeping bag, I felt on my face the cold east wind blowing into the shelter and the faint scent of wood smoke.

Sleepily I awoke enough to hear Mary and Robert, between Claud and me, arranging their sleeping bags and quietly whispering as they settled onto their Ensolite mats. Robert, I could see, had protected his bag from the wind with a big sheet of plastic which gave off an artificial rustle as he pulled it around him. Mary shushed him and he turned toward Claud's sleeping form. Beside me Mary fell asleep, apparently, as easily as a tired child. This soothing example and her presence lulled me sound asleep.

I awoke to a commotion of snores, gasps, and coughs from Claud's side as his circular saw snarled through a hemlock knot. Flatulence added to the racket, which went on and on.

I could also hear a crinkly rustling and a slippage of what I assumed was the nylon of Robert's modern sleeping bag against the plastic as he moved restlessly under his plastic tarp. Next to me Mary, from her stillness, slept peacefully.

Claud's gasping gulps for air continued unabated. Mouth open on his back no doubt. I couldn't reach him for a poke in the ribs. I couldn't get at him as I might have done if we were alone. I wondered why Robert didn't stir up Claud till he faced the wall on his side. A stretch of silence from under the tarp made me think that Robert's exhausting day had won out over the disturbance, and sleep was blessedly resting him.

No, there erupted a tremendous flapping of plastic sheeting. I was amazed at how crisp it sounded, and loud. Then crawling noises and rustling footsteps, flutterings, silence from Robert if not from Claud.

I pulled the hood of my bag tighter around my head. Like Mary, I slept.

MOST DIFFICULT MILE OF THE APPALACHIAN TRAIL

WHEN IN THE DIM LIGHT OF THE MORNING DRIZZLE I STARTED FOR water down the steep trail, I almost stumbled over Robert under his plastic tarp. He had escaped into the spruce woods.

Last night he could not find solace in sleep during Claud's nearby reverberations. Today if I accidentally put a boot in his ribs I doubt he would have stirred. I was carrying kettles and cans. The clatter failed to rouse him. My legs functioned enough to let me step over him. A dragging boot rattled the plastic. Not a move from Robert.

He continued motionless when I puffed back with the dripping kettles and cans. A sound sleeper in the morning, maybe he was a midnight-oil scholar accustomed to morning slumber. Or maybe exhaustion held him.

How about Mary?

Claud, bending over the fire to add sticks, held a twig to his lips and nodded over his shoulder. In the shelter a curved mound of orange quilting contained Mary, lost in the sound sleep of youth. She remained quiet as Claud and I puttered about cooking breakfast.

He sliced bacon on a log. I selected a big envelope of pancake mix from supplies he had laid out beside our packs on the bunk. Mary's black hair hid her face.

Claud fried slices of bacon. He dropped tea bags into the boiling water of the coffeepot and set it aside. I added water to the envelope of pancake mix. Stirring with a spoon made batter quickly—some poisonous additive blended it fast?

Claud forked limp bacon from the frying pan onto an aluminum plate. He had cooked four slices long enough to kill the trichinae, but not so crisp as to waste any of, as he called it, "the full food value." The fat in the pan he poured into an old tin he'd saved from the fireplace, burned and rusty. He handed me the frying pan. We squatted like savages at the fire.

I held the frying pan over the flames till jets of smoke rose, then poured in some batter. It was too watery, so spread at once much larger than I liked. I wanted my first attempt to be small, a pancake, not a broad flapjack, on a theory of mine to start easy on all projects. Too late now.

But after flowing, the batter set immediately. The edges began to bubble. I relaxed my belly to steady my arms, in the old trick of rifle shooting. I was afraid of flubbing the flip. Still the left hand with the spatula remained tense. The right hand with the frying pan trembled as I brought the pan away from the fire and examined the bubbles all over the batter. The bottom must be a satisfactory toasted brown.

I skimmed around the edge with the spatula, shook the pan, and thought I detected the flapjack's sliding just enough for the flip. Now, quickly lower the front of the pan, snap the wrist up, prepare to catch the descending, turned flapjack and hear the rewarding sizzle as the uncooked batter meets the hot pan....

My flapjack lifted partway, caught on the bottom somewhere, and draped itself over the edge of the pan. It resembled a drooping Salvador Dali watch.

The spatula and I clumsily shoved the mess back into the pan, browned side up, but wadded.

Claud was adding water to an envelope of dark powder—syrup-to-be. Another benefit from Chuckwagon. He eyed the flapjack as I prepared to tip the gob of my error into the fire.

He grunted, "Ununh," and held out a cup.

"It'll be raw inside," I protested. "If I cook it more it'll burn."

I was wasting my breath against his conditioning by Depression days of scanty food at home in a large family. Hadn't they eaten an eel we caught in the Connecticut River? And all the fish and game he brought home?

He consumed the flapjack with syrup and apparent relish.

I greased the frypan using the spatula dipped into the can of bacon fat, and heated it to smoking before pouring in more batter. An errant breeze blew smoke in our faces. Mutually groaning we stood up as our cramped knees creaked. I flipped the flapjack with expert perfection and felt the glow of accomplishment. Beauty is in a delicately browned flapjack. I stepped upwind and squatted again.

Behind us a sleepy voice spoke two words.

"Good morning."

I slid the flapjack onto a warmed plate, and not looking at her, said, "Morning."

Claud, chewing, gave a double-barreled Canuck greeting, "Bo-jou, bo-jou."

I heard a zipper grate metallically but muffled by quilting. Wool-stockinged feet appeared on the orange sleeping bag. In jeans and sweater, Mary crawled to the bunk log and pulled on her boots. Undisheveled, she had no need to fuss with her hair. Her eyes were bright with wide-awake interest.

She said, "My dad took me fishing once with two Maine guides. That scene out there reminds me of them."

"We could be guides," I boasted, "except maybe running rapids in canoes."

She smiled. "And where's Robert?"

"Sleeping out in the woods," I told her. "Didn't our snoring bother you?"

"I go out like a light. Well, he can't sleep late this morning." She shrugged into her down parka and gathered up their kettles and water bottles.

She must have shaken him awake as she went by, because he appeared blinking, an untidy figure in jeans and blue sweatshirt, dragging his tarp and sleeping bag in one hand, in the other his Ensolite pad. He stared at Claud and me on the bunk log where we sat gobbling our flap-jacks and syrup and fat bacon washed down with Claud's authoritative tea.

Claud spoke to him first. "Have a cup of tea. Plenty in the pot there."

"Thanks no. Did I see Mary going for water?"

"Yes," I told him.

"Thanks. I don't wake up fast."

He dropped his sleeping equipment and wandered off. Somehow he had put on his sneakers—or maybe slept in them. I felt the abrupt fore-knowledge that something enduring in him would turn him into a hardy mountaineer, or at least into one of those tough and wiry Boston Appies of yore. Suitable for Mary.

He evidently met her coming back from the spring. When they reap-peared he was carrying their water bottles.

Mary asked, "May we have some of your hot water? This is icy from that little pool."

"There's boiling in that black pot," I said.

Claud with a stick of wood lifted it off the coals by the bail.

They waited not for fire-cooked food. With our hot water they breakfasted on instant coffee, cups of instant oatmeal from those little packets with fruit flavors. Powdered milk and sugar stirred in with more hot water for each of several envelopes I suppose added to a good break-fast. Substitute orange juice powdered and mixed with water washed down Danish pastry. I was so interested I almost forgot the beginning of a headache.

We offered bacon and pancakes. Claud said, "Better take on some fat. Stamina, you know."

Mary declined for both. "Thanks, can't spare the time."

Their breakfast in this backwoods setting suited their modern equip-ment, such as the aluminum packframes, the little gas stove, and the gleaming kettles. The latest quilted down parkas topped their narrow jeans—dungarees, as I thought of them, although I knew the name was now "jeans," an absolutely necessary piece of clothing.

Mary, however, went away and reappeared in her red shorts. I thought, "Must have taken off her boots. Those dungarees were painted on her." I noted a hardy lack of goose flesh on her thighs. In contrast Robert leaned over the fire nursing another cup of coffee.

Not for long. Mary began packing. "Come on, Robert. Time to hit the trail."

He, as the saying goes, was galvanized into action.

They shouldered packs. Mary said, "So long."

I flipped a flapjack to show off and said, "Good luck." Robert and Claud raised hands to each other. After a few steps Mary dropped off the ledge that Claud and I had struggled up the previous afternoon. Robert hesitated, then backed down.

They were gone.

We talked about their day—easy for them to Gentian Pond. We might be old, but we felt good. I think association with youth was beneficial. My headache had eased. Claud looked rested, because as I watched him pour his third or fourth cup of tea I noticed that his frown had left him. We were silent, maybe happy.

After a while I broke both quiet and tradition. "That was some girl."

Claud tossed dregs of tea leaves from his cup into the fire and blew bits off his tongue. A tea bag had come apart in the pot. "We were born too early. No liberated girls."

"Oh, I don't know about that."

"Well, looking back, I suppose I missed some at Galehead." He added thoughtfully, "Guess I was slow to recognize the symptoms." He began loading his pipe. "Looks like clearing."

I stood in front of the shelter and gazed about. The clouds had lifted almost to the upper spruces on Fulling Mill Mountain. The day might indeed open up and give us the view. I had anticipated wide vistas, and now longed for them. Maybe Claud too, for he said, "I've had enough plodding along in the rain."

I went looking for the shelter's throne. It was located on a promontory, which instead of oceanic water jutted into a sea of trees, mostly evergreens. The wooden box protruded above the low scrub. A seat on the throne provided a magnificent view to the valley of Goose Eye Brook, all the way, I judged, to Bull Branch and maybe as far away as Sunday River's drainage, of which Bull Branch was a part.

Clouds swirled about the peaks. Stray wisps, off to the east, caught brief sunlight. My remote location was relaxing in contrast with the tension normal to defecating in such an exposed toilet. The east wind, however, threatened. Besides, it felt cold and it suggested more wet weather. I didn't sit long drumming my heels on the box and admiring the view. I plucked a swatch of wet ferns, fragrant and turning brown. Scrubbing my hands, I took a final look around.

The prospect was so wild that it made me want to get nearer civilization, or at least to Speck Pond Shelter, from which I figured I maybe could make the summit of Old Speck, the high one of the range, and down to Grafton Notch and a ride home with Don and Ruthie. I needed to escape from the confinement of the mountains, and from their demands on my shallow reserves of strength and energy.

That phrase, "Maybe could make the summit of Old Speck," began to haunt me. Self-confidence, like energy, has a well that needs filling up, and it's slow when you're really tired at age fifty-two. We should rest for a day. Full Goose Shelter was the right place to loaf around and eat regularly. We could smoke our pipes and talk, doze, work up some more wood. Claud's mushroom collecting and studies would benefit. His interest, and my checking birds and plants, were important to our Mahoosuc adventure, and neglected. I convinced myself for the day of rest.

Claud was packing when I returned from the throne. I watched as he rolled his sleeping bag to squash out the air, then folded it into a pad for his back. He slid it carefully into his Duluth. I felt abruptly a flash of tiredness. It destroyed my dream of lazing around the shelter all day. The good feelings of breakfast time emptied away; I realized we couldn't rest. We were trapped by an endurance contest. Voluntary servitude. Our spare day was entirely theoretical. It might be required at Speck Pond Shelter to recover from total collapse.

We had an obligation to arrive in Grafton Notch, if we could—oh Jesus!—by tomorrow! The spare day was for unforeseen complications such as sickness or a blizzard. Of course, Don and Ruthie were prepared to wait a day, *if* we couldn't make the appointed day. I must not squander the spare in loafing.

So I packed while Claud lit his pipe and went for a walk. I thought of deceptive distances along the Mahoosuc Trail. We had envisioned a ridge walk, not this constant up and down. Too late to regret not getting topo maps and counting contours and thus learning what we would get into. Yes, far too late.

I hefted my pack, and told myself it must be lighter. In my head little hammers were beginning to tap. When Claud came back I said, "Marchons!"

"Non, vee moost take ze photograph."

We had the usual exchange:

I said, "This time I'll take your picture."

"Naw, I always look sour as swill."

"You could try saying 'cheese.'"

"No use. Get over by the goddamned shelter."

He took, as it turned out, the last picture of the trip—the primitive old logs, me in red parka (rain shirt to me), still-wet green pants, and beat-up green hat, trying to look strong and fit to shoulder the Duluth pack, a feat I put off till the last second.

In anticipation of sweating up Fulling Mill Mountain I took off the red parka. Why keep out rain only to be soaked with sweat that could not escape?

The pack felt lumpy as always when first on my back.

We looked around the shelter walls for any clothing we might have hung on nails. The bunk's packed fir branches were brown and vacant with no suggestion of the comfort they had provided.

Claud said, "Good place to camp. Well, I don't suppose I'll be here again."

His words would have ordinarily caused me to attempt a cheerful comment about returning next summer. I wasn't up to it, although I felt sympathy diluted by impatience.

I knew about leaving places I never saw again, dangerous to dwell upon, necessary to lock out of consciousness. Maybe I first experienced it the evening before I left Iowa City for good—was it June 1922? We were leaving for an Orford summertime, then Rochester, New York, an unknown place, a city, where Father would have the Unitarian Church. A little girl next door and I ran about our darkening yards catching fireflies. We put them in a jar and pretended we had a lantern.

I think sometime after that I recognized the paradox of nostalgia, because I didn't like my two years in Iowa City.

Claud's remark was a door opened to pessimism. Quickly I stepped to the ravine from which Mary and Robert had climbed the previous dusk. I lowered myself into the wooded col. The trail eastward among the evergreens led upward.

With the possibility of a dose of gloom from Claud I kept slogging on as fast as allowed by my joints and muscles. This left behind any comments he might have about the Bomb's destroying the world, Overpopulation (though he and Louise had seven children), Disease rampant out of Africa or China, and general Human Stupidity, Crimes, Follies, and Misfortunes. Hail, Mr. Gibbon!

I kept at Fulling Mill Mountain until I could hardly see the rocks in the trail. So I stopped. Claud caught up but was too winded for vocal pessimism. My tapping headache had given way to a sort of light-headedness.

We began again, keeping a slower pace through the spruce-fir woods, with frequent pauses for breathing due to steepness. I hoped they would also reduce the chance of our wearing out early.

Maybe they also caused in me the illusion that I was going farther between the last gasps. This was a good sensation. Almost cheerfully I would stare off into the green, dripping branches through which clouds crept, while my heart slackened its pounding.

At last we stepped out into a high alpine meadow. It spread between two wooded summits. I supposed we had climbed, as I remembered the map, about 400 feet from our first rest.

I felt good and said, "Maybe my wind's improving, compared to the first day on Mount Hayes."

"You're lucky. Mine's worse." He moved on. "Pick 'em up and lay 'em down. What's the title of the book by Fred Allen?"

"*Treadmill to Oblivion.*"

"I like that."

No suitable reply came to me. None was needed. He kept plodding ahead.

My thoughts as I followed mulled over pessimism. In the classifications laid down by William James, I would belong in that of the "healthy minded." I regarded pessimism as slow death, while acknowledging that it's a rational philosophy—if you want to sour all the enjoyment of life's delights and possible significance.

For instance, how sad for Claud never to admit that he had made a success of his life. To wit: Self-educated in the sense of working his way through UNH and Michigan University vet school to a DVM, now an excellent and respected veterinarian (if known for non-white-smock methods and attitudes, cryptic humor, gentle caring with gruffness, and reasonable fees), fine wife and family, solvent, and as sidelines, expert woodsman, authority on the Civil War and firearms, soon to be on mushrooms—the list never seemed to give him any satisfaction or sense of achievement. Belittling was perhaps first a pose, then a habit. I felt helpless in the face of it, or at times disgusted. Occasionally I would point out, "You never had it so good." And he'd grin.

We crossed the foggy meadow or heath with its low bushes and sphagnum moss. Supposedly we were below the South Peak of Fulling Mill Mountain. Again evergreens enclosed the ribbon of trail. The cloud thickened. The trail dropped out of sight. I had not read ahead in the *Guide* pages to know that we would drop 1,000 feet in a mile.

The steep falling away of the mountain made us grab trees if available. If not, then spruce branches. Kick heels to stop a slide. Soon came that ache of thighs from knees to hipbones. Call the malady "descent-pang."

I said, "How in hell could those two climb this after the notch and all?"

"They're young. When I was at Galehead I didn't think anything of skipping up to South Twin for the hell of it and the view—a thousand feet." He added, "Not now."

"You ought to be glad you had it once. Look, we're below the cloud. Down there must be Mahoosuc Notch."

"I've heard it's the worst mile of the two thousand of the AT."

"Then this'll be a record day for us." I realized that my optimism was too, too much, besides being hollow.

So did Claud. He made no comment.

The trail slid us to the bottom at a sign board in a little valley so comparatively open that it appealed to me as a sylvan vale near civilization. We shucked packs and sat down for a smoke and to consider our progress and the signs.

The Notch Trail to the northwest connected with the Success Pond Road. I had given up any idea of escape by that route. I was aimed for the road through Grafton Notch. Or bust! Somehow I wanted to be able to say I had lugged a pack through the notorious rock debris of Mahoosuc Notch.

This was our first complete rest of the morning, and a junction, so I checked distances and times in my *Guide* pages, compared to my watch readings. Elapsed time for us had been one hour and 25 minutes. Distance was a mile and a half. The allowed time statistic figured to—wow!—an hour and 25 minutes! I felt a silly pleasure. We were right up there with the experts, or so I thought of the Appies.

There in the harmless vale I read on. The text made me feel poised at the edge of a desperate venture. I was told to use care in the notch, to avoid dangerous patches of moss over deep crevices. I must scramble over boulders and crawl under others. Watch the white blazes.

I needed to express disdain for Mahoosuc Notch threats. I said to myself, "Pooh-pooh." Probably it wasn't much worse than Polar Caves near Plymouth, suitable for tourist capability.

I figured the *Guide*'s mileage and got .95 M. Impossible to measure that close. Must be a guess. Time one hour, 20 minutes. Another guess. For us, two hours?

The cause of this snail's pace turned out to be huge slabs fallen from the cliffs above the narrow slot of the notch. We came to them after knocking out our pipes and shouldering packs for the gentle descent into the closure where the cliffs rose toward the sky. The white blazes and arrows led over and between the slabs and boulders. Yes, and under some.

Mahoosuc Notch, I decided, is no place for claustrophobics. Up the craggy cliffs, tenacious evergreens clung to invisible cracks. The rock walls seemed to slant inward, almost over us. Which section, like the great blocks we clambered over, might next crash down?

Claud passed me at an upturned slab. His boots disappeared around a vertical edge.

I continued to study the cliffs in an attempt to convince myself they wouldn't fall on me. I'd never felt this impending crush before.

Then I saw a large bird slice through the high air and tilt sideways on narrow wings showing a flash of pale, barred feathers. It was a hawk, all right, but which? Another swoop emphasized the pointed wings and tapered tail. It couldn't be an ordinary soaring hawk. It certainly displayed a falcon's silhouette. Too large for a sparrow hawk, the bird must be a duck hawk, a peregrine.

Yet how long since I had seen one? Fifteen years, at Greeley Pond, off the cliffs of East Mount Osceola. Or, really long ago, circling Fairlee Cliff during my boyhood.

But peregrines were facing extinction. The poison DDT had indirectly softened their egg shells.

The falcon vanished low in the cleft.

I stared up at the gray slit of sky. It remained empty. I couldn't wait long enough for another sighting that might not occur. I'd never know whether I had seen a peregrine.

I looked down to study moss in great patches, soft, green, inviting. Concentration on the moss would moderate the wild instant of ecstasy left by the flashing bird.

The moss couldn't be dangerous. It was lovely. I trusted one section of green carpet. It gave way into a crevice that might have broken my leg had I not grabbed a little spruce to keep from falling sideways. I could feel no bottom to the crack.

Thereafter I avoided stepping hard on moss until I'd tested a patch that I couldn't avoid. I followed Claud carefully. I looked up not at all unless I stopped firmly…no falcon.

A half an hour of negotiating the mossy slabs brought on a growing urge to get out. I felt trapped, and beneath that, panic sought release. I had to tell myself that sometime I would get free of the slabs and caves and moss and overhanging cliffs. Patience, patience. But the white blazes and arrows led into more and more difficult passages.

I stopped at one mammoth block that seemed precariously balanced over a low tunnel. Animal sounds came back to me, growls and moans of pain—or rage. Yes, rage, and a scrabbling slithy sound of rubber and cloth on mossy stone. Hollowly reverberated profane language. It commented on the ancestry and mental warp of the guy who blazed the so-called trail.

I saw no way around so crept into the slot. Soon I felt my pack scraping on the stone roof, but daylight ahead and Claud's boots and vertical legs kept me wriggling along on my belly and knees. I stood up when my head and shoulders and pack cleared the monster slab.

Claud was brushing off wet moss. He snarled at the rock with a ferocious grimace. "No goddamned need to squeeze under there. Bad enough without a pack."

"I don't see how the kids managed with those frame packs above their heads."

"Must have taken them off and pushed 'em to each other."

"These Duluths are bad enough."

"Well, I'm a sonofabitch if I'll follow blazes into a cave like that again. Damned foolishness."

We continued in the mossy gloom of shattered rocks, which formed a corridor leading deep down to a trickle of water and a pool under an overhang. We stopped to drink from the envelope. The water was so cold my teeth conducted the feeling of paralysis to my jawbones.

Climbing up into daylight we came to a jumble of massive stone over a four-foot opening. A white arrow pointed there as if to an entrance. Not for Claud, although he took to action instead of remarks. Lurching at his first step of detouring ripped moss, he pressed up and around through gaps in the rock pile, using handholds of spruce roots and branches and crannies. His boots tore into blankets of moss interlaced with rootlets.

He called down, "You won't suffer through the Lemon-squeezer this way."

He was referring to a narrow hole so-named in the tourist attraction known as "Lost River" near Kinsman Notch. The constricting gap, so I'd heard, was closed after a plump lady, despite the coveralls provided, got stuck.

Claud's struggle upward and over and into difficulties that caused anguished vituperation urged me to take my chances with the cave, but I hesitated.

The decision was difficult. I too questioned the placement of the white paint, the marked route. Yet without the blazes, I might lose my way forever in the labyrinth of rocks. Mahoosuc Notch did that to me. "What's more," I thought, "you must maintain our way for Claud, too. He could soon be lost and need to know where to find the so-called trail." I took off my pack.

I felt a chill breeze from the cave. It suggested mid-winter. If in September, ice lay below me somewhere, then it had to stay all year round. I'd probably find out, because I pushed my pack ahead of me into the tunnel.

Creeping into the chill dark, I felt an acute pain in one knee, sharp as the stone that delivered it right through my pants and long underwear.

The pack caught on another protuberance so I couldn't move it. I rested and rubbed my knee. I couldn't be sure whether the moisture was blood or water. Probably water, because my blood vessels were full of ice, and I was freezing to death. That prospect drove me to yanking on the pack until it came loose and I could lunge ahead. Jamming my boots against rock behind me I slid into daylight and lay with my face on the pack out in the open. I looked upward.

Rubber soles showing smoothed chain-treads eased toward me down a long mossy slab.

I could hear Claud muttering, "There, I sarcumvented the bastid, him and his white blazes. See him sneering as he painted that arrow back there and talked to himself like this, 'Heheheh, I'll make 'em a route they'll remember, heheheh.'"

Claud himself grimaced with a satanic leer such as would have twisted the mouth and eyes of his fictional trailblazer.

When we stood on our feet together, I told him, "I've just been through a refrigerated cave. Let's get out of this place."

"What's the matter? Ain't you enjoying this?"

I lifted my pack. If you balance a pack on your thigh, it's halfway to your shoulders while you make up your mind to swing it up for the final balance on your back.

There was other balancing which continued to strain my entire body. I came to think of our progress as the "Mahoosuc Notch Dance." The steps were slow and wide. A mistake in judgment and rhythm meant teetering toward a toehold that would eliminate a spine-jarring drop. The dance included arm movements, sometimes desperate, as hands grabbed for holds.

I kept looking for a white arrow or a streak of paint. None were visible. I worried. Claud didn't care.

"Can't miss the other end in this bloody unroofed tunnel."

Often several possible routes appeared among rocks as big as one-car garages. So we went left, right, up, down, and past an occasional white blaze. I hoped we didn't dead-end at an insurmountable face of rock where a whole section of the cliff had collapsed.

And then...I was leading the way and stopped short. Where were the huge rocks? Gone. Joy be! A narrow carpet of green grass, a miniature meadow, stretched into fresh daylight. The cliffs opened away from us. I welcomed leafy little trees growing beside the meadow. Their leaves had turned yellow. They were mountain maple saplings, sunshine trees. Beside the grass a trickle of water flowed into a pool.

A mass of sticks and mud held back the water. The ends of the sticks showed teeth marks. How could the icy water appeal to beavers? It was running water and beavers had to stop the flow. The tiny model of a dam consisted of sticks retaining the bark, so this was not made from remnants of meals. The dam could serve no purpose as a home pond. The project must have been just for the merry hell of it, to satisfy some young beaver's instinct. He had to plug trickling water.

An axed pole driven into the dam marked the path into taller swale grasses. This swished against our pants and boots. The trail became hardened, slippery dirt.

We stopped to rest.

Looking up I realized that clouds shrouded the upper cliffs. How long had we walked without the morning drizzle? I couldn't remember, hadn't noticed. My watch told me we had sojourned among the rock slabs for one hour and 55 minutes. Seemed longer.

A damp wind was blowing at us into the notch. I hoped it wanted to keep the rain suspended in the clouds. This pathetic fallacy of sorts began because I was suspecting the wind and clouds of waiting till we were more exposed.

Claud looked up at the overcast and said gloomily, "I got enough weight in this pack without rain water." Then he appeared to transfer his pessimism to an amusing memory. His face lost its drawn look.

"One September at Galehead, closing up for the winter, I lugged out a packboard of blankets stacked two feet above my head. Weighed seventy pounds on the hut's scale. I should have laid a tarp over the blankets before I roped 'em on. Right in the middle of that steep part, rain came on like the proverbial cow and flat rock. Those blankets weighed in at the supply shack at a hundred and twenty-six pounds." He almost smiled. "I thought they were getting a mite heavy. They had about four miles to soak up the rain."

This day's rain began again by pattering on leaves, which contrasted with the sibilance of rain on evergreen needles. We came to a larger beaver pond. The cliffs had dwindled to ridges of spruce above the leafy forest we were entering. Heavyset yellow birches surrounded us in their awesome loftiness. They were the first such trees of our trip, and somehow had escaped the ax and saw. We walked past the beaver pond under a green canopy turning yellow.

I judged our elevation as somewhat below 2,500 feet. This seemed to be the dividing line in the Mahoosucs between spruce-fir and birch-maple-beech, assuming I had been counting right the map's contours.

We began to follow the small outlet from the pond. It was fortunately only a step across because the trail turned abruptly left. I stopped to check the *Guide* pages.

We were heading up the side of Mahoosuc Mountain to Mahoosuc Arm. Why "Arm"? The map and I didn't really understand each other. Maybe "Arm" meant "Ridge." No matter, we were aimed correctly and could expect an old logging road, also "ledges and deer runs to the bare summit."

My downward glance as I tucked the pages into my shirt pocket hesitated at a fanlike object, white with brown initials and numbers. It was obviously a shelf fungus broken from its dead or rotten host, probably a maple. Another fungus, also dated and initialed, lay nearby on the same rock. Claud picked it up. We stood there in the drizzle examining them.

About eight inches across, brown above the white underside, they were medium specimens, which we knew could grow three times that size. Every country kid has broken them off and has drawn upon the snowy side with a twig, leaving brown lines. You must be very careful not to touch the sensitive white, except as you intend to mark it permanently when it dries.

I asked, "Does yours have the figures nine dash four dash six six?"

"Yes."

"That's today!"

"You sure?"

"Damn right," I said. "And does it say age eleven?"

"No, age eight, sort of crude." He squinted at me.

I nodded. "Those tracks on the ridge off Goose Eye."

We were silent. This evidence of real, live children kept us staring at the fungi and turning them over, as if the shell-like, layered upper surface might tell us why children were here. I felt the forest around me, and around the children on this rainy day. A tremor of concern came, and a vision of them lost and comforting each other by drawing with twigs on the white underside, so they could leave a record of their passing.

I said, "Kids that age can't be in this Godforsaken wilderness."

"Well, sure not common, even with their folks."

We set the fungi back on the rock and began the upgrade. The drizzle seemed wetter. Then, as my Grandmother Wilson sometimes claimed the rain liked to do, it let up to get a better hold. We climbed on. I kept thinking of the fungi and the children, as if I could do anything about them.

Claud was thinking the same way. "They must be getting wet."

"Hellova place for kids," I said.

"Not to mention the notch," he pointed out. "How'd they get through those rocks to here by this time of day?"

"If they're up ahead, where'd they spend the night?"

"Beats me."

We moved slowly up the steep slope. I happened to be in the lead by several yards enjoying the soft duff underfoot while I pondered the mystery of two kids. How pleasant the leaf mold after the rocks in the notch, and the treacherous moss—bad place there for children.

After 15 or 20 minutes the gradient eased as the trail began slabbing the side of Mahoosuc Mountain. I could look about.

Up ahead a patch of red moved. I thought, "Two months from now that might be a deer hunter's red hat. If he shot one in here he'd have to camp and eat it—no way to drag it out. Must have been an early red leaf of a maple."

The trail had begun to follow an old logging road. We came upon a side-hill spring of clear water.

There a woman sat quietly on a small square of black plastic, maybe a folded trash bag. The color of her red parka had caught my eye. Beside her lay an orange packbag and its aluminum frame. Two little girls perched on a nearby log, also black-plastic protected from damp bottoms. They had pulled up the hoods of their orange parkas. A man offered them a cup of water.

This came to me in a dream. I could have sworn it. I spoke anyway, "Hello," and trudged on, a step at a time. I noted that they seemed in no trouble. Indeed, quite the opposite, as they were too relaxed for difficulties. They rested in leisurely attitudes. Confidence almost emanated from them. Parkas could be one reason. There were others, such as being at home in the woods—ephemeral but very important.

Their boots were sturdy leather meant for hiking. Lug soles certainly were the latest improvement, and a far cry from the hobnails and edgenails of my youth. The boots were not new, however, because they looked broken-in. The modern packs and frames lying on the ground, four of them, included cases under the flaps, surrounded by rolled mats such as Mary and Robert used. In the shiny blue cases, I realized, fastened with drawstrings and protected from the weather, must be their sleeping bags. Eventually I learned that the cases were "stuff sacks" of waterproof nylon.

The woman smiled. The girls uncertainly followed her example, so I assumed she was their mother. The smiles were nice and friendly, considering we looked like wild old men of the mountains, dirty, unshaven, and strangely dressed with grimy shirts and pants and misshapen hats.

The man nodded as he bent to fill the cup and drink. He eyed us over the cup. He was strongly built, maybe 35, in a green parka and sensible hiking pants. His heavy boots were worn but oiled. He called after us, "What kind of packs are those?"

Claud answered, "They're called Duluth packs."

"Never saw them before."

I felt too tired to mention their use in the canoe country of Minnesota. My headache had become a tight band with a stone under it near my left temple. But he was friendly and interested. I paused on a little rise and looked back to tell him.

His eyes brightened. "I've heard of the Quetico-Superior. You been there?"

"No, maybe someday."

"Me too."

Then we climbed again. On and on into a downpour that really drenched us. But the wetting didn't quite destroy the excitement of climbing through the forest of first-growth red spruce. Massive dark trunks rose to branches overlapping high above us. The interlaced needles resembled a remote roof. It failed to shed the rain.

Old fallen trunks were logs rotting for the benefit of seedling spruces. The infant trees rooted in the moss of the logs, the adult spruces overhead, may have been going through the same cycle for 10,000 years since the ice sheet retreated north. We were interlopers.

From a practical standpoint, I asked myself, how come the trees remained? Saved from the ax by economics? Too remote and too steep for loggers to make a profit? A few such patches still existed in the White Mountains. Or *was* this truly a primeval forest?

I gave up the problem to enjoy the trees. The mysterious world of life beyond my understanding created a profound mood of humility toward something outside my limitations.

Shifting again to practicality, I luxuriated in the fallen leaves and the resiliency of a steeply angling path. My boots told me I walked on many inches of humus. We must be climbing through the "fine forest" mentioned in the *Guide* pages, which were a wet mass in my shirt pocket. We were ascending Mahoosuc Arm and regaining the thousand feet we lost when we dropped into the notch—a typical Mahoosuc arrangement.

We didn't pause for lunch. We kept onward, munching chocolate and crackers. I tried sticking my tongue out for water to moisten the crackers. This helped some. The delicious chocolate flavored the crackers. I chewed slowly. The aroma rising up the ducts to the nose reminded me of Mount Katahdin. We had eaten chocolate in 1931 on the Hunt Trail.

I stopped. Although we never followed each other closely, I could sense him behind me, stronger, so I let him by. At this stage of our fifth day I could follow better than I could lead.

The rain pelted down as cold as hail.

I began thinking of the little girls back near the valley. Could they climb this steep trail? How far was protection from the deluge? I wondered whether I could have handled such a crisis with Ruthie and Penny 16 years before, supposing we got into such a dangerous predicament.

We left behind, gradually but inevitably, our protective forest. Claud said over his shoulder, "I'm going to miss those trees, in more ways than a windbreak. Wish I could have taken a picture. Too dark I suppose."

"Yes." I added in an attempt at humor, "No sun up in the sky, real stormy weather."

Claud snorted and led us into scrub spruces.

We had climbed a thousand feet to about 3,500. Now the rain arrived on the force of a strong wind. I stopped to pull on my parka. It cut the wind some, but let through the water. I should have spent the money needed for a new one.

Underneath the parka my shirt was heavyweight cotton. Under that my union suit provided a final bulwark. I was, compared to Claud, well-clad. His striped shirt might have originally served at weddings, funerals, or veterinarian meetings. Plastered to him, its thinness revealed the neckline of his usual white undershirt whose shoulder straps were hidden under those of his pack. His tanned forearms showed through the sleeves of the shirt, the white skin above. At least he had rolled down his sleeves. The old gray hat dripped water that might soon form icicles. His worn cotton pants must have been funneling water into his boots.

At the edge of the scrub the trail stopped, or rather disappeared in cloud and the "deer runs" predicted by the *Guide* pages...as if any sensible deer would venture onto that blasted heath ahead of us. Stopped, too, was Claud, with his hipshot stance and slanty shoulders. He turned to me. Because he held one elbow, his right one, and stroked his jaw with his right hand, I knew he had seen no clear route for us. Unlike some of these barrens in the Mahoosucs, this one offered no worn turf or shredded twigs or scuffed rotten rock. No cairns on the ledges, and now when we needed white blazes, none.

He asked, "Well, what do you think?"

"I think you're freezing." I took off my pack, then my parka, and held it out to him. "Put this on. You're shivering. It leaks but it'll keep out the wind."

"Naw, I should have brought a parka myself."

"I don't need it. I've got on my winter underwear."

"All the same, you lugged that parka damn near twenty-five miles. I didn't." His scowl was stubborn. "My wool shirt's in my pack. Saving it dry for the shelter. I'm all right."

"Like hell you are. Look, we're in this together. Put the parka on so you can lug me to the shelter. You may have to."

He shook his head. "Nope, I already owe you for loaning equipment way, way back...well, back to those moccasins of yours I wore so I could walk out from Isolation Shelter when I burned my boots."

"Not altogether burned. There were some eyelets on the rocks of the fireplace and a few nails."

"I remember. Seems as though it struck us funny."

On Mahoosuc Arm in the rainstorm we couldn't joke about that result of the great fire he'd built to dry us out before we wrapped up in our blankets for the night. We had laughed enough the next morning 35 years before. Being 17 helped.

I said, "You're probably the only guy in the world who ever wore Indian moccasins over the rocks of Boott Spur and down into Tuckerman Ravine to Pinkham Notch Camp."

He still looked stubborn.

I talked on. "Don't forget loaning me your shotgun so I could shoot my first partridge on the wing, out there in Quinttown. Now take the parka and let's get out of this hellish place. I'm damned if I'll stand in the stream of a firehose any longer."

He shed his pack and took off his hat. He tried to pull on the parka. It was too small for him. I had to help. His arms came out of the sleeves too far, even before he attempted to draw it over his head.

If a parka is big enough, the pullover style makes sense. Numb fingers sometimes can't join and start an open zipper, because hands paralyze before you realize that you're chilled while climbing hard into bitter wind.

After Claud pushed his head through the opening, we yanked the red fabric to his hips, which it failed to cover.

I began giggling at our difficulties.

This adolescent silliness brought an unrelated scene from our Orford boyhood, and my uncontrollable laughter of excitement at the flames from the town dump, which drove back firemen and spectators as the red plumes set fire to a telephone pole by the road above Jacobs Brook. We stood by our bikes close to the little fire engine, and he hissed at me, "Shut up! Someone will suspect us."

I was silly now but aware of the narrow boundary between laughter and hysteria, as though laughter could be a friend or an enemy.

Was it infectious? I had once noticed it to be dangerously so. And this time Claud didn't shut me up. Instead he let himself go with a snorting guffaw.

For some reason this choked off my giggles and scared me.

Wind rushed us. Rain sluiced us. Scudding clouds opened and closed.

In that driving fog we faced a flat, bare ledge. Our direction could be anywhere onto the misty heath. No indication of a route appeared as a cairn or path.

I felt panic in my belly. The chill that climbers take on unawares reached me. Clumsy fingers, as they would act at a divided zipper, fumbled for the topmost buttons of my union suit to snug up the neck.

My wet hands could hardly open my compass case.

Claud leaned close and asked, "Where to?"

"The *Guide* said something about a zigzag from the summit. Southeast. We don't know if we've reached the summit."

"Gotta get out of here fast, then figure where we are."

We shouldered our packs. His thin canvas Duluth, I knew, soaked more rain than mine, which weighed a ton. I followed him into the cloud. We came to a pile of rocks. The name "cairn" might have applied once.

All the same, I wanted to kneel down and express gratitude. It had to mean we stood on the summit of Mahoosuc Arm.

I said, "Southeast from here."

We huddled over the compass. Claud raised his arm at an angle across the direction of the arrow on the floating dial between E and S. We stared at the tangle of spruces and rocks beyond his pointing finger.

"Shit," I said, closing the compass case.

He bent to examine a patch of mud. "Deer tracks."

I could see faint points heading north. The hunter began walking slowly along beside the tracks.

They led to a trace of a path, not southeast, but a way among rocks and through little patches of scrub spruce. We passed pockets of heath plants and cotton grass growing in black humus.

I noticed a feathery, flattened evergreen. No, not evergreen because the needles had a yellowish cast to them. Tamarack? Yes, and growing close to the ground in this exposed location, maybe a foot up and two feet across. It revealed adaptability, all right, also endurance and will to live.

It made me happy.

A quotation seemed to rise from it out of an essay on the White Mountains by Justice Douglas who himself was quoting G.M. Trevelyan to catch some of the mystic aura of the mountains, the natural world. "And to the young who have no pain, who have not yet kept watch on man's mortality, nature is a joy responding to their own."

Something of this joy came to me crossing that blasted ridge. I had pain and awareness of mortality enough, yet part of the response, the joy, was the flicker of a younger notion that I was equal to the wild elements and to the challenge of the earth's elevations here. It was a sweet yet poignant delight, and fleeting.

Rhapsody ill-suited that cold, wet, gale-lashed heath. The instant passed. I wanted desperately the protection of trees.

We pushed steadily on with the wind at our backs. This meant that somewhere we had taken a zag of the zigzag. Pure luck, and Claud's recognizing traces of trail. I didn't stop for a compass reading. Several times I thought we should orient ourselves because the trail became obscure. We might indeed have been following mere "game trails" leading God only knew where.

Then assurance and certainty were ours as the trail became visible between edges of turf and black soil, which exposed to our boots either bare rock or crunchy gravel.

This disintegration of the primordial world-mass supported plants far advanced from the first lichens. This beginning of dirt lay before us to be inspected. Thoughts irrelevant to survival comforted me thus: "We'll have to return someday and gather samples of the process, and should we include the toad who seems too blissful in the rain to hop aside? Maybe. Not blissful—numb with cold. And describe the slate-colored junco that flitted away from two unadapted bipeds tramping along? Maybe."

Meanwhile the two bipeds (evolved in such a complicated way) dared not stop for intellectual pursuits. Their delicate systems would succumb to death by cold.

We had to escape. Claud wiped the rain from his face with his sleeve and plodded on.

I longed again and again for woods. Instead of descending toward them, we seemed to be walking upwards. I was short of breath so we must be going uphill. We had become lost.

Out of the fog loomed a big cairn and post, both set on a barren ledge, the true summit of Mahoosuc Arm. It had to be.

No attractions detained us. Our eyes were only for the trail. It turned abruptly right. We followed it to—oh, goddamn it—to a fork. The left path must be the wrong one. This place was not for lingering. We faced the path to the right. Did I see worn rocks, and boot impressions almost washed away?

In clear weather all would have been simple. Now I could only look a question at Claud. He nodded. In the wind I didn't try to tell him why I thought we should go this way. Aside from the intimations of a trail, I noticed the east wind against my left side and cheek, so the southeast trail must be this one and our route. I was aware of specious reasoning, but stepped out into what I hoped would be the last zag of our zigging.

When scrub evergreens protected us a little I stopped and took out the pages of the *Guide* from my shirt pocket. The wet sheets stuck together or flapped in the gale. Lucky for us the AMC used tough paper. I fumbled out my glasses, which at once streamed water. With my green hat pulled down I leaned over the blurry pages. I could read "windings…above .5 mile, SE, NE, and N, then drops steeply .25 mile to Speck Pond…at about 3,500 feet, said to be the highest in Maine…reputed to be 250 feet deep…east side of pond about .25 mile to Speck Pond Shelter."

I pocketed the pages and my glasses while adding mileage in my head.

I announced to Claud, "Only a mile to go."

"Let's hope the guy with the wheel for AMC measured it longer than it is."

"Oui, mon cher Gaston, mais ce n'est rien. MARCHONS!"

We did.

The trail became a path in gravel and turf. On bare ledge a white blaze reassured me, and yes, the windings seemed to conform to the bearings in the *Guide*.

Wind and rain blasted across that down-tilted, exposed heath, which supported occasional scrub spruces. Rivulets crossed the trail and formed mudholes in the pockets of the ancient bog.

I tried to stay on the turfy borders to prevent black humus from sucking into my boots. Claud, in his rubber-bottomed boots, squashed along behind me without much regard for the footing. Sometimes we picked our way over exposed, tangled roots in spruce thickets. The brown tentacles lying just below the gunk were slippery.

Then abruptly the trail slanted away. Down we went and soon we had escaped most of the wind, because the head-high spruces interlaced their branches, feathery and impenetrable, like two green walls. We walked between them. The trees became taller.

I straightened up from the crouching fight against the wind. The spruces gave me safety and relief. I breathed easily. I relaxed into a comforting assurance that we had made our way through the worst the Mahoosucs could throw at us. Despite my legs telling me to mistrust the tendency to exult at our success—hubris and all that, my legs warned me—I confidently anticipated the complete protection of the log shelter ahead.

Not alone I felt untimely jauntiness. Behind me in the rain, Claud managed to start whistling "March Militaire."

We failed to step out with the peremptory beat. Our weary legs continued their swinging pace, slow but steady. He changed the tune to "The Barcarole" from *Tales of Hoffman*.

Ahead the cloud and rain thickened. Emerging from the evergreens into an opening I saw ahead of us a mirage of dark waves where the ground should be. The realistic thought came: "Not yet Speck Pond, too soon."

Then the trail brought us to rock-strewn water, narrow and almost still. Stepping across on the wet stones was easy. I walked several yards without realizing I had crossed the outlet to Speck Pond. I stopped to look back. Claud was splashing through and called out, "Roof and four walls not far?" It was both a question and a statement. We hurried on, drenched but hopeful.

The trail curved along the shore. We were passing a strip of gray water that blended into fog. Cold waves showed the wind blowing hard in our direction. We walked for a longer time and distance than seemed necessary. My confidence nevertheless delivered patience. This made me wonder about exhaustion. I had learned that my body's dregs were liars, for they often paradoxically told me that I could go on forever. I suppose Claud was wondering, too. He stopped whistling.

The rocky trail ended in a clearing.

Our crude shelter, its overhang darkening the interior of the log walls, appeared as a low, empty cave. We approached. I noticed two signs on single trees. The arrows pointed into the woods. Lettering announced on one: "Water," on the other: "Toilet."

We sloshed through mud surrounding the circle of stones and wet ashes.

Claud's reaction to the dreary scene demonstrated some of the relieved satisfaction that I felt. "By God, there is a shelter. For a while I thought we were walking into the final joke of these bloody mountains—nothing for the night but wet woods and rain."

We bent under the overhang, packs still weighing us into our tracks. Out of the rain at last, I was nearly ecstatic from the protection, yet his words "final joke" made me fear they caught the attention of the gods of the Mahoosucs.

I said, "Final joke hell. You better knock on wood or we'll find out what is final between now and Grafton Notch."

He didn't bother. Other actions came automatically.

Drop packs on the bunk's brown fir boughs. Sit on the front log and shiver. Think of fire. Survey the small heap of broken branches in the corner.

I have never seen Claud so cold, not even when he joined me after a two-hour wait on Crystal Mountain when I shot the deer we'd been expecting to approach the scent of a buck's scrapings in the dead leaves and duff. This time Claud was too cold to light his pipe. With cramped hands he began breaking fir twigs from the bunk.

I sorted through the junk wood in the corner, where the dripping log walls splashed on rotten limbs that someone had collected. The wind whipped between the unchinked logs. No wonder our night's shelter gave us the shivers, like tired hound dogs in zero weather and only snow for warmth.

Claud knelt in the mud and reached below the bunk seeking dry wood.

The only possible place for a fire was under the overhang and in front of the sodden ashes of the fireplace. So in that mud I laid a foundation of rotten sticks. I placed on it the twists of fir twigs that Claud had collected from the bunk. I was in a mood to burn all the bedding if necessary for a flaming fire.

My numb fingers fumbled in my pocket for my waterproof match safe. The size of a 10-gauge shotgun shell, it was a "Marbles," so old that the company must be unknown to members of the younger generation, such as Mary and Robert. I finally managed to unscrew the hinged cap with its inner rubber gasket that closed the nickel-plated brass cylinder. The knurled sides for striking matches had worn smooth from use, and besides, my hands had wet the surface. I found a dry stone under the bunk.

The match flared. Windblown rain doused it. I used match after match. No matter how I cupped them, the initial flashes went out.

Claud, adding dry chips and bark to the twist of fir twigs, said, "Wait." He reached under the bunk until he was almost flat in the mud. He pulled out a basket. "Here, try this old trout creel to protect the match."

I hesitated, confused by bewildering unreasonable reluctance. The willow creel curved in an obsolete shape. Modern creels were woven square and bulkier. This relic, narrow and shaped to fit your hip when you adjusted the shoulder strap to the right length, resembled my father's trout creel. I couldn't hold a lighted match near it.

I said for an excuse, "It's not ours."

"Jesus, it's falling apart."

"Just the same it might catch fire...."

After my father died, his creel, like this one, hung by its strap from a nail in the shed of the Orford house. I carried trout in it. What the hell now gripped me? Inexplicable sadness rising out of a time 40 years past. Not right—Father lived a joyful life for his fifty years.

Claud was explaining something, patiently, as if to a child. Age 13 is not a child and I'm 52. I seem to have lost a year—40 from 1966 is 1926 and he died in 1927....

Claud said, "Listen again. I'll hold it against the wind and over the match and twigs for protection, that's all. Now strike one."

It fizzled out.

Claud muttered to himself, "Half-assed modern matches. If we had the good big matches before the war...."

I was still in Orford, taking down my father's creel to go trouting alone, but I said, "What we need is the empty tar barrel from the dump that day."

My next match flared. Claud held the creel closer. Among the fir twigs a wisp of birch bark gave off oily smoke as a red flame caught the tinder. Fire leaped up. I thought the rain and the gale would kill it. Claud dropped the creel into the little blaze, just as I knew had been his intention.

Now I was glad he dropped it for the creel became a torch. But he tried to divert my attention and concern.

"We were damn fools to light a fire in that barrel and take off on our bikes. We should have gone home and come back through the woods to do it."

"The dump was fouling Jacobs Brook."

"And it made a great fire that shook up the damn town."

"What's more, we got a fire here."

It was burning up my sadness.

He said, "The creel burns hot but will for only about two minutes."

In that time we piled onto the flames every stick of wood not part of the shelter, including dry branches from the bunk, leaving the deep cushion of needles. Claud collected odd logs lying around partially burned. I dragged in tangles of brush left outside by previous hikers. All this junk wood protected our flames from the rain. The wind acted like a giant bellows.

We sat down on the bunk log and returned to the Orford dump. Claud said, "I think Henry Patch saw us pedaling by on our bikes like the devil was after us. I saw him sitting on his porch. I always figured he knew we set it. Funny he never blabbed."

"His wife was a friend of Mother's."

"Well, I wouldn't have guessed. You know she was a Mosely."

"Yes. I think Mother may have taught her in school."

We sat there on the bunk log, both of us seeing in the flames the towering fire of the Orford dump.

And we took heart, though not from the warmth. The wind carried away in the waving red plumes and gray smoke and sparks the abundant heat we needed. Frustration must have driven Claud to desperate activity. He lurched out into the whirled smoke. He dragged in more junk wood. He piled on stumps, logs, and branches until the heap rose big as a beaver lodge.

Under this tangle burned enough small wood to boil a pot of water, which I brought from the pond. We were in no condition to look for a spring beyond the sign "Water."

Kneeling on the bunk among the fir needles, which stuck to everything wet, such as boots and pants, we put tea bags in tin cups, poured steaming water, and added sugar. Wind seeking us through the gaps in the log walls instantly blew away the steam. We stirred our cups with trembling fingers as I said, "Never mind the milk." We were shivering uncontrollably.

Both of us remembered wool shirts in our packs and dug them out. The shivering moderated. Two more cups of tea helped. We didn't talk.

The fire died down. Claud tucked his hands into his armpits. I tried to shrink myself out of the wind. The fire under the wet wood faded back to red coals fast turning to gray ash. Claud reached into the bunk for boughs to catch the last flare. He stood up and yanked at the mass of branches above, so he could stamp them down. The hissing blaze would soon burn itself out.

Need of wood brought me an urge similar to the drive that had sent Claud into frantic activity. I took off my wool shirt to keep it from getting soaked. I crouched out into the horizontal rain. If I didn't find some wood we might die of exposure in that log crib.

Downwind of the fire, through the billowing smoke, I stumbled against a projection. Then in a few steps, another. Stumps! I felt around in a drapery of ferns and kicked loose from the ground a small stump. Rotten roots but solid wood above. Must be resinous spruce that would burn though wet. Cut years ago by unknown hikers, perhaps by the builders of the shelter.

I rushed armloads of stumps back to the shelter. The desperate work thawed my bloodstream. Claud was nursing the fire back to life and heaping on stumps.

But we needed more wood. I grabbed the ax and ran out to chop down little dead spruces I had found. I laid down several and began staggering back with two gripped in fists and tucked under elbows. I stumbled into the shelter.

Claud growled, "You better quit charging around out there like that."

"Two more," I protested, and dragged them in before his words stopped me from dashing out once again. I stood huddled under the overhang. He added stumps to the fire, and it flared, but I became aware of terrible cold and wind. He handed me my shirt. I managed, "Thanks. More tea."

He poured two cups from a pot he had brewed—almost black, so three teaspoons of sugar were necessary, and filled to the brim with powdered milk.

Pulling on my wool shirt I noticed that my inner shirt pocket no longer held my glasses case. Fell out, leaning over, I assumed, and didn't care. Why hadn't the flap been buttoned? Other pocket still contained the soggy *Guide* pages. I was too cold to worry about the glasses.

We stood under the overhang to drink the tea, as close to the fire as we could get and still be under the roof. Water streamed from the eaves, splashed in the mud, and spattered our boots and lower pant legs. The wind blew the smoke and flames off to the left almost flat, like a picture of a bonfire in a storm.

The optimist said, or maybe Pollyanna, "One thing about the wind blowing between the logs, it clears out the smoke we might be choking on."

"Better than Hermit Lake Shelter in Tuckerman Ravine, when that snowstorm in June thirty-one holed us up."

We stared into the fire. I was never quite sure whether he took as much comfort from memories good or bad as I did, even smoky shelters, so I improved the recollection. "Two days later at Isolation Shelter we had no smoke inside."

"Open gable end at Isolation, no overhang."

"Tight logs, too, all caulked with oakum," I added, and thought of a solution, attractive but impossible, for these drafts laden with spray. "Here if we had our Forester tent, we could set it up inside on the bunk."

"I hope that family had a tent," Claud mused, "and knew enough to stay in the woods after the storm hit."

"With a tent and an ax they could make themselves more comfortable than in this goddamned wind tunnel."

Claud poured into his cup the last of the tea, a distilled tannin solution. "Maybe we ought to go see if they need help."

"Up that steep ridge? You must have more strength than I have."

"I know, and I ain't."

"If we had a good-sized tent to take for them—and us."

"We'll have to wait till morning," he said. "Tough on the girls."

There was nothing more to say about the family.

The thought of the little girls persisted. I didn't know how Claud thought of them but to me they were wet and cold, huddled on the deadly summit while their mother attempted to shield them from rain and wind, and their father searched for the trail. I stared out to windward of the flames and smoke. Driven cloud obscured the pond and trailed through the spruces.

The face of a little girl floated into my vision, as though she had just stepped around the log wall. Framed in a green hood, her unsmiling mouth, her pale cheeks, her questioning eyes were a fantasy of my deranged mind. Her figure must also be a dream. She was standing there in front of us, and when she turned to look behind her, she exposed the back of her hood. It extended like a dark cloak over her poor deformed shoulders. She was a hunchback.

A billow of smoke engulfed her. The vision reappeared closer, under the overhang. I detected inside the hood a gleam of orange—another hood drawn tight, a parka hood, yes, the color of the parkas on the little girls at the trail-side spring.

This was beyond belief. She was so small, if perhaps the older of the two....

Her sister, even smaller, came trudging into the shelter, also hunch-backed.

I realized that they wore ponchos. The skirts flapped in the wind about their legs, and the green fabric extended over their packs.

The younger girl clapped her gloved hands. "Oh boy, a fire!"

Her older sister, less enthusiastic, inspected us and the shelter before she perched on the bunk log.

Next appeared a poncho-clad woman, their mother, and stepped inside.

Arousing ourselves, Claud and I helped the girls off with their ponchos and packs. Mother took off hers. We quite filled the area in front of the bunk.

Outside, hooded father stood streaming rain water from his poncho, which gave him the same humped silhouette over his high packframe. Apparently waiting for space inside, he calmly surveyed the scene, smiling a little at our blazing fire. He probably knew that the wind whipped away most of the heat, but the flames had to be a cheerful sight.

Claud and I looked at them and at each other. A verbal exchange would have been, "No need to have worried about this family...and how come we had such a bad time up there?" But we said nothing about our thoughts. Mine came clearly. These people were fabulous, incredible. Confidence and composure emanated like visible strength. In me they caused both relief and wonder. They had conquered the terrible storm on the exposed heights that had nearly overcome us—us, two experienced mountaineers and woodsmen, the hardy characters from an era of roughing it. Ha-ha!

Besides all this, they were wearing ponchos longer than the relic of World War I that I once used for my blanket roll and as a ground sheet. A rubberized canvas square with a slit in the middle for the head of anyone who wanted to get tangled in the army contraption; I didn't. But these ponchos that kept your pack dry! I was learning several innovations from this competent family.

The girls scrambled onto the bunk and pushed back their parka hoods, revealing the smaller girl as blond, the older girl as dark brown and wavy. Seriously, dark brown head bent over her pack and arranged contents. Blond head turned to us as the younger girl hugged her knees and looked at us brightly, then called out to her father, "Come on in, Daddy. Why are you standing out there in the rain?"

"Just enjoying the sight of you and your mother under a roof."

Daddy took off his poncho and pack before he ducked under the overhang and leaned his tall packframe against a wall. I guessed the weight at 60 pounds. He nodded to us, saying, "Thanks for the tracks you left up on the mountain."

Claud said, "You'd have made it all right."

I was thinking of the last time our tracks had been followed, in snow on Crystal Mountain by two lost hunters who began firing shots after dark below the clearing around Claud's tar-paper shack.

Daddy shrugged a modest "Maybe," and bent over his pack.

Now began family camping as I had never seen it done. While we moved our packs and kettles to the windward side so the girls would be out of the flying spray from the unchinked logs, Daddy, Mama, and their daughters settled in with steady organization that appeared to me as expertly offhand.

First Mama helped the girls change into flannel pajamas, dry wool socks, sweaters, sneakers, and the orange parkas. Then she herself changed into dry jeans and sweater. Claud and I watched the flames and steamed close to the little heat that the wind left us while whirling away most of it.

Daddy unpacked sleeping bags and air mattresses. He said to our backs, "Great fire."

Mama added, "Yes, it's a fine blaze."

Her voice was quietly lilting. I got the idea she was laughing at our backs, at least to herself, for she said, "You can turn around now. I'm decent."

Her smile matched her pleasant face and easy manner. Her appreciation of the fire meant more than the windblown heat, or so I felt sure. I sensed a feminine reaction and made a tentative, dubious generalization about womanhood and the glowing, though smoky, presence of this ancient household necessity.

Daddy's appreciation took a sharing role. He said, "I'll bring in some more wood."

He pulled his poncho back over his head and shoulders, then turned his back on his wife, saying, "Please, my dear." She bent over to take a tuck in the long rear skirt that trailed on the ground without his pack. She fastened up a foot or more with the snaps provided. A very modern poncho to me, sophisticated.

Daddy unsheathed a hatchet with a metal handle. He ducked under the overhang and vanished into the woods.

I noticed that Claud watched, shook his head, and sucked on his cold pipe, not at the poncho but at the hatchet. I knew that he regarded the hatchet as any axman would: hopeless, dangerous, and Boy Scoutish.

He said to me, "Remember that time on Smarts Mountain when a boys' camp counselor came to our tent with a cut in his new boot?"

I wished I could say, "Damn it, Claud, you do sometimes speak before you think." I also dreamed up a remark that I hoped would dismiss the hatchet connection between daughters and Daddy, saying, "That counselor envied us lying in the Forester tent out of the rain. I won't repeat his words."

The younger girl piped up, "What were they? Tell us, tell us!"

My excuse was thin. "I've sort of forgotten. Long time ago."

The older sister said, "He won't tell us. They were naughty words."

I asked her, "How do you know?"

"By your expression."

"Well, you see, he was wet and tired, but he just said, 'Golly, you guys look snug in there.' We were in an open-front tent out of the rain, whereas he and his camp kids had bivouacked all night in the rain."

I waited for one of the girls to ask about the cut boot. I was trying to devise more talk that left out the hatchet similar to the one her daddy was wielding somewhere out in the woods, except, back then, hatchets had wooden handles, not steel.

The younger girl asked, "What's an open-front tent?"

"Susie," said her sister, "don't show your ignorance. It hasn't a door."

Claud put in, "Less than that, no front wall. We set it up on two crossed poles and a slanting ridge pole like a tripod with one long leg, so the tent had the shape of a tall pyramid cut in half and the bottom tipped up to form the open front."

The girls lost interest. Mama was unrolling their sleeping bags. I didn't have to explain that a camp kid chopping with a hatchet had let it slip. Flying through the air, the blade cut the instep of the counselor's left leather boot. He used language as assumed by the older sister. New boots, expensive-looking, Russell shoepacs. The lack of blood seemed to him small comfort.

Still thinking about the snug Forester tent on Smarts Mountain, and the counselor whom we encountered once more with his kids over on Mount Cube just before he took them down into trackless woods toward the boys' camp on Baker Pond, I realized that Claud was holding up an envelope. I could read "Macaroni with Hamburg." I nodded.

He tore open the envelope and dumped the dried contents into a kettle. He was squatting, I was standing, so I lifted a pot of boiling water, and added some of it to the mess.

He said, "Directions say to reconstitute for three hours. I figure simmering for an hour could make it edible. Pour in some more water, will you?"

I did. He kept stirring, then held up the fork to stop me.

The remaining hot water I offered to Mama.

"Oh, thanks. I'll make hot chocolate for the girls and coffee for myself."

I didn't reply. I was shivering and had to clamp my jaws tight together. For the wind I used silent words like those of the long-ago counselor. The wind must be picking up the pond and hurling it at the shelter. In one corner I spotted a bundle of old rags, dishcloths, and a washcloth. I began plugging them into the widest cracks between the logs on that windward side.

Claud used his fork to drag from under the bunk a pair of torn shorts. I ripped off swatches and jammed them into more cracks. If only I had a roll of oakum, or a bushel of sphagnum moss.

Daddy had been gone a long time. I heard no whacking of the ineffectual hatchet. But I heard the serious sister ask, "When's Daddy coming back?"

Mama answered, "Pretty soon, Jane. Your chocolate's getting cold."

Jane was doing the worrying. Susie sat quietly in her sleeping bag. Jane moved restlessly in hers. Mama sipped her coffee.

Jane asked, "Is he all right?"

"You know he can take care of himself in the woods."

Soon I knew that, too. He emerged from the gathering darkness, smoke, and rain. Behind him he dragged two dead spruce trees about six inches through at the butt where he had chopped them off with the hatchet, which I now began to respect. Wow! Here indeed was a man to take care of himself in the woods.

He walked off into the rain twice and dragged back two more pairs of dead trees, six in all, each about 15 feet long. He proceeded to wield the hatchet with accurate strokes that made the chips fly as he limbed out two of them and chopped fire lengths.

Claud said, "That's a mighty sharp hatchet."

"I carry a little carborundum stone." He shrugged deprecatingly and drove the blade into the end of a log for safekeeping. He came into the shelter and said to his wife, "Now I'll clear the feedline in the stove."

Claud suggested "We can rake out some fire so's you could cook away from the blaze."

"Thanks, I'll get this going." He picked up the little gasoline stove from beside his pack.

It resembled the stove that Mary and Robert used at Full Goose Shelter. Quite evidently Claud and I were behind the times. Maybe we looked puzzled when Daddy declined our fire. Perhaps Mama thought our feelings hurt. She explained, "We have a system and get mixed up if we don't stick with it."

I said, "And you have clean shining kettles."

"Yes, there is that." She pursed her lips in amusement.

Daddy said, "There are trade-offs. I carry two or three pounds you don't—the stove and two gasoline bottles. Also remember this little gem needs loving care." He was searching the side pockets of his pack. "Dear wife, where's my glasses?"

"Should be in the left pocket."

"Don't seem to be. I'll try the wire without them."

The girls began to talk about the wind and rain they had endured up on Mahoosuc Arm.

Susie announced brightly, "I'm glad I had my pack on to hold me down or I'd have blown away." She giggled. "That was when Daddy had to find the trail."

Said Jane, "My poncho blew right over my face." She made a pout. "Everything happens to me."

Susie tittered. "You were awful funny, walking into a tree before Mama uncovered you. Tell them about our night in Mahoosuc Notch."

My eyebrows must have shot up, because Daddy said, "I miscalculated and we were caught in there with darkness coming on. I thought a bivouac was the wisest decision. Too risky trying to get through with flashlights."

I remembered a charred pile of stubs on a ledge. "Did you camp under a rock and build a fire?"

"No, we cooked on our stove."

Jane put in, "I almost rolled off my air mattress into a deep crack during the night. My place slanted."

"Yes," Daddy said. "We always give you the worst place to sleep."

Jane's voice took on a plaintive tiredness as she sat up in her sleeping bag. "So tonight you put my sleeping bag under a leak in the roof. See? That drip right there." She stretched out her legs and pointed to moisture in her lap.

She received only casual comments from her parents. Daddy was trying again and again, without his glasses, to slide a tiny wire into the feedline of the little stove. Mama was methodically sorting through the contents of his packbag's pockets. She shook her head. She didn't frown. "I'm sure they are here somewhere. When did you use them last?"

"I looked at the map with them, right after these gentlemen passed us."

"Ah yes, that gives me an idea."

He continued to probe with a hair-thin wire at the orifice of a valve in the stove's tubing.

Jane asked, "Why do you always put me in the worst place to sleep?"

He answered, "It's my diabolical nature, sweetheart."

Claud, stirring the macaroni-hamburg, looked at Daddy and smiled. The answer was one he might have made to one of his daughters.

Mama handed Daddy a leather case, the type that clips on a shirt pocket. "It was in with the trail snacks and your Sierra cup."

"I remember now. I was thinking about the map and time for Mahoosuc Arm when the girls asked for hard candies. I'm getting absent-minded." He put on the glasses and looked like a college professor. He added, "Now I'll have the stove going in a minute."

Mama was unfolding a plastic tarp, red on one side, silver on the other. She spread it over Jane's sleeping bag. A drop of water fell on it and ran off. "There," said Mama. "The Space Blanket will keep you dry."

So I learned about another item of new equipment. A Space Blanket! I could not picture astronauts in the primitive log shelter as antiquated as a trapper's lean-to. And Daddy cleaning the wonder of the stove...scientific-industrial-commercial. His glasses seemed to have put him in control....

Glasses?

I'd lost mine, oh damnation, somewhere out in those darkening woods.

Taking off again my wool shirt I told Claud, "I forgot to go find my glasses." I ducked under the overhang and dashed across the clearing. I had to locate the little knoll where I had kicked loose the stumps and beyond where I had been swinging the ax against the dead stub. My case was the old-fashioned style of covered metal that snaps shut...maroon-red...I'd never find it. I started to panic as I strode about trying to recall at which clump of spruces I'd bent over last. The trees were threatening me—a limb snatched at my hat and I bent down lower to thrash my way free. The case lay in plain sight at the toe of my left boot, inches from stamping it into the ground forever.

Relief swept through me with the nearly tearful reaction of exhaustion.

I was uncertain where to find the shelter, but knew enough to follow the smoke upwind.

Claud motioned me to stand in his place nearest the fire. "Did you find 'em?"

I held up the case and felt blessed, for a change, by the mountain gods.

Daddy and Mama bent over their stove, whose flame, a constant blue flare under a clean aluminum pot of water, caused him to say to us, "Great invention. Smart people the Swedes."

I thought their rig looked like nothing hot, yet steam began to escape the lid.

I nodded to Daddy and pulled on my wool shirt. Claud said, almost in a whisper, "And dynamite. Great invention."

Mama selected a clear plastic envelope whose contents she shook into the pot of water. How fast it came to a bubbling boil.

I was witness to modern techniques of camping out—to use the term that meant for me an escape into the wildwood. This shiny gadget and its blue flame, the silvery kettle, the transparent envelope of grain or dried meat held in a white-gloved hand—this wasn't camping out. The glove was a clean white cotton workman's glove to protect Mama's hands from the heat. Camping out was done around a basic principle known as a fire. I was going to think about this contrast, but where to begin?

Once upon a time when the world and I were young, I had immersed myself in woodcraft. Yes, even to starting a fire with a bow, a slab of balsam wood notched for the maple drill, and the fist-size, hemlock knot gouged as a socket for the drill. Left hand held the socket, right hand sawing the bow and its thong around the drill, smoke curling up from the pile of brown dust on the tinder under the slab of balsam. Then boil water in a birch-bark vessel. Who now reads Kephart, Nesmuck, Seton, Beard?

For this addiction of mine Claud felt an amused tolerance. He relied on his innate at-homeness in the forest, a woodsman's ease there. Hunter, fisherman, lone explorer of remote New Hampshire mountains, he had camped out with a blanket and a tin can to cook in.

Claud and I were anachronisms, 40 years out of our time. We cooked in sooty pots—one at least blackened first in 1929. We built fires using an ax of the same age. We drank from tin cups.

I counted up all the equipment of our new friends. Four sleeping bags, four air mattresses, four aluminum packframes and nylon bags. Then there was group equipment like the stove, two metal gasoline bottles, a light tent (carried for emergencies, Daddy later told me), an aluminum cooking kit to serve four. Not to mention four sets of clothing, boots, and unseen gadgets. I arrived at an estimated cost of $500. More careful recollection of prices in outfitting catalogs revised this figure upward to $700.

What an extravagant sum just for camping out in the mountains!

Before I quit Scott and Williams those dollars were a month's pay. Now as a writer, $700 was an unlikely sum for any of my efforts—or so I feared.

The counting and evaluation left me with a sense of lost innocence, of simplicity overwhelmed by modern technology, and yes, admit it, of lost youth.

Claud and I were seeing new efficiency. Comfort, sure, but nevertheless, gadgetry—and for all I knew, Big Business.

I should welcome all this, but I couldn't. I remained pensive—while shivering.

Still, we were all settling together. The smell of beef stew wafted from the aluminum pot on the gasoline stove. I could almost taste it. Mama was arranging belongings and packs. Daddy sharpened his hatchet with his carborundum stone.

Claud kept chopping wood.

He knelt in the mud under the overhang, near the outside seat-log he'd rolled into our corner. Using it as a chopping block, he wielded the Hudson Bay ax at an angle against sticks, usually managing his one-blow slicing. He could see by the light of the fire. Sticks fell in a heap below the bunk where our sleeping bags lay. The trick is to chop against the side of the log in the direction you want the piece to go.

Daddy asked, "Do you fellows work in the woods?"

Claud replied, "Not really. Just enough to get out my winter's wood."

I said, "He's a veterinarian. His sons get out the wood."

"When I can drive them to it, or bribe them."

If Daddy asked me what I did, I couldn't claim to be a writer as I wasn't making any money. I forestalled the question by saying, "We've camped out since we were kids."

Daddy raised twinkling eyes from the hatchet and stone. "When was that?"

"Almost forty years ago. Started in nineteen twenty-nine."

The conversation was slow and progressed formally. Claud needed food and his pipe. I felt diffident because we were so primitive.

Their supper consisted of beef stew and crackers, then dried fruit from one of Mama's little plastic envelopes.

Susie grimaced, and Jane asked, "Sour, Susie?"

I had the feeling they were doing a routine. Mama said, "Apricots are good for you."

"Sour," said Jane, making a face.

Mama took their cups of fruit and added sugar, then hot water. "There you are. Instant stewed fruit. Stir for a while."

Daddy said to Claud and me, "I came through the Mahoosucs about fifteen years ago. Remember that little spring where we met? There's a brook, and a stone basin down below the trail. I was alone then and in no hurry, so I took a bath. Talk about cold! Well, you know mountain streams. I probably wouldn't do it now." He chewed an apricot and looked into the fire. " I had been hiking the White Mountains. Someone at Carter Notch Hut told me about the Mahoosucs. You ever stay in the huts?"

Claud and I, steaming away in the firelight, considered the question. I recalled three or four nights in the huts but waited to hear what Claud would say.

He replied, "Not since I worked in them."

"Were you at Carter?"

"No, Galehead."

"Sure. Over near South Twin. When was that?"

"Summers of nineteen thirty-four through thirty-eight."

"No helicopters then."

"The worst load was a five-gallon tank of gasoline on my packboard. Always leaked down my back. We used it for lanterns and the water pump."

"Hard way to earn a living."

"Well, yes, looking back, but it was a job, and I wanted it enough to keep trying to be hired. Served me right, I guess."

"It got you through college?"

"Through University of New Hampshire but I had to work one winter at Pinkham Notch Camp to save up for one of my years at vet school out in Michigan. Had to work there in thirty-nine to graduate in forty."

Susie asked, "What's a packboard?"

"It's two wooden slats riveted onto two crosspieces, and held on your back by two shoulder straps, same as your packframe, only they were leather. A man named Roddy Woodward built them for us."

"And you carried all the food to the hut?"

"Well, me and one other guy. About six miles with eighty pounds or so."

Susie said, "Holy cow!"

Jane thought a moment and said, "Feeding hikers, you must have run out of food sometimes."

"Once I had nothing but flour, bacon, and onions to feed eight hikers."

"What did you do?"

"Made six loaves of bread, then fried up two big pans of onions, bacon, and liver."

"Ugh, where'd you get the liver?"

"Six hedgehogs."

Jane, scrunching back away from the drip, asked, "Hedgehogs?"

"Porcupines," said Claud patiently, and I thought of his wife's remark that little girls could twist him around a finger so easily it was comical.

"You see," he explained, "we had just opened the hut for the summer, I guess June of thirty-six—a log cabin really—and these porcupines had wintered under it. They were chewing the place to pieces. Tried to bore up through the floor. So that day I'd been shooting them."

Daddy asked, "Did you…that is…." He stopped in laughter. "Did you tell the hikers?"

"No, I figured if they thought it was calves' liver I better not disillusion them."

Neat, careful Mama had a question. "How did you dispose of the carcasses?"

I held my breath, waiting to hear the reaction to his probable statement about cutting off the noses for the 20-cent bounty.

"Why, first," he began, and glanced at me. "Well, you see, there's quite a drop toward Twin Brook so I pitched the remains over the edge."

Jane said, "That was polluting."

"In those days nobody was down there for miles except wild animals—coons, foxes, bears, and deer. Besides, the paper mill below in Lincoln was polluting the Pemigewasset River. Of course," he went on,

"I could have buried them, except the ground was all ledge. And my boss, Joe Dodge, hadn't then let me use dynamite for garbage and trash holes."

Susie's eyes widened. "Wow, dynamite!"

"It worked good, but one day I touched off a charge that blew some rocks over the spruces and onto the trail. Showered some Appies."

"What are Appies?"

"Old-time members of the Appalachian Mountain Club. They had quite a lot to say to me and they complained to Joe. Don't know why. T'wan't anything but gravel and a few bits of rocks the size of golfballs— well, a few bigger."

Claud held out to me a plate of macaroni-hamburg.

We began to eat the soft but crunchy, delicious hot mess.

Daddy and Mama stopped laughing after a while. We lapsed into silence. I chewed meat not quite reconstituted and stared at the fire. I figured that Claud's summers at Galehead had been maybe very happy times.

Gradually talk resumed. We got acquainted. We talked about camping. Mama explained her food system. Claud and I learned that they had been on the trail almost a week, just moseying along, staying in the shelters, enjoying the wild mountains.

Having driven to Gorham from Ithaca, New York, and from AMC Pinkham Notch Camp, they hired a taxi to follow them to Grafton Notch. They left their car and taxied back to Shelburne, where they started hiking the AT up Peabody Brook Trail.

We hadn't noticed names as a family in the register at the Mahoosuc Trail junction. Yes, they had signed.

Mama spoke about her concern for their car. "Out West we've done a lot of pack-camping where cars at trailheads are sometimes broken into."

Daddy added, "Or dismantled. I hid ours away from the trailheads in woods. Couldn't find an opening in Grafton Notch away from the parking area."

"Well, don't worry," I said. "Grafton Notch is pretty remote—not that I've ever been there."

Daddy asked, "Ever been on the AT farther north, well, and east?"

I shook my head.

"We hope to follow more of it next summer."

Claud put in for us, "We climbed Katahdin."

Daddy asked, "When were you there?"

I looked at Claud. Did he feel young again? The recollection of that episode made me feel young.

He took his pipe from his mouth. "Nineteen thirty-one."

Daddy laughed. "I was four years old."

I could see in memory the peak ahead of Claud and me, and we'd already walked about 10 miles that day to the Hunt Trail. I said, "It rises right out of a swamp to a rocky pinnacle above a massif."

Daddy and Mama exchanged glances. She told us, "That's our kind of mountain. We met in Glacier National Park. We'll have to go climb Katahdin."

"Yes," Daddy said, "and before we do any more of the AT here. Next summer. Have you been there lately?"

"No," I said.

Claud surprised me. "Maybe we will."

He must really be feeling strong and youthful.

Come to think about it, maybe we would.

Talk lingered on the mountain's Baxter State Park, modern access routes, and trails we'd read about.

After a time I realized that the girls had fallen asleep. Jane slept soundly under the leak, protected by the Space Blanket over her sleeping bag. I heard the occasional tap of the drip. Susie lay curled behind her mother. They looked warm and cozy.

I still felt an occasional shiver and began laying out my sleeping bag. The soft accumulation of balsam fir needles would ease aches, and the balsam scent would be the essence of the wild forest.

I supposed that the fragrance for the girls would be memory-evoking all their lives. Firelight touched both their faces and in them I could discern Mama's girlhood features for Susie, and for Jane, perhaps Daddy as a serious little boy.

Conversation had dwindled into silence, a companionable quiet.

Daddy and Mama, wearing their sweaters, jeans, and socks, crawled into their sleeping bags and settled onto their air mattresses.

"Good-night," half-asleep Mama. "Night now," from Daddy.

We replied, "Good-night."

Claud had been tending the fire with steady addition of sticks. I was nearly dried out. Yet the bottoms of his pants refused to give up their water, as he discovered sitting on the bunk log to take off his boots. Because of the leather tops he had not noticed his cold, wet pants.

He knelt on the bunk, then stood up crouched under the roof.

Whispering, he told me, "I can't stay awake any longer."

He took out his jackknife and cut off the bottoms of his pants. When they were free, he tossed them onto the flames. He sat down to pull off his wet socks, which he draped on the bunk log.

So into our sleeping bags we wriggled, zipped up, and lay still.

I relaxed on my back to revel in the warm comfort. My so-called mind declined to relax. Calculation added up the hours I had been shivering—six and one-half. Shivering was said to be a body's method of fighting cold. Now the contest was over—not even a twitch. I snugged the hood around my head.

Claud snorted and gulped a few times, then might have died.

Although muffled inside my hooded sleeping bag, I could yet hear the wind and rain lashing the shelter. I began to worry about getting out to Grafton Notch the next day. Slowly, however, I rested. Aches subsided. My body knew it had reserves of strength never fathomed in simpler experiences. Nothing could stop me from reaching that road in Grafton Notch. Nervous concern faded. I dozed.

Gradually an illusion suffused me. I understood its nature. It was a reality in the realm that memory reserves as paradise.

I lay not in a log shelter on balsam boughs but in a double bed against my sleeping wife, when we were young, or maybe later when we were middle-aged. Outside our blankets our room was icy cold. The little cottage sturdily withstood the winter storm. I felt warm. I knew no fear of anything in the world or beyond it. I dozed in the perfect security offered by womanhood. Without desire I gave myself to deep slumber.

TO THE BITTER END

PARADISE BECAME AN UNREAL ILLUSION WHEN I AWOKE NEXT MORN-ing. Gray light appeared in my opening eyes. I raised on an elbow to stare outside. The wind still swept wet clouds across the pond and waved the spruce boughs threateningly at me. I felt desperate enough to fight my way through that weather to escape from the Mahoosucs. A spasm of frenzy came as hysteria and made me want to burst out of the strait jacket that was my sleeping bag. Get out! Get out!

I tried to rip open the zipper but couldn't find the leather thong looped into the metal tab. I must kick free, release arms, sit up, anything for freedom. But how? I'm the only one awake.

My companions lie still. Don't make a fuss. Endurance is the solution.

My face felt hot against the gusts of wind seeking a way through the shelter. I looked out again. The blasts tore open the fog above the pond. More clouds poured in to fill the gaps. I couldn't be sure whether rain fell or whether water blew off the spruces. The wind carried moisture from somewhere, perhaps off the waves dashing against the shore, or from the dripping eaves and dank stones surrounding the fireplace. I could smell wet charcoal, a dank charred odor. No chance for a breakfast fire.

A gust in my face chilled like a handful of snow. I blinked wet, so not snow, not sleet, temperature above 32 degrees. I couldn't start out. I'd freeze to death as soon as I became soaked.

I lay back and stared at the shadowy poles of the roof. Over toward the family I could hear the wet tap, tap, tap on Jane's Space Blanket. This was distinct from the eaves-water slopping into the mud near the fireplace.

Jane stirred. She whispered loudly, "My sleeping bag's wet. My pajamas are wet."

Her mother answered, "They can't be, not under the Space Blanket."

Daddy's low voice explaining was contrite. "Condensation. I should have realized that your body moisture couldn't escape. I should have rigged a little tent with stakes."

Mama said to moaning Jane, "Good thing the night wasn't hot as well as rainy. You'd have steamed like a turkey roasting in aluminum foil."

I heard a giggle, then three together.

Mama said, "I'll pull on my parka and get out so you can slide into my bag. Take off your PJ's inside and I'll pass you a shirt and pants."

I was restless but had to lie doggo till Mama and Jane reorganized their clothes against cold and a leaky roof.

At last, time for me to get up. I had to get up. Locate the zipper and thong. Bend knees up to the opening. A cramp grabbed my left calf. Quick, legs outside the bag. I managed to pull a boot on the left foot so I could sit on the bunk log and stamp away the stricture in the muscle. That leg contained my skiing knee, as I termed the occasional "arthritis" resulting from being a less skillful skier than I thought.

I pulled on the second boot, jammed my hat to head, and hobbled into the woods cursing the Mahoosucs, the weather, and especially the rain, which was forming droplets on my wool shirt. Oh well, wool was warm when wet, because of some fortuitous arrangement by God Almighty for sheep and men without raincoats.

At the pond's shoreline I rinsed my hands with ice water and sand. A splash on my face was enough. My red bandana failed as a towel, but everything was wet anyhow, including my wool shirt. I stopped on the way to the shelter to gather underbranches from a spruce. A white birch provided, as I passed, a wide curl of hanging bark.

On the bunk log, Claud sat lacing his boots. He couldn't tuck in his pants because the lower portions lay as wet envelopes of charred cloth on the charcoal.

Because Mama and the girls would hear, he kept his voice low. "Another hellish day."

I nodded. "Socked in for another three days probably."

With the wadded spruce branches and the birch bark I began the ritual of the fire, whether it burned or not in the wet charcoal. After several matches, fire crept up. Claud passed me sticks from under the bunk. For a wonder he hadn't burned them all the night before. The wind blew the flames sideways so I had to pile the sticks to windward, or the fire would have left them behind and gone out.

A rustling above me sounded interesting. Claud was holding my red parka over the flames.

"Something I got to tell you. There's a mite of a tear in this, and we better stick it together with adhesive tape. Or sew it first if you brought your needle and thread."

The rent extended from one arm across the back to the other arm.

"You see," he went on, "taking it off last night when you were getting wood, so's I could put on my wool shirt, well, it was kind of tight. I'll buy you a new one."

"No, you won't," I whispered. "We'll burn it and forget it. I'm warm enough. I still got on my union suit. That parka doesn't owe me anything. Neither do you. So for Christ's sake let's not talk about it."

I was pretty sure that someday soon a rain parka would appear from a package in my mailbox, but for now he merely handed me the coffee-pot full of water. Set to windward of the fire, the pot blocked some flame. I needed tea bad, so poured most of the water into another kettle. Two cups boiled would do for now. I piled sticks around the pot. We sat on the bunk log and waited.

The family next door, so to speak, began their morning routine.

Jane and Susie snuggled in sleeping bags. Tousled heads, one dark and one blond, rested close together for whispering. Daddy laced his boots, then added gas from a metal bottle into the little stove. Smelly process. Mama sorted envelopes of food for breakfast. She set one aside, made four piles, picked up the special envelope, and with it crawled along the bunk to Claud and me.

Briskly, she began, "Last night's talk about prepared foods, remember?" We nodded. "All right, you two should lighten your packs the next time. Here's an example of modern backpacking food. It's an omelet with green peppers and herbs."

I was mentally comparing the word "backpacking" with "camping out," when she went on, "I remembered this extra mix I have. I always bring spares. I'd like you to have it."

She handed Claud the plastic envelope. Yellowish contents and green bits showed through. Cautiously he took it. I put sticks on the fire while he eyed the envelope's printed data. His behavior followed a pattern I could have predicted.

"Are you sure you don't need it?"

"Certainly I'm sure." Her expression showed concern for his reluctance, but not yet impatience. Her eyes widened as she emphasized, "Really."

Daddy, tending to the flame under the kettle, said, "Believe her. She's our expert in provisioning."

"Yes," she said, "I'll accept that. He speaks from experience. I always bring plenty of extras."

Still Claud hesitated. She eased him into acceptance by turning to her pack for several empty envelopes. "Here's a few we've eaten. They'll give you an idea of the variety. There are the addresses of companies that sell specially dried backpacking foods."

"Thanks, but this omelet...." He was reaching toward his hip pocket where he kept his wallet. "We'll pay for it."

She shook her head. "I should have taken off the price tag."

"But it says one dollar and thirty-five cents. That's a...a..." The words almost formed and I could guess: "...a hellova lot for an omelet." But he said, "We want to pay."

I added, "Of course we do," but I wished he would drop the necessity never to owe anyone, not ever.

Daddy, amused, winked at his wife with the eye away from Claud and tipped his head toward our fire.

She followed his nod with a glance. Her face broke into a radiant

smile. "Don't be silly. The omelet is for having that glorious fire to welcome us."

I expected Claud to say something about our lighting the fire to dry
out, but she had soothed his insistent pride. That was a feat.

I thought to myself, "We are both of us putty, easily molded by a
charming woman."

Claud's putty softened visibly. "Well, thanks. My wife says I've got
to learn to accept a present gracefully. Thanks for the chance to modern-
ize our camping out."

"Enjoy it," she said, and crawled back to their side of the bunk.

The directions on the envelope told us to shake the yellow powder
and the green bits into a container and add one-half cup of water. That
meant mixing with a fork in one of our tin cans, the water guessed at
from a tin cup.

I held over the fire our frying pan and a pat of butter. Claud waited
till the butter hissed before he dumped in the eggs and peppers. At once
I worried about burning it. Should I raise the pan higher off the flames?
Yes, and a good move because I couldn't see for the smoke.

I turned my head and blinked away tears. I saw Daddy sitting on the
bunk log watching the little stove and the shiny pot. Steam rose up. He
lifted the pot with a clamplike pliers and set it down near Mama kneeling
on the bunk. She was emptying envelopes of oatmeal into four cups. I
heard her say to the girls, "Which? Apple-flavor or banana-flavor?"

Like Mary and Robert, these expert backpackers patronized a supermarket for cereal. As Mama began pouring hot water into the cups I
faced back to the smoky fire and the omelet. I heard Mama's spoon stirring the instant oatmeal.

When the omelet looked firm I figured the pieces of green peppers
would bind it together. I didn't dare try flipping it like a flapjack. Claud
turned it for me with the spatula.

He said, "We better eat it hot. I'll fry the bacon later."

I held the pan while he divided the omelet in half with the spatula.
Normally I'd have slid his portion onto a plate and eaten mine out of the
frying pan. Mama was watching us, so I avoided crudity and served myself on a plate. The omelet was browned enough for us to pick up like
toast, but we used the short-handled forks.

Mama said, "Hope you like it."

"Just like fresh eggs," I lied.

"It's good," Claud added.

The taste suggested eggs all right, though the dehydrated flavor of spoiled vegetation lingered in the green peppers. The problem was to get a forkful past your nose. It smelled like a fried woolen sock.

Our friends were completing their breakfast with rectangular pieces of bacon, and scrambled eggs from another envelope Mama opened. I watched the girls; by some miracle of conditioning they failed to turn up noses at the eggs and confirm my reaction. But they had hot chocolate for a chaser; Mama and Daddy, instant coffee. So a mocha scent arose from their cups.

Claud began slicing the last of our slab bacon.

I said, "No improvement in the weather."

"Bad day for Old Speck." He looked out at the clouds shrouding the pond. "Couldn't see off—not more than shotgun range."

Daddy heard our exchange. "We'll rest up today."

The girls had been subdued. Now came cries of relief.

Susie clapped her hands. "Daddy, you read my mind!"

"Oh goody," declared Jane. "I can go back to sleep."

Claud finished slicing our bacon and left it on the log. I was still squatting by the fire. To hand him the frying pan so he could fry the bacon I stood up straight. BASH! The top of my head struck the log support for the overhang.

I though I was going down. I dropped the frying pan. Flashing spots before my eyes flickered like blue and red chips in a kaleidoscope.

Claud spoke gruffly. "Sit down before you fall down."

Mama gasped and Daddy started up.

"You better lie down," he said.

I couldn't even shake my head to indicate my need to keep going. I knew enough to bend over as I staggered out of the shelter, so missed another bashing...must be recovering to know that much.

Anger came like a flash of heat against the cold wind—utter fury at the shelter, at the Mahoosucs, at my stupidity, and at the goddamned weather. I kept walking until water in my boots brought me to a stop in the pond.

I backed out and said my say to the adjacent world. That took some time.

Well, my boots had been soaked in the dripping woods.

When I returned to the shelter a chorus of "You all right?" brought out a reply about my hard head.

Claud, fork in hand and squatted by the fire, was turning the bacon. I sat on the bunk log and watched. He would pierce a slice with the fork, inspect it and either put it on a plate or return it for more cooking. At last he took out the thickest slice and poured the fat on the fire. The smoky flare meant finality—not for cooking, not for flapjacks, not for shortening in biscuits or corn bread. With the fork he lifted the hinged lid of the coffeepot. Tea bags and water simmered. Still using the fork, he hooked the bail and set the pot aside from the dying coals.

I wrapped my wet bandana around the folding wire handles before I filled our cups. Claud spooned out sugar and dried milk. I needed that tea. It was too hot. I stirred and sipped cautiously. No, be patient, or burn your tongue.

We ate the chewy bacon while our tea cooled. Claud had cut the slab through the rind without trimming. He hated to waste the least bit. We held each slice in our fingers and chomped to the edge of tough hide, which we nibbled clean of fat. Had I been starving I'd have eaten the hide, but I balked at eating pigskin. Claud's saving nature made him crunch up the hide of the first two slices. Thereafter his edgings went into the fire with mine.

Tea, hard bread, and raw prunes completed our breakfast.

No talk passed between us. We knew we'd be leaving Speck Pond Shelter.

Mama was cooking more eggs and bacon for Daddy. Their bacon seemed to have had the fat pressed out of it in that cube, which Daddy had sliced. Maybe it was made with soy beans and flavors by a company specializing in expedition foods.

I recalled the "dynamite soup" once sold by David T. Abercrombie, when Claud and I first camped out, called *erbwurst*—pea soup for the German army, pressed into a sausagelike cylinder of cloth. Well, damn my wandering mind.

Their bacon, whatever it was, smelled only slightly smoked compared to Claud's home-cured product. He burned maple-tree sawdust for the smoke in his smokehouse.

I noticed that Jane and Susie had settled into their sleeping bags after hurried trips to the woods. They shared a map and talked. How fine for them to be young and sit at ease in sleeping bags with no cramps or aching backs. Mama and Daddy sat on the bunk log as if at home. She was darning a sock. He wrote with a pencil in a little notebook, then put it down to take from the stove a pot of boiling water. Again chocolate's rich smell came to me as Daddy proved to be versatile with their supplies, so I figured he sometimes cooked the meals. I could sense family conviviality joining them for their day of rest. Probably the girls would eventually squabble, but not now.

The prospect might be great for our friends, but I had to escape the mountains. I think that Claud felt the same need in a different form, not so much escape as determination to achieve the final summit of our excursion, maybe just to get it over and into his past.

As tempting as was a day to recover and wait out the weather—and Don and Ruthie prepared to spend a night in Grafton Notch—I found myself hurrying to finish the bacon and to moisten my hard bread in the tea so I could choke it down quickly.

Claud began folding his sleeping bag. He poured himself more tea and poised the pot over my cup. Often I didn't drink the final powerful brew, as he remembered. This time I nodded.

We kept on packing and drinking the last of the tea. I dumped the tea bags hissing into the coals and wiped the pot with my bandana—inside. Its torn paper bag would once more protect my pack from soot. A rag from the chinking served to clean the frying pan well enough for the final bagging of it. Urgency took me. I sheathed the ax.

Packs shouldered, we could have started right off, but we lingered. I looked about for anything forgotten. My head throbbed. Claud loaded his pipe. I hoped he wouldn't say, "Well, probably won't see this place again."

I puzzled about why I now hesitated to begin ridding myself of the Mahoosucs. Not the soggy woods—I was soaked anyhow. I saw the red parka hanging on a nail. No fire remained to give it a ceremonial end. I tucked it under the flap of my pack.

Once more waiting to leave, I said inanely to Daddy, "We won't douse the fire."

"I may use it. A camp isn't the same without a fire. Too bad you have to go out into that weather."

"It's best we meet our ride on time."

"Well, good-bye. Glad to have met you both."

Mama smiled. "Maybe we'll meet again on the trail. Hope so."

"Me too. Me too," came from Jane and Susie, who added, "And more stories." Jane said, "Maybe we'll go to Galehead someday."

Claud nodded and turned to Mama. "Thanks again for the omelet. It'll give us strength for Old Speck." He raised one hand in a tipping salute to the brim of his hat.

I felt the useless and ineffable sadness of parting with friends to go separate journeys. Also I was leaving behind the romance of camping out. Years and age haunted me.

What was to be said? "Good-bye and good luck."

We took off into the wet woods along the last of the Mahoosuc Trail, heading for Old Speck and whatever adventures might await us there or while descending the steep Warden's Trail to unknown Grafton Notch.

My watch showed 7:45.

We faced only two–and–three-quarter miles for the day, including about a mile and a quarter to our highest elevation of the trip at 4,180 feet. We moved right along.

First we climbed over two wooded humps. They seemed a farewell extra requirement from the Mahoosucs—up, down, up, down; and up once more. In one of the hollows, we came to a sign on a tree. It pointed left to a spring. Claud said, "I'm absorbing enough water," and kept plodding steadily on.

We left behind the forest and achieved the 4,000-foot scrub evergreens, then missed not at all their wet branches as the trail led up a bare ridge of rock. My boots and legs gave me the sensation that I was walking on the foundation of Old Speck, which I was, but not just a mountain, a foundation of the earth, the world. And this felt familiar. I was understanding a pervading quality of the Mahoosucs, and it formed in my mind as "Mahoosuc Earth Magic."

This barren ledge lifted us into driving clouds that no longer shed rain, while at the same time they contained moisture for us. The wind was veering around to the west. We pushed our boots against rock. Scarred by the boots of other hikers, it was our only course. There were no cairns or paint blazes.

"Old Speck"—Maine's third highest peak. The *Guide* pages had told me the name "distinguished it from the Speckled Mountains in Stoneham, Maine." Once upon a time "Old Speck" must have been grouped with them, but why or where I didn't know.

We kept to the long crest. The crevices of the rock supported vines of mountain cranberry. We leaned over to pick the pea-size fruit. I reached too far and my pack gave me a shove. I nearly pitched headfirst so rested my hands on my knees. Wisps of clouds wafted across the rock and green vines.

Claud was dropping berries into a plastic envelope. "I told my wife I'd bring her some. Just want her to know I remembered."

We continued to climb the narrowing ledge up which scrub spruces reached. At the end of rock, a path opened into the woods as though we had known where we were going. The trees protected us from the wind. We walked softly on the needles and silently in the gloom of a taller forest. White signs appeared on two trees. They stopped us abruptly at a trail junction.

Here I began to realize that we had been hurrying, or maybe we had become, on our sixth day, toughened to the Mahoosucs.

The junction was the end of the Mahoosuc Trail at the Warden's Trail. To the left that level stretch must suddenly pitch down to Grafton Notch, the end of our voluntary servitude in the wild Mahoosucs. On the right must be the summit, and our last. I hoped not much higher.

I asked, "Taking your pack?"

For answer he slipped off the shoulder straps. He took out the camera and a bag of snacks. Away he went. I shucked my pack and followed him. I had to hurry. The light-footed ease of packless walking didn't account for his pace, surely. Maybe he wanted to get it over as much as I did.

We loped along the almost-level trail, which was an aisle in the evergreen forest. Claud stretched into his flowing stride. This made me scurry to keep up.

Of course, Old Speck and anticipation were incentives. A new summit, and longed for.

We stepped into a clearing. Ragged edges of spruces surrounded the misty open space. Its center was a decrepit steel tower. No ladder. At one time we could have climbed the girders. The cab was gone. In the grass at our feet lay pieces of sheet metal and shards of glass. Over against the north side of the forest, someone had built a shelter from boards, poles, corrugated roofing, and spruce branches.

The summit of Old Speck was a mountaintop slum.

We looked into gray cloud. We stared at the surrounding evergreens pointing into the cloud. I finally said, "Even in good weather we'd have no view unless we climbed the framework of the tower. Not me. Not now."

"Too risky, and no point looking closer at that cloud."

We poked disconsolately about. Claud investigated the crude shelter. I prowled into the scrub east of the tower. The *Guide* pages had mentioned a trail and cliffs.

Yes, the mountain's summit fell away into a foggy void. I could look down on misty pointed spruce tops vanishing into opaque gray. I turned back into the clearing.

Persistently the urge to reach Grafton Notch hung with me, and now added was the possibility of failing strength. Fatigue, gloom, cold, and the various aches made me fearful, as though I must get off Old Speck while I was able.

To hell with the highest Mahoosuc. Without the energy and agility to climb the tower, I saw no sense in waiting to see if the cloud would lift. We had time to spare, because the descent was only a mile and a half. If we should wait…but I could hardly think clearly about anything, certainly not coherently about maybe the weather clearing, and Claud wouldn't climb that tower either, so give it up, forget it.

A feeling of guilt assailed me. I was beginning to disbelieve that giving up was a sin.

I walked across the clearing to join Claud at the junk shelter. We squatted under a sheet of corrugated roofing and munched zwieback and chocolate.

He asked, "What about a picture?"

"Not much light. Hardly even for black and white."

"Then I don't care enough to waste film on our final destination."

"Some destination. Grafton Notch is my destination."

He continued to mull over—what? Disappointment, or more likely the experience gained in living, because he gave me a conclusion, "I guess you shouldn't think of a special place too long before you go there."

I pulled myself upright by a pole. I said, "Maybe the going there is what matters." As I chewed chocolate, I watched him stand and look around.

He said, "Not very wild after all. It's like any other wooded summit with an abandoned tower."

"There have been better moments back along the trail. I had a few up top of Mahoosuc Arm. I felt equal to it."

He nodded. "Peculiar, those times take over for no reason at all." He started toward the tower and said over his shoulder to make his words seem completely casual, "I had a spell on Cascade Mountain that first morning, with mountains all around, sun on the fog in the valley, and five days ahead to explore and enjoy it with nobody to bother me."

"Gentian Pond was all right." Then I had a vivid thought about him. "You should have been born in eighteen-fourteen instead of nineteen-fourteen, and gone West with the mountain men as a boy."

"Maybe." He stared at the tower and shook his head.

I asked, from my guilt at giving up, and from duty, "Should we wait a while?"

"Naw, we're in a spell of bad weather."

"Let's get out before the rain starts again."

"That wind goes through me like a thousand icicles." He looked around once more. "Well, we made it."

We left behind the misty clearing surrounded by pointed spruces, the summit of the long Mahoosuc Range. We were heading out. The aisle through the forest seemed shorter, maybe because, up ahead, Claud loudly whistled the "Triumphal March" from *Aïda*. Well, we had triumphed.

We swung up our packs.

I was so eager to get off the mountain that I didn't wait for him to light his pipe. And I went down suddenly. The Warden's Trail fell off the ridge. I went down and down. The footpath became a mere gash in the mountainside. Filled with small rounded stones and with larger ones as big as bushel baskets, the trail without them would have been a deep gully eroded by rainwash and snowmelt. All soil had been cleaned down to the stones except where crumbling rock had collected in pockets with treacherous angles that gave my legs twisting jerks as my boots slipped.

Careful! Too near the end for a mishap. I began to move more slowly. Claud caught up with me. We crept down, concerned with survival.

"Steep like this," I said, "I bet on a clear day we could see the Rangeley Lakes like nowhere else."

"If we hung onto trees so we wouldn't fall off."

"I'm not sure I care about the view. The fronts of my thighs are made of aching jelly." I stopped and sat down beside a pool of clear water under a rock. "Let's eat."

We shucked off our packs. I just dropped mine. Claud unstrapped his and took out a hunk of cheese and a box of pilot crackers, saying, "I'm too dry for this fodder so I'll mix up some pink lemonade."

"Water's all right for me."

"You'll need the food value in this sugar and chemical lemon flavor."

While he was busy with cups and a kettle and spoons, I took from my shirt pocket the soggy *Guide* pages. I figured that we met the *Guide's* time from Speck Pond Shelter to the summit, which gave me some sort of grim satisfaction.

How about our descent of the Warden's Trail? I read aloud, "This trail is, and I quote, '...almost uniformly one of the steepest in the mountains.' Ummm, our pool here must be the one that's about a third of a mile above the fire warden's cabin and a small brook, ummm...allowed time going up from the cabin to the summit, one hour for six tenths of a mile, and some of that, and I quote again, 'nearly level on top.' So it says, and I say, Ho, ho ho."

I wanted to laugh because our situation and past days struck me as comic in a silliness I couldn't believe. I knew enough to stop talking.

The pink lemonade was horrible, but sweet.

Maybe the sugar would drive some energy into me, assuming my pancreas could provide enough insulin to burn the sugar...or whatever the hell was wrong. Time to move on.

Stepping down again under the pack, I kept belching that lemon flavor. Gas on the stomach and ache in the head. The gas was eliminating itself, but how about the headache? I formulated words with which to ask my doctor about it. I wouldn't mention the knock from the log in the shelter; headaches had become part of my life for over a year...there seemed to be a relation between them and physical activity. Two years ago the doctor had diagnosed my diabetes and put me on a diet which took off ten pounds. I would ask him, "Doctor, are headaches normal for diabetics of the late-onset variety? If the answer is Yes or No, what the hell are you going to do about it? I get the feeling more and more that you guys don't know much about diabetics. The trouble with you medical men is that unless an ailment is life-threatening, you don't know what to do about it. Oh, you think diabetes is life-threatening?" Et cetera, as the king of Siam said, et cetera, et cetera....

If nothing is to be done, I decided, I've taken my last camping-out excursion in the mountains.

The trail dropped us into a clearing. We scarcely paused at the abandoned fire warden's cabin of boards and tar paper near the brook. I did remark, "Looks as though the Dead End Kids had been working it over. Not a pane of glass left. And they had twenty-two caliber rifles to shoot up the stove pipe."

Claud, the firearms expert, disagreed. "The holes are too big for a twenty-two. More like a thirty-thirty deer rifle. Or maybe forty-four."

Here was civilization.

Yet I felt relief, and was ashamed of myself for it. Some mountaineer, some woodsman.

Civilization seemed to clear my head, because after I had carefully placed boots on stones to cross the brook, I realized I could have waded and not soaked up much more water. I noticed a sign on a tree for "East Spur." That must be the route off the cliff where I'd looked into the cloudy, spruce-studded abyss near the tower.

Our trail left the little pocket in the woods, which had protected the cabin—and the warden. Nearly vertical progress began again, but not on stones. Instead, mud.

The forest of spruce and fir merged with the leafy trees of lower elevations. There came from them a sensation of less exposure to the elements, although wind still blew cloud through the yellowing leaves of the birches. Sugar maples and beech were the green color of early autumn, which I thought of as stationary green, when seasonal growth was over, or waiting green, before orange and brown. An occasional red maple earned its name on some of its glowing branches. In the cloud the leaves were the dull red of hardwood coals.

From great yellow birches, roots extended across the mud of the trail. Without them we descended by sliding in a mud flume. Or we made our way with handholds on trees down the side of the trail. Heel-digging into the mud kept our feet under us most of the time. Often we chose the woods as easier and safer. We made critical comments on the condition of the trail and on the judgment of whoever laid it out straight up.

Two teen-age youths passed us going up. Legs pumped, arms swung, hands gripped trees. Breathing hard, they had none for greetings, but smiled, and the leader, slipping in the mud, laughed. They were enjoying themselves. I stopped to rest—going down!—and admired their strength and speed.

Claud said, "Once we used to run up mountains."

I was too tired for an effort to moderate his regret by reminding him we were damn lucky to have had it at their age. Besides, I'd never thought much of running up mountains. Not my style.

Descending again, I noticed that I could see farther among the trees. This seemed like a miracle after days of spruce-fir forest. It indicated the approaching end of our trip. I said, "Look, we're below the cloud. Down there over the treetops must be Grafton Notch and the road."

"That's the most we've seen since the ledges before Carlo Col, two days ago, almost three."

The boys evidently reconsidered their attack on Old Speck. They passed us leaping down without a good-bye. But their whoops echoed up as they skated down a mud slide.

We, too, slid enough. Grasped branches controlled us down through the hardwoods. I felt a pleasure almost solid from the certainty that there was a world below the clouds. The Mahoosucs were releasing me. I was convinced of my escape when I heard a distant whooshing of a car in the depths, a four-wheeled vehicle with an internal combustion engine, on a highway with a number, Route 26.

Happiness gave the final strength to my legs.

Our down-spout descent had been cautiously slow—two hours for 1.6 miles. We walked slowly the last 100 yards, with the level earth hitting our boots hard. In the open space of the parking lot I stood and blinked. Claud walked toward a pickup truck and the two young fellows who had passed us.

I had forgotten the distance that remained up the road, Route 26, to the continuation of the AT eastwards. In another era in another world I had arranged to meet Don and Ruthie up there. So I had, and how long ago! None of us then had known what Grafton Notch was like, except that a shelter existed along the AT, not far from the road.

Claud remembered the distance up the road. He was talking to the boys, then waved me toward him. I trudged over.

He said, "These fine young men have taken pity on two old codgers and offered us a ride up to the next section of the AT."

We threw our packs into the back of the truck, climbed in, and sat on them. I saw another car by the edge of the woods, a large station wagon, doubtless belonging to our friends of Speck Pond Shelter.

Our driver took off like a hare. We braced hands behind us on steel.

Oh, blessed wheels! I slumped and watched the black asphalt unroll behind us. On either side the trees blurred. We looked at each other and nodded, then again stared at the road, which seemed to be speeding under us.

That half mile to the sign for the AT and a turnout came in another two seconds, and with an abrupt halt. We struggled over the tailgate and dragged out our packs.

The boys left in a spray of sand and a squeal of tires on asphalt.

We stood in a little clearing, where trail signs pointed east to Baldpate Mountain, the Bigelow Range, and on toward Mount Katahdin, which was impossibly far away.

So this was Grafton Notch. Closely wooded, it might have been on any secondary highway in the Maine forests. It reminded me of boyhood tours through the unopened notches of the White Mountains when branches interlaced over the narrow roads. Along these roads my father slowly drove the big Studebaker with the top folded down behind me and my three sisters, while Mother sat up front with Father. In Franconia Notch to see the Old Man we had to pile out and run down to the shore of Profile Lake. Here Grafton Notch was just a pass through wild mountains.

I knew in general where we stood. South of us was Route 2 along which Claud had driven the Model T Ford in 1931 on our trip to climb Katahdin. Yes, I knew that highway because it was the only east-west, or west-east, route between northern New Hampshire and Maine. Northward Route 26 led to Errol, New Hampshire, known for its rainbow trout in the Androscoggin River and for the turn to Wentworth Location and then a branch road to Dartmouth College Grants.

I knew where I was all right. I looked at my watch. The time was noon.

I said, "My kids won't be here for a while. I'd lie down and take a nap if I could find a dry place."

Several cars passed by. Joy riders of Labor Day, tourists, weekenders. The people stared at us as though we were strange animals in a zoo. I felt a sudden and vast contempt for the occupants. "They think they're seeing a rare species."

"Maybe they are." He began loading his pipe.

"They think they're seeing the mountains. They don't know anything about 'em."

An old man came wandering down the trail, which was apparently a passable road for Jeeps. The old man came toward us eagerly. I thought perhaps he was lost but he only wanted company and talk. He wore a Hawaiian flowered shirt that hung out square, green and yellow, over his tan slacks.

"Where you boys from? My family is climbing up to Table Rock so I'm killing time. Our car's down at the parking lot. I walked all the way up here with my grandchildren and that's enough for a man my age."

I started to tell him I was a grandfather, and instead almost said that I was too pooped to care.

He had a determined expression. Yes, determined to talk. "Where you boys from?"

Claud looked sourly at him. "Laconia." And applied a match to his pipe.

"Laconia, well, well. Maybe you buy furnace oil from me. My trucks service the Laconia area. My business is located in Franklin but I have Laconia customers. I'm Walt Winton—Winton Oil. Well, my son has it now."

"No," I said, "Chet…" I couldn't think of my oilman's last name. Claud helped me out. "Chet Gardner."

I sat down on a stone. The position allowed Walt Winton to plant his loafers right in front of me. "So you get your oil from Gardner Fuel. I knew Chet when he was a young fellow just starting out. What's your name?"

"Doan." I stood up and went to my pack, from which I fumbled pipe and tobacco pouch.

The kindly old man followed me. "Doan. Sounds like Dutch."

"English." I might have overwhelmed him with talk, if I had the energy to start in about how my family was once named Donne, which became Doane. And how the Quakers dropped the "e" after they got kicked out of Massachusetts Bay and moved West to Ohio.

Walt Winton said, "You look about worn out."

"I am. We walked the trail from Gorham."

"Gorham? You can't walk here from Gorham. I think you're kidding me."

"No. We walked the Appalachian Trail…well, the Mahoosuc Trail."

"Where's your car?"

"We're to be met here. Soon I hope."

My pipe kept me busy, and Walt Winton walked over to Claud. I waited with interest, remembering Claud once telling a gullible youth in Guyot Shelter about working in a salt mine.

Walt Winton said to Claud, "If you had a shave I think I might know you. What's your name?"

"Henry Hilton."

I waited for something about the hotels.

But Walt Winton pursued his idea. "You remind me of a vet over to Laconia. Well, he lives on the edge of Belmont. Name of Doc Sharps."

"Never heard of him. I'm a stranger here myself. Spend most of my time traveling around the family hotels. Hilton Hotels, you know."

Our kindly old man wasn't a gullible youth. He gave us a disgusted look and started down the road, to his parked car, I supposed. We smoked and watched him go.

Claud removed his pipe. "That's the only way. Otherwise you hear all about their animals and symptoms of ailments and what should be done and what do I think his wife should do about her little poodle, on and on, ad infinitum."

I looked at my watch. Only 12:30. I felt grimy when I thought of meeting Ruthie, so I told Claud, "Maybe there's a stream along the trail. If you'll stay here, I'll go wash my face and hands. Flag down a white Volvo."

"I'll wave it in here."

I walked along the track with my boots high-stepping as they still tried to support the pack. A pool gave me water, perhaps rain water, and in my mood I thought of the home mechanics who once put out glass bowls to catch rain for car batteries and saved the cost of distilled water. No more. Rain wasn't what it used to be.

I wiped with my bandana. The operation couldn't be called drying off.

When I returned to Claud and the edge of Route 26, I found him lying on his back, his head propped against his pack. Beyond caring about wet ground I also stretched out against my pack. We watched three cars slide by.

The next was a white Volvo sports sedan.

From the little car a laughing girl jumped out and came toward us. A solid young man joined her and they stood looking at us. Ruthie seemed smaller than I recalled, and younger than was possible. She had been born in the year of our old secondhand Ford Mercury, 1939, and I was reminded of that car because the Volvo looked like it, but not gray— white, and through the wrong end of a telescope.

I said, "God, I'm glad to see you two." I stood up by rolling to hands and knees.

Ruthie kissed me. "You made it! We looked up at the mountains coming over from Gorham and wondered."

I asked, "How's your mother?"

She gave us strict instructions if you didn't show to call state police, game wardens, AMC, and the National Guard."

"Ah, glad to know she wants me back."

"Going home, we'll stop and see Penny in North Conway. Also your granddaughter."

"Good."

Don solemnly shook hands with me and then with Claud. "Congratulations."

Ruthie giggled. "I'll tell you what he really said as we came along Route Two."

"Now Ruth," Don said, "that's not necessary...."

Ruthie kept on by informing us, "Don's not a mountain climber so you can imagine, when he saw those peaks, how he reacted."

Claud told them, "From the road you don't see the real high ones."

I asked Ruthie, "What did Don say about our excursion?"

"Well, as he looked up and up, while more unrolled ahead, he kept saying, 'The damned old fools, the damned old fools.'"

"He named us correctly," I said. "But you didn't have to wait a day for us to arrive."

"We were ready to," Don said, "especially after seeing the Mahoosuc Range. We had all the gear and food for a night in the shelter."

Ruthie said, "An adventure we'll try some other time."

Don asked, "How in the world did you manage it?"

"Simple," I said. "Same way a friend built a house. First he nailed on one board and then he nailed on another. First we climbed one mountain and then we climbed another. I'll write it all down some day."

Claud announced, "I'd just as soon feel some wheels under me." He picked up his pack and walked toward the car.

Don carried my pack. I didn't protest.

He lifted the rear deck and arranged the packs with the camping equipment that he'd tidily fitted in. Then he opened the right-hand door of the car because on that side the bucket seat tilted farther forward.

I said to Claud, "After you, my dear Gaston."

He didn't move. He was looking up and with reason. Sunlight lay on his stubbly jaw and brought out tired lines under his eyes, which were focused upward toward Old Speck.

His gaze turned mine. I realized we were standing in sunshine.

High above us the clouds had vanished. Cliffs marked the mountainside. Above the sheer crags and rock slides the summit loomed green in the outline of pointed spruces. I couldn't make out the tower.

Claud looked at me, expressionless, and back again at our destination, our high point. He shrugged before he leaned over to crouch into the back seat.

He said in his phony French accent, "C'est la vie, my dear Alphonse. C'est la vie."

I crawled in beside him. We peered out the windows for last views of Old Speck as Don drove off.

Claud warned the distant cliffs and spruces, "We'll be back."

I didn't think so.

*   *   *

Fourteen years later he was right.

GOOD-BYE

IN 1980 CLAUD AND I WENT AGAIN TO SPECK POND SHELTER AND Old Speck.

The route of approach was by Success Pond Road to the Old Speck Trail. We would stay overnight, climb Old Speck, and head home.

Why did we go? Because Claud had said we would be back.

During those 14 years, we had kept on climbing mountains while significant events took place in our ordinary lives.

One event stands out for me, and its name is insulin. I was lucky that my Laconia doctor moved away. On diet, exercise, and medication, Orinase, he had reduced me to 127 pounds. But I was also lucky that before he left he first made me an appointment with Dr. John Milne of the Hitchcock Clinic, who put me on ten units of long-lasting insulin. Soon I began a new life of fitness.

Although we carried packs for this overnight to Speck Pond, we did not consider it a backpack. Speck Pond Trail was about four miles of varied terrain culminating near the end in a look-off down to the pond, to the shelter, and over to Old Speck. The descent to the shelter was steep. AMC termed the place Speck Pond Campsite. The new shelter was spacious, made of boards, and facing the woods, not the pond. We remembered wind-driven rain off the pond. The roof wouldn't leak. Great improvements.

After sunset, which came early, hikers drifted in, until accommodations began to look inadequate. The weather was threatening. By bedtime a steady misty rain began to fall.

We lay down to sleep like the proverbial sardines in a can, but only one layer.

Claud and I had no tent. Who needed a tent at a shelter 'way to hell and gone off, like Speck Pond?

I had put my sleeping bag as far away as possible from Claud's to avoid his classic snoring. The rain continued to fall.

To make the situation terrible indeed, someone down the line was unbelievably flatulent and laid down a gas attack every few minutes.

The breeze, as in all such open-front shelters, blew toward the interior.

The entire evening had been peculiar.

Of course Claud had built up a glorious fire. Nobody but us used it to cook over. Ten or a dozen little gasoline or propane stoves appeared with shiny aluminum pots. Our blackened teapot proclaimed us as has-beens. But we feasted on a whole roast duck that Louise had baked and Claud had packed in, along with a bottle of wine. Was it the wine that made me drop my lower partial plate while brushing my teeth? Hilarious when the group learned why I was poking about with my flashlight. Fortunately I didn't step on the plate before I found it in the dirt.

Sleep was impossible for me. Also for Claud. He was next to the flatulent young man. I heard talking but couldn't make out anything except Claud's disgusted comment before the shushing of others dropped his voice to a whisper: "Mushrooms? And you didn't know what kind they were?"

I could imagine the rest, and next day after talking to Claud I pieced together his subsequent remarks: "You thought they were edible. So you ate some, being very hungry. Well, you keep it up and you won't make Katahdin or even Grafton Notch. You're one of those bold young mushroom-eaters. Didn't anyone ever tell you that there are no bold *old* mushroom-eaters?"

If there is any accommodation more discouraging than getting up in a shelter on a rainy morning, it's getting up in a crowded shelter. Excessive politeness covered growls of discontent that verged on bitching. We got in each other's way. The fireplace and spare wood were soaked. Claud and I had no ax for dry wood and a fire. Like the others we went for our backpackers' gasoline stove, a concession to modernity.

Everyone squatted and boiled water or fussed with a stove or ate instant oatmeal flavored with fruit. But Claud had to have his bacon slices, and he'd also brought four eggs. Then there was a movement afoot to climb Old Speck.

My attitude was dubious. I had no trouble containing my enthusiasm. Wait for better weather. Old Speck again in the rain?

Claud's attitude was to go and get it over with. A group of five or six gradually gathered. We started out, I with a disconcerting sense of being crowded on a familiar trail once before wet, but uncrowded.

Then I remembered that in the early confusion I had forgotten to take my insulin. Besides, the weather was worsening. Another ascent with no view. I told Claud, "I give up."

He went on. He returned with a comment, "Same as last time." But I could see the satisfaction it gave him.

And I knew a little distaste for myself, but not much.

When he and the others got back, soon one of them, a young girl, appeared in a swimsuit and plunged into the icy water.

I felt old.

The highlight of the trip was a bypass trail that took us out to the summit of Mahoosuc Arm, where we had nearly lost the trail in 1966. This was a nostalgic moment. The wind was not blowing a gale.

We descended to the car and drove back to Berlin on the rough road, dodging potholes, and so home.

*　　　　　*　　　　　*

Ernie, my wife, grew more and more crippled with arthritis. Then she was found to have cancer of a lung. She died in June 1982.

Claud and I were nearing the end of our many years of hiking together. One cold and windy day we climbed good old Mount Chocorua, scanned our mountains all around, and soon left. It was our last hike.

I remarried, and Marjorie and I moved to Jefferson where, from our house and 10 acres, we look to the Northern Presidentials and Mount Washington.

Claud seriously injured his back. An operation repaired his spine but resulted in a crippled left leg. Then he realized he had oral cancer. He took his own life in September 1984.

I shall miss him all the rest of my life.

After two strokes, I hobble around on a cane. I watch Mount Washington, Jefferson, and Adams off our deck or through our big windows.

The mountains seem, now I know I'm all done climbing them, to be more distant.